MW01126424

BAD
COMPANY

BAD COMPANY

PRIVATE EQUITY
AND THE DEATH OF THE
AMERICAN DREAM

MEGAN GREENWELL

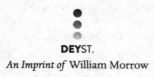

DEYST.
An Imprint of William Morrow

DEYST.

HarperCollins books may be purchased for educational, business, or
sales promotional use. For information, please email the Special Markets
Department at SPsales@harpercollins.com.

FIRST EDITION

Designed by Alison Bloomer

Library of Congress Cataloging-in-Publication Data has been applied for.

ISBN 978-0-06-329935-1

25 26 27 28 29 LBC 5 4 3 2 1

For Dad, who was always the first to believe I could do it.

Jim Greenwell, 1942–2021

CONTENTS

INTRODUCTION

UNTIL IT COST ME MY DREAM JOB, I HAD NEVER GIVEN PRIVATE equity much thought.

When a Boston-based private equity firm called Great Hill Partners bought Deadspin, the digital sports magazine where I was editor in chief, and its sister sites in 2019, it hardly seemed like the worst possible outcome. Our company's previous owner, Spanish-language broadcaster Univision, had mostly operated the company through benign neglect, never interfering in our coverage but not trying particularly hard to boost profits, which meant the sites punched far above their weight journalistically, yet were losing a reported $20 million a year. Great Hill Partners, though, had invested in trendy, successful brands like Wayfair, Bombas, and the RealReal. The firm's partners said their goal was to shore up the business side of our company, bringing in more revenue from ads and e-commerce and subscriptions. My colleagues and I *wanted* our publications to make money. If these finance guys were going to bolster our finances, we'd get to continue producing deep investigations and funny blogs. A win-win.

I had a vague sense that private equity had caused trouble in other industries; the downfall of Toys R Us had become a global news story just a year before, and Alden Global Capital had been the bogeyman of local newspapers for a decade. But everyone knew the retail industry was sinking under Amazon's weight, and that newspapers had sabotaged themselves by failing to adapt to the internet age. We weren't a failing company: more than twenty million people read Deadspin every month, many of them multiple times a day. I knew private equity was a problem. I just thought it wasn't *my* problem.

It didn't take long to realize how wrong I was.

At first, I couldn't figure out why none of my new bosses' ideas seemed like they were designed to serve our large, almost disturbingly loyal existing audience, even though large and loyal audiences are generally considered the holy grail for media companies. They told experienced product managers that quality-assurance testing and other best practices were unnecessary because they cost too much money, which meant things broke constantly. They forbade Deadspin from publishing several types of stories that were among our most popular, then got angry at me when I pointed out that eliminating popular stories would mean fewer readers. They were so busy micromanaging how the company's journalists worked—not just what stories we reported but what we wore and during what hours we were sitting at our desks—that they never seemed to have time to follow through on their plans for the business side.

After I read yet another story about yet another newspaper driven into the ground by Alden Global Capital, it finally dawned on me that the disconnect I was experiencing wasn't accidental. Alden was destroying newspapers because it didn't care about newspapers, and because it could make money off their ashes. Similarly, Great Hill Partners did not care about Deadspin. The firm's goal was never to make our website better or grow its readership. Great Hill Partners, and private equity at large, exists *solely* to make money for shareholders, no matter what that means for the companies it owns.

In the simplest terms, "private equity" describes a system in which a firm bundles money from outside investors—including university endowments, public pension funds, state-owned investment funds, and ultrawealthy individuals—which it uses to buy and operate companies. The firm and the investors have a symbiotic relationship: the firm gets to use the investors' cash for its own business goals, while the investors earn returns when the firm's portfolio companies are sold or taken public. Sometimes the way to make the most money involves strengthening the portfolio company itself. But even then, the benefit is only incidental, the company's success a mere side effect of increasing profits for the private equity firm and its investors.

And often, making money for the firm and its investors doesn't require making any money for the portfolio company. Private equity firms earn management fees, transaction fees, and monitoring fees that typical companies do not. They benefit from tax breaks that allow them to keep much more of their profits than other types of businesses. They can sell a company's assets and pocket the proceeds rather than reinvesting them. There are stunningly few limits to the methods a private equity firm can use to profit off a company it owns, whether or not the company profits too. Even the company going out of business entirely can be lucrative for its private equity owner.

In other words, the point of Deadspin wasn't to make money for *Deadspin*. It was to use Deadspin to make money for Great Hill Partners and its investors. In private equity, shareholder value is the only measure of success.

By that standard, Great Hill Partners is thriving. While it does not release detailed information about its financial performance, it did boast about ranking tenth on a list of the midsize private equity firms that generate the best performance for investors in 2019, the year it bought Deadspin's parent company.

Three months after Great Hill took over, I submitted my resignation, explaining that my bosses' micromanaging what we published was hurting our traffic and making it impossible for me to develop a coherent editorial strategy or lead my staff effectively. Two months after that, following another showdown with management over what they were allowed to write about, the rest of the staff followed me out the door. Great Hill attempted to rebuild the newsroom, but the audience had disappeared. In 2024, the firm sold Deadspin to a Maltese gambling company, which now uses the site to drive traffic to online casinos. In less than five years, Great Hill's executives had turned one of the most popular sports sites on the internet into one that draws slightly less traffic than a Pennsylvania dog breeder called greenfieldpuppies.com.

Great Hill Partners itself avoided any fallout from the Deadspin debacle. In 2024, the year it sold the site, its partners announced that it had risen to number four on the list of the midsize private equity firms that generate the best performance for investors.

=====

AFTER I WALKED away from Deadspin, I couldn't stop trying to puzzle out what had gone wrong—not out of spite, but out of pure curiosity. I had assumed that a private equity firm made money when the companies it owned made money, and that when the companies lost money, the firm did too. Once I began to grasp how misguided that assumption had been, I grew hungry to understand how it worked, how exactly destroying a flourishing website made for a profitable strategy.

I also needed to know how private equity worked in other industries. As much as I had loved my job, our snarky sports blog wasn't exactly curing cancer. But now, everywhere I looked, I saw other companies being acquired, with terrifying repercussions. Shortly after I quit, a close friend discovered that both her children's daycare and her Brooklyn apartment building were owned by major private equity firms. Her primary care physician had recently, and narrowly, fended off an attempt from a different firm to buy her practice. Business-press headlines trumpeted the skyrocketing number of private equity deals in hospitals, mobile home parks, and public utilities; those same publications also reported on dozens, hundreds, thousands of layoffs at private equity–owned companies. Private equity was transforming much more important businesses than Deadspin, and costing scores of people their jobs.

Few Americans have any idea how deeply private equity is ingrained in their lives.

Twelve million people work for companies owned by private equity firms—about 8 percent of the employed population, collectively generating $1.7 trillion of the nation's gross domestic product. Because of the industry's fondness for byzantine corporate structure, many of these people have no idea their jobs are ultimately controlled by financial giants like Blackstone, the Carlyle Group, Apollo Global Management, KKR, or Cerberus Capital Management.

These firms' influence, though, is far more powerful, and widespread, than individual paychecks. Eight percent of private hospitals are private equity–owned. America's production of oil, gas, and coal is increasingly dominated by private equity firms, which have invested at least $1.1 trillion in just over a decade—twice the combined market value of Exxon and Shell. Four of the five largest for-profit daycare chains are owned by private equity. So is the University of Phoenix. It controls supermarket chains, pet stores, voting machine manufacturers, local newspapers, nursing home operators, veterinarians' offices, fisheries, fertility clinics, autism-therapy practices, lumberyards, plumbing companies, luxury fashion houses, and prison service providers. It owns Cirque du Soleil and the rights to Taylor Swift's first six albums. The industry manages highways, municipal water systems, fire departments, and emergency medical services in towns across the country, and owns a growing swath of commercial and residential real estate.

Private equity executives, meanwhile, are not only among the wealthiest people in American society, but titans of politics and philanthropy. The central branch of the New York Public Library, the computing school at MIT, the forthcoming humanities center at Oxford, and the performing arts center at Yale are all named after Blackstone cofounder Stephen Schwarzman—the richest man in the industry, with a net worth *Forbes* estimates at $49 billion, and an influential Trump donor. KKR cofounder Henry Kravis has served on the boards of the Metropolitan Museum of Art and Mount Sinai Hospital, where the children's hospital and a cardiovascular center are both named for him. Apollo Global Management cofounder Leon Black was chairman of the Museum of Modern Art board until journalists raised questions about the $158 million he paid to Jeffrey Epstein. Dozens of people have switched from private equity to politics or vice versa, most notably Bain Capital cofounder Mitt Romney but also at least one cabinet member under each of the last six U.S. presidents.

Yet despite all that power and influence, private equity's workings remain opaque to most people. That's by design: the "private" in the industry's name distinguishes it from publicly traded companies not just in terms of their respective sources of funding, but also in terms of transparency. Even the biggest private equity firms must report far less about their structure and operations than other types of companies.

(Until the 2010 Dodd-Frank Act, they generally didn't have to report anything at all.) They need not disclose how their portfolio companies perform, how their own payment agreements are structured, or even which companies they own. Hundreds of millions of dollars spent on lobbying and political donations have helped keep things that way; Republicans and Democrats on Capitol Hill benefit from private equity contributions in roughly equal measure, and neither party has demonstrated interest in further regulating the industry.

The result is that it can be almost impossible to tell what a private equity–owned company is up to: how much money it is winning or losing, what its strategy is, what its executives are paid. That means workers have far less information about their employers than their counterparts at other types of companies, which can leave them in a precarious position if their employer begins to flounder without warning. It also means that the community—or communities—in which the company is based may no longer know whom they're dealing with, much less how to reach them.

THROUGHOUT MOST OF the twentieth century, nearly all major American companies were publicly held: their shares were listed on the stock exchange, available to anyone. Whether an individual bought a single share or ten thousand, they were an owner, eligible to voice their approval or dissent of company strategy in shareholders' meetings and vote on important decisions. Federal regulations, meanwhile, limited the ability of banks and large public corporations to control other large public corporations through huge stock purchases.

In practice, however, that meant few stockholders had any real power; as companies expanded, ownership diluted further and further, until being a public company meant having no meaningful ownership at all. Instead, professional managers were functionally in charge of companies they did not own, a phenomenon first described, disapprovingly, by Adolf Berle and Gardiner Means in their landmark 1932 book, *The Modern Corporation and Private Property*. The separation of ownership and management was not just unfair to shareholders, they wrote: it undermined the entire philosophical basis of American capitalism.

Berle and Means were several decades ahead of their time; the system they saw as so destructive in the early 1930s would only increase its dominance until the 1970s. Then, thanks to the expanding influence of the conservative Chicago school of economics combined with concern over declining corporate profits, their arguments went increasingly mainstream.

Milton Friedman had outlined his objections to managerialism in his 1962 book *Capitalism and Freedom*, but it was his *New York Times* essay eight years later that popularized his "shareholder theory," revolutionized MBA curricula across the country, and set the stage for the rise of private equity. "The social responsibility of business is to increase its profits," the headline announced; the three thousand words that followed warned that any corporate executive who concerned himself with any factors *other* than making his business more profitable—including "providing employment, eliminating discrimination, avoiding pollution and whatever else may be the catchwords of the contemporary crop of reformers"—was a socialist with no place in American capitalism. The sole interest of shareholders is to make money, he argued; the sole job of the CEO is to carry out their wishes. The interests of workers, suppliers, customers, and communities, much less any larger mission, were unworthy of consideration.

Taken to the extreme, this logic—arguably the most important economic theory of the twentieth century—means a company doesn't even need to exist at all. If driving it out of business while selling its real estate and collecting its management fees will make more money than actually producing goods, liquidation is not just the best option, but indeed the only one.

IN THE BEGINNING, the promise of the private equity industry was that it could turn losers into winners.

Financial firms began taking out loans to fund what they called "bootstrap deals" in the 1960s, acquiring companies that were doing well enough but remained too small to go public. The concept was something akin to house flipping: the investment would provide capital to grow and strengthen the company, eventually resulting in an exit that allowed everyone involved to win. These deals became known as "leveraged buyouts," the engine of the private equity machine.

Unlike venture capital firms, which make investments in exchange for minority ownership stakes, private equity funds typically purchase companies outright, assuming full control over their operations. The investors, meanwhile, cede control to the firm. If the leaders of a pension fund are dissatisfied with the performance of a company their money helped buy, they cannot sell their shares; they must wait until the private equity firm makes its "exit"—either taking the company public or selling it to another buyer—or until a specified termination date in their contract.

Most of the money used to acquire a given company, though, doesn't come from these endowments, pensions, and the like. The vast majority of it comes from bank loans—the "leverage" in a leveraged buyout. Between 2013 and 2023, 74 percent of the purchase price for the average leveraged buyout deal was funded by loans.

Large amounts of debt, of course, make for riskier investments. If a company is responsible not just for increasing profits, but for paying back massive loans and *then* increasing profits, the path to success begins to look more like a tightrope over a canyon. The threat of bankruptcy and liquidation increases exponentially. With those kinds of odds, it might seem like a wonder that the private equity industry exists at all. Why would the smartest guys in finance choose to work in a system where the risk of catastrophic failure is so high?

The answer is that the risk of catastrophic failure *is* high—but not for private equity. When a firm acquires a new company, it borrows money in the *company's* name, not its own. Even though the firm is the company's sole owner, even though its executives are the ones who decided to take out the loans, it is not legally responsible for paying the money back. If the acquired company runs into financial trouble, its owners need not bail it out. Even in bankruptcy, when a company declares in court that it cannot pay all of its creditors, the private equity firm that owns it—a firm worth orders of magnitude more than the company itself—won't step in to cover the costs. As secured creditors, banks are the first to be paid back with the money that remains after a bankruptcy, so the threat to them is low too. The company and its employees shoulder the risk.

Some leveraged buyouts still look very much like those early bootstrap deals: stable family-owned businesses that are strengthened by the infusion of cash a private equity firm can provide. These are the deals industry leaders point to when they argue that private equity is a boon to the American economy, and research does indicate that many of them work out well for all involved. But in terms of the number of people affected, these small local companies represent a tiny sliver of the pie. According to a report commissioned by the industry's chief lobbying group, private equity–backed "small" businesses—defined as those with fewer than five hundred employees—employ 1.4 million people, roughly 12 percent of the 12 million total who work for private equity–owned companies.

In the mid-1970s, three executives at investment bank Bear Stearns were frustrated by the firm's unwillingness to back as many bootstrap deals as they wanted. They left in 1976 to form Kohlberg Kravis Roberts & Co., or KKR. There they started to scale their ambitions, targeting large public companies in addition to small family-owned ones, and taking out bigger and bigger loans to finance their acquisitions. They also made sure to maintain sole control over the operations of companies they acquired, despite putting up small fractions of the purchase prices.

Two years after they struck out on their own, KKR executed the deal that would launch the modern private-equity industry. Houdaille Industries had grown from a local auto parts manufacturer in Buffalo, New York, into a Fortune 500 company producing a much wider range of products. Before the acquisition, the company was stable, if hardly exciting, with slow growth in profits and stock price. What it did have was $40 million in cash and just $22 million in debt—until KKR assigned it $300 million in loans to finance a $390 million buyout. KKR itself put up just $1 million. The rest of the finance industry took note. "The public documents on that deal were grabbed up by every firm on Wall Street," one executive later told the *New York Times.* "That showed everybody what could really be done. We all said, 'Holy mackerel, look at this!'" (Later that same year, KKR received a gift to make its system even more profitable: Congress voted to lower the maximum tax rate on long-term capital gains, including private equity profits, from 49 to 28 percent.)

When a recession arrived in the early 1980s, Houdaille was ill-prepared, in part because manufacturing jobs were moving to Japan and in part because KKR had spent $35 million of the company's $40 million in cash to pay down its debt. A 1985 "restructuring" cost 2,200 jobs; two years later, KKR sold what remained to a British company, which swiftly sold back all but one Houdaille division. The vast majority of the company's 7,700 jobs disappeared.

From KKR's vantage, though, the pioneering deal was a success: when the firm sold Houdaille after nine years, it earned a 33 percent return on its investment—not including its management fees—according to two KKR consultants who wrote a history of the firm's operations. In a report commissioned by the firm a decade later, the Houdaille acquisition was described as a triumph, for the simple reason that all its investors made money. "All of the Houdaille 'constituents' . . . fared well in the LBO [leveraged buyout]," the report concluded.

All of them, that is, except for the workers and the towns in which they lived in New York, Iowa, Colorado, and Florida.

So KKR had not turned Houdaille from a loser into a winner, but that hardly mattered, because the shareholders had made money. The leveraged-buyout industry grew quickly after that. Nearly 2,600 buyouts occurred during the 1980s, 7.7 percent of all mergers and acquisitions. Increasingly, these were aggressive maneuvers: about one in three companies on the Fortune 500 in 1980 were subject to hostile takeover attempts over the next decade, almost 90 percent of which were successful. The deal sizes, meanwhile, ballooned. Just a decade after KKR stunned the industry by spending $390 million on Houdaille, the firm shelled out $25 *billion* for RJR Nabisco, still one of the largest leveraged buyouts in history even before adjusting for inflation.

Today, less than four decades later, private equity firms control $8.2 trillion in assets—more than the gross domestic product of any nation on earth except the United States and China.

———

PRIVATE EQUITY EXECUTIVES explain what they do by saying they improve companies to prepare them for a profitable exit—either going public or a lucrative sale. Blackstone, for example, describes its mission as creating "long-term value for our investors . . . by strengthening the more than 230 companies, ~12,500 real estate assets and other investments in our portfolio, equipping them to thrive." Such language has helped create the impression that private equity operates like an intensive care unit, saving companies that would otherwise wither away. Firm executives, then, play the role of highly trained specialists with expertise in each company's operations and ailments.

Yet private equity executives are not experts in each type of business they buy, but in *finance*—mergers and roll-ups and restructuring and real estate plays and tax write-offs. (While firms have divisions specifically dedicated to the core industries in which they invest, the leaders of each division are finance professionals whose focus is financial engineering within the industry, not the work of the industry itself.) Private equity firms own companies for an average of seven years; they're trying to sell for a profit, not grow the business over the course of decades. Investing in research and development, improving products or services, ramping up sales strategies—these are all yearslong processes.

Cutting costs, on the other hand, pays off almost instantly. Unsurprisingly, this philosophy often means shedding jobs. A 2019 paper found that employment shrinks by an average of 4.4 percent in the two years after a leveraged buyout, and 12.6 percent when the company was previously publicly traded. (Two finance professors argued that those figures actually significantly *understated* job losses by miscategorizing different types of buyouts, suggesting that employment shrinks by more than 25 percent in the five years after a public company is bought by private equity.)

Dramatic cuts to a company's staff often don't work—that is, if success is defined by the company staying alive. Researchers found in 2019 that companies acquired by private equity firms are much more likely to go bankrupt than their peers: 20 percent of them enter bankruptcy proceedings within ten years, compared to 2 percent of other companies. That seems an all-but-inevitable outcome of the debt involved in leveraged buyouts; if market forces or increased competitive pressure causes a downturn in revenue, loan payments can easily become overwhelming. And while declaring bankruptcy is not the same as going out of business, research shows that more often than not, companies that go bankrupt do not survive.

But bankruptcy doesn't prevent private equity firms from making money for themselves. Private equity deals typically follow a structure known as 2-and-20: when outside investors commit their money to a private equity fund, they promise 2 percent of their total investment as an annual fee to the firm in charge. The firm also takes 20 percent of all profits from a deal beyond a certain threshold. Additional fees apply for "monitoring" the portfolio company, as well as for transactions like mergers or refinancing. While earning the 20 percent requires the company to turn a profit, the fees are not dependent on performance.

The 2-and-20 setup guarantees a steady source of income to a private equity firm no matter how its portfolio companies fare. The high amounts of leverage and the firm's insulation from a company's debt, combined with tax breaks and other legal protections, mean it wagers very little on any given deal. Taken together, it is very, very difficult for private equity firms to lose money. The only real risk is to the companies, their employees, and the communities they serve.

In Milton Friedman's hypothetical world, focusing only on shareholder value creates an unstoppable network of thriving companies providing goods and services that Americans can't live without. In the real world, the goods and services are, at best, beyond the point—and at worst, an active hindrance to shareholders' larger goals. If a private equity–owned retailer can make more money by selling fewer products, that's what it will do. If a private equity–owned hospital can make more money by eliminating all but the most lucrative services, patients whose care won't increase revenue will be turned away. The profit is the only point.

========

COMMUNITIES, THOUGH, REQUIRE businesses to exist.

Even Berle and Means, the spiritual godfathers of shareholder value theory, reserved some concern for the public: "The economic power in the hands of the few persons who control a giant corporation," they wrote, can "bring ruin to one community and prosperity to another." Even *Milton Friedman*, who argued that businessmen who believed themselves to have social responsibilities were "preaching pure and unadulterated socialism," allowed that there might be exceptions. "A group of persons might establish a corporation for an eleemosynary purpose—for example, a hospital or school," he wrote in his famous essay about shareholder value. "The manager of such a corporation will not have money profit as his objective but the rendering of certain services."

All three men recognized that an individual company does not operate in a vacuum; it plays a role in society. If a store closes, the societal problem isn't just that local residents are inconvenienced by the need to shop farther away, but that its hometown loses out on valuable tax revenue that it uses to pave roads, maintain parks, and buy textbooks. If a hospital closes, the societal problem isn't just that sick people will die without treatment, but that high-paying jobs will disappear. If an apartment building evicts all of its lower-income tenants, the societal problem isn't just that people will be left homeless, but that their government will spend more money on safety-net services.

For private equity, though, the *only* definition of value is return on investment. The inevitable outcome of this philosophy is that a disproportionate number of leveraged buyouts make wealthy finance executives wealthier at the expense of the places where the buyouts take place. In 2024, an economist and a sociologist synthesized a wide range of research to evaluate how private equity affects local communities. Citing data on everything from wage stagnation to increased rents at private equity–owned apartment buildings, the researchers described how private equity undermines the economic power of locally owned businesses, as well as some of their harder-to-quantify benefits. "Local businesses sponsor local sports teams, hire local workers, and benefit the local economy through multiplier effects," they wrote. "When [private equity] acquires firms, these networks are disrupted, and the community experiences a loss of wealth and fragmentation."

The vast majority of the existing books about private equity focus on the macro level: the number of companies that shutter, the number of jobs that disappear, the number of dollars that are won and lost. In the pages that follow, I take another tack. When we talk about how private equity affects communities, we're really talking about how it affects *people*, the individuals who have no choice but to rely on firms for their jobs, their homes, their essential services. Understanding the destruction wrought by this all-or-nothing system requires looking closely at what it has meant for those who have lost out.

This book follows four workers: Liz, Roger, Natalia, and Loren. Each of them saw a private equity firm upend one of four businesses—a retail chain, a small-town hospital, a newspaper company, and an apartment complex—and with it, his or her life. Taken together, their individual experiences also pull back the curtain on a much larger project: how private equity reshaped the American economy to serve its own interests, creating a new class of billionaires while stripping ordinary people of their livelihoods, their health care, their homes, and their sense of security. At heart, this is a story about the hollowing out of the American Dream, and the people trying to do something about it.

When the only worth of a local grocery store, a newspaper, or a hospital is the short-term profits it can generate, the company becomes little more than a mine awaiting extraction. Businesses that were once pillars of a society founder and crumble. In the best-case scenario, money that used to flow continuously through town is redirected to a gleaming office tower in Manhattan. In the worst case, grocery stores and newspapers and hospitals disappear altogether. Workers lose their jobs. Customers lose the services they rely on. Little League teams lose their sponsors. Communities lose their institutions.

Only private equity wins.

BAD
COMPANY

PART I

BEFORE

ONE

LIZ

———————————

ONCE, YEARS AGO, LIZ MARIN WAS TALKING TO A FRIEND WHO HAD recently been laid off. The friend, Annmarie, was fretting because her husband needed insulin to treat his diabetes and she needed an inhaler to treat her asthma, but she had recently lost her health insurance along with her job, and they could only afford to cover the cost of one of the two medications out of pocket. Liz was enraged—at the company that laid her friend off, at the American health care system for failing to provide an adequate safety net, at rich people generally for fighting to preserve the status quo.

She couldn't fix any of those problems, but, she figured, she *could* get her friend an inhaler. Liz didn't have much money either, but she did have health insurance, and she also had asthma. So she did what seemed to her like the obvious thing: she called her doctor, lied that she had lost her inhaler, got a new one, and mailed it across the country to her friend. "Yeah, I know it's insurance fraud," she said later. "But the thought of her dying because she couldn't afford a three-hundred-dollar fucking inhaler, I couldn't fathom that. I have the power to do something, and just because the government calls it illegal is not going to stop me."

Liz can't help herself from speaking up or butting in when she sees injustice in the world—*especially* when someone she loves is involved. Most of the time, it doesn't involve violating federal law. But it doesn't matter how much or how little she has; she won't be happy unless she's sharing it with family, friends, and strangers. Several years ago, her in-laws, who had never lived outside their home country of Colombia, moved to the United States to live with her and her husband, Henry, in Washington State. More recently, her own father, Loren, whom everyone calls Buddy, came from Alaska to the American mainland and began splitting time between Liz's home and her sister Mindy's, a couple hours south in Portland, Oregon.

The Marin house, which sits on a quiet street of cookie-cutter homes atop neatly manicured lawns in University Place, a suburb of Tacoma, is designed to take care of people. In the kitchen, next to stacked cases of Kirkland water bottles, sit value-sized boxes of individually sized snacks—mixed Frito-Lay chips, chocolate and vanilla pudding, Ensure, apple chips, fruit cups. Just above that, on the kitchen counter, is a first aid kit teeming with Band-Aids, face masks, rubbing alcohol, gauze, and painkillers. When Mindy's family comes for the weekend, which happens often, Liz's office is swallowed by an air mattress, the living room overtaken by video-game controllers and kids' shoes, the bathrooms drowned in other people's toiletries.

Like many women socialized to put everyone else first, the one person Liz often forgets to take care of is herself. Sometimes it's because she's too busy. Sometimes she's just too broke from providing for everyone else. A few years ago, the Marins had a little financial breathing room for the first time in their adult lives. When one of the kids outgrew their sneakers, she'd sprint to the store to buy them a new pair, but she hadn't bought herself a new item of clothing in years. Henry encouraged her to go shopping for herself—demanded it, basically—but she didn't see the point. So he threw out her entire wardrobe.

Liz still sounds a little shocked about it all. Henry is the soft-spoken one of the two, the one content to sit quietly, awaiting further instruction, while people mill about. He *adores* his wife. So when he and their children began carrying armfuls of her clothing to a dumpster near their house, she couldn't quite make sense of it. *Now you have no choice but to buy some new things,* he told her.

He didn't realize he had missed a bucket—a literal bucket—full of her oldest, most worn-out clothes. *I'll go shopping tomorrow*, she promised. Instead, she took the clothes from the bucket, folded them, and put them in her dresser. Aside from a few holes and the fact that most of them didn't fit particularly well, they were perfectly wearable. But Henry realized pretty quickly that the holey clothes that didn't fit were not in fact new. The resulting argument lasted for days.

Eventually she bought some clothes. She didn't, however, shake off the guilt. Sitting at the dining room table recounting the story, she wore a threadbare pair of jeans and a six-year-old T-shirt from a Native Alaskan tribal celebration, her long salt-and-pepper hair cascading over the print on the front.

The Marin home is also a monument to the people Liz loves. Family pictures aren't sequestered to the mantel or a single gallery display. They cover every table, shelf, and wall, and feature every imaginable combination of relatives. On the few patches of wall that don't hold photos, traditional Native Alaskan art hangs instead. Often the two are combined: two paintings above the dining room table depict Buddy and his sister in traditional dress at a powwow.

One room, though, is devoted to a different kind of memorabilia. Behind the desk and above the air mattress in the office/guest room, a waist-high bookcase houses dozens of giraffes. Large stuffed ones and bronze ones are surrounded by smaller ones made from plastic, rubber, and wood. Photos rest among the animals, most of them of Liz grinning with friends. In one, her son, Daniyel, holds yet another stuffed giraffe. This giraffe, with the tuft of dark brown hair between its ears and the stars that stud its neck, is recognizable to anyone who has ever stepped inside a Toys R Us. The display is a shrine to Liz's six years at the company, a shrine to what was the best job she ever had until it all came crashing down. The giraffe in the photo, *Geoffrey* the Giraffe, is the one that upended the Marin family's entire life.

———

BEFORE HE LAUNCHED THE TOY store that transformed retail, Charles Lazarus was a poor kid with a dream.

Lazarus was born in 1923 in Washington, D.C., where his father, Frank, owned a not-particularly-successful used-bicycle store called National Sport Shop in the Adams Morgan neighborhood. The Lazaruses, one of the few Jewish families around, lived behind the store: their home was connected to the shop by an opening in the dining room, so someone could get up quickly and help a customer who happened to show up during dinnertime.

The family rarely had money for luxuries. There was always food on the table, even during the depths of the Great Depression, but Charles wanted more. He wanted to be rich. He didn't dream of Madison Avenue or Wall Street. He wanted to sell things to people.

Lazarus, who died in 2018, once told an interviewer about a pivotal conversation he had with his dad while helping him fix up an old bicycle. Charles asked Frank—who had grown up in a Jewish orphanage in D.C. and, by his son's account, never aspired to anything other than the ability to care for his family—why they never sold new bikes, which would bring in more money. His dad responded that new products required too much money up front, and they would never be able to compete with big retailers like Montgomery Ward and Sears, Roebuck & Company. "I just didn't believe that," Lazarus said. "I just thought that you had to have a defeatist attitude to always sell used goods. And I told him, 'I'm not going to do that.'"

When the younger Lazarus got his first job delivering newspapers in elementary school, it didn't take him long to spot a business opportunity. None of the other kids liked collecting subscribers' payments, which often required multiple visits to every home. Lazarus offered to handle that part for them in exchange for a portion of their income. Soon he had six boys funneling him a cut. He quit delivering his own papers; he was making a lot more money than he ever had on his route.

After high school, Lazarus was eager to start his own business. He worked briefly for the U.S. Treasury Department, earning a relatively luxurious $25 a week, but his goal was $10,000 a year, a fortune by American standards at the time. First, though, he knew he would have to serve; it was 1943 and World War II was in full swing. Looking to avoid being drafted into work he didn't want to do, he voluntarily enlisted in the Signal Corps as a radio operator and then cryptographer. Military life brought an important perk: there was nothing on which to spend his salary of about $100 a month. Instead he sent the money home for his mother to invest on his behalf.

When the war ended, an honorably discharged white man with a healthy savings account had plenty of options. The GI Bill offered tuition assistance for college or trade programs, low-interest loans, and unemployment payments. Lazarus, who married his girlfriend, Udyss, almost immediately after returning home, skipped higher education. With a $5,000 wedding gift from his father-in-law, the profits from investing his salary, and a government-backed business loan, he had enough to start a business. The GI Bill's homeownership program also allowed him to buy his first home, in the tony town of Chevy Chase, Maryland, north of D.C. (Until the war, Jews had been banned from Chevy Chase, which was created by the white supremacist developer-turned-senator Francis Newlands in the 1890s.)

Now Lazarus just had to figure out what kind of business would earn him that $10,000-a-year salary and put him in the upper echelons of society. The winning idea came to him as he observed his fellow veterans. After being discharged from the Army, they all followed a similar path: move home, marry your girlfriend, buy a house, have a child or two. Lazarus saw the baby boom coming, and he realized all those new parents would need to buy cribs, rocking chairs, changing tables, and playpens. Frank Lazarus had just about paid off his mortgage on the Adams Morgan building that housed his bicycle store and three apartments, so Charles convinced his dad to retire and offered him $320 a month for the building. National Sport Shop became National Baby Shop, a purveyor of all types of baby furniture.

From the start, Lazarus fixated on how to make even a small neighborhood store a one-stop shop. He expanded his offerings vertically, building shelves to hold chests of drawers *above* their coordinating cribs instead of side by side, which allowed him to display significantly more products at once. He started with about $8,000 worth of inventory, but when his concept proved successful, he used the profits to stock up on new goods. It didn't take too long for him to start doing well—not $10,000-a-year well, but making more money than his father ever had.

Lazarus was always on the lookout for new opportunities, and one day he stumbled into one that would shape the rest of his life. "Somebody came in one day and said, 'How about a toy for my baby?'" he said. "'You know, to play with in the high chair or in the playpen or in the stroller.'" The idea surprised Lazarus, who recalled thinking, *What do you mean, a toy?* He sold essentials, not frivolities; toys didn't fit the model. But he decided to stock a few as an experiment, and from then on, National Baby Shop offered toys along with all its other baby goods.

Until then, people mostly bought toys in department stores. In the 1920s, Macy's opened the country's first permanent toy department in its midtown Manhattan store. The chain also started its Thanksgiving Day Parade, which ended with Santa Claus standing outside that Herald Square building, ginning up excitement to buy Christmas gifts. Not long after, Sears, Roebuck & Company followed suit with a toy department of its own, and quickly became the biggest toy retailer in America.

These big department stores sold more than half of their toys between Thanksgiving and Christmas. But after the woman asked him about toys that day, Lazarus started to think maybe he could show parents that they could use toys year-round. In fact, he thought, toys might actually be a better business than furniture. After all, babies only needed *one* crib, one rocking chair, one changing table, and one playpen, and younger siblings typically got hand-me-downs. Toys, though—no kid could ever have enough toys. Children would out-grow them, wanting new ones designed for their new ages. Or they would simply get bored with what they had and demand something new. And with the prosperity of the postwar era, selling nonessential goods, especially ones that delighted the children of the baby boom, just made sense.

Soon after adding toys to the National Baby Shop inventory, Lazarus went all in. Initially he renamed his store Children's Supermart, with reversed R's to make it appear childlike. But that name didn't look catchy on a sign, and it certainly didn't spark joy in kids. So in 1957, he renamed his company Toys R Us.

⸻

LIZ KNEW WHAT IT WAS like to want more. As a child in Alaska—the state most associated with the American myth of rugged, individual-istic bootstrapping—she heard all the legends about how anyone can will themselves to a more successful life, about how everyone has a chance to make something of themselves.

Her Alaska, though, is very different from the ones written by Jon Krakauer or Jack London. Liz, or Łáxhshaadoosti, is part of the Tlingit people, an Indigenous group who have lived in the southeastern part of the state for centuries. Her family's history as members of the Eagle/ Wolf house in Angoon, a community of a few hundred mostly Tlingit residents on Admiralty Island off the coast of British Columbia, goes back generations.

As Liz likes to say, the fact that she, her family, or the village of Angoon exists at all is pretty close to a miracle. Almost exactly a century before Łáxhshaadoosti was born, her own country's govern-ment attempted to wipe her homeland off the map. On October 22, 1882, a Tlingit healer named Teel' Tlein was killed in an accident on a Northwest Trading Company whaling boat. The United States had purchased Alaska fifteen years earlier and placed the territory under military control, so when the Tlingit reacted angrily to the company's refusal to make amends in accordance with tribal practice, the Navy moved in. They shelled the coastal village with howitzers and Gatling guns mounted on a tugboat before sending troops to raze Angoon on foot, destroying the village and killing six children.

Many Tlingit who were born generations after the bombardment, including Liz and her family, still speak of the event as if it were a fresh memory. Though Alaska was removed from military control in 1884 and became a state in 1959, the Tlingit and other native Alaskan peoples have continued to be discriminated against, cut off from many of the privileges associated with the American Dream. As a child, Liz's mother, Miranda, like generations of Tlingit before her, was taken from her family in Angoon and sent to a boarding school designed to forcibly "civilize" and assimilate Indigenous Alaskans, stripping them of their native language and culture. Liz's father, Buddy, was adopted by a white family who lived on a farm in Missouri, and returned to Alaska as an adult.

As a result, Liz was born in 1979 in Anchorage, not her ancestral homeland of Angoon. She didn't grow up understanding the Tlingit language, because her father never learned it and her mother had been brutally punished for speaking it. Miranda had moved her family to the city so that her children would blend in. In a majority-Tlingit community, they would never escape the risk of prejudice, persecution, or worse.

Life in Anchorage wasn't easy either. Buddy wasn't around much, and Miranda struggled to pay the bills for her own three children and the four she adopted when her sister died. When Liz was in elementary school, her mom remarried, to a man who sexually abused Liz from the time she was eight until she was fifteen. He abused multiple cousins too. All the while, Liz excelled in school, particularly in math. But she also struggled with trauma and relentless feelings of worthlessness.

When Liz was fifteen, her stepfather was arrested for sexual abuse of minors. Liz thought it might be a chance for a fresh start, but soon afterward, Miranda died suddenly from a seizure. Liz tried to care for her younger siblings herself, until an aunt intervened and took them all in. Soon after, the state assigned the kids to different living arrangements: some moved in with relatives, some went to foster care. Liz and her sister Mindy were sent to group homes in Juneau.

Liz completed her high school coursework there, but she missed out on a diploma because she left a few weeks early to care for a now-pregnant Mindy. She gathered up her sister, left the group home, and moved in with their father, who happened to be living in Juneau too. She got a job at Costco to help pay the bills. In 2000, she had her first child, a daughter she named Alleah.

In 2004, Liz was assigned to train a new Costco employee named

Henry Marin on the overnight shift. Henry was from Bogotá, Colombia, and had moved to Alaska to live with his birth father. Liz thought Henry was cute, but he was also six years her junior, and she didn't want to date someone so young. They became friends, though, and she loved how he cared for Alleah. They married in 2005, when Liz was twenty-six and Henry nineteen. She soon gave birth to a daughter they named Aracely.

Liz also loved Henry's ambition. After his night shift at Costco, he would go work days at Burger King. He had plans to become a pharmacist. Liz was used to scraping to make ends meet on a minimum-wage income, but pharmacists make six figures; she knew he could care for a family. The trouble was, there was no pharmacy school in Alaska. Following Henry's dreams and catapulting their family into the middle class would require living thousands of miles from the only homeland she had ever known.

She was terrified at the idea of moving away from Alaska, and hated leaving her family behind, but she knew it was the right thing to do. She hadn't found much in the way of opportunities in Angoon, where the median household income was under $30,000 a year and her family usually made a lot less than that. She hadn't found them in her mom's apartment in Anchorage, or in the group home in Juneau. She lived in a world that had been systematically starved of resources over a period of centuries. Perhaps life on the mainland would be different. Perhaps moving to the West Coast like a twenty-first-century gold rusher would unlock the American Dream she had heard so much about.

Relocating would require Liz to single-handedly support the Marin family—which in 2012 grew to include a son, Daniyel—for four years while Henry was in school. All of her work experience was in retail, so that's where she focused her search. She wanted to be able to easily transfer to any city where her husband got into pharmacy school, so she looked for a job in Juneau that would allow her to move elsewhere when the time came. She needed a company with flexible transfer policies, because Henry would have to do his internship in a different city from where he was studying. She needed opportunities for career growth. She needed daytime hours so she could be home with her family in the evening. As she worked her way down her checklist, one company name seemed to tick every box. So Liz applied to work at Toys R Us.

———

ONCE HE CREATED TOYS R US, Charles Lazarus set out to grow it.

His key strategy was discounting, setting prices so low that no other store could compete. That practice, and the existence of chain stores that could afford to use it, had long been controversial; a 1937 federal law carved out an antitrust exemption to allow a minimum price for retail goods as a way to defend mom-and-pop stores against chains. But by the late 1950s, when Children's Supermart became Toys R Us, minimum price laws had largely fallen out of favor. A 1962 *Time* magazine cover credited Korvettes, a New York–based department store, with making discounting "respectable," reporting that the company kept operating expenses to about half that of a traditional store and turned over inventory about twice as fast. Throughout his career, Lazarus would cite Korvettes founder Eugene Ferkauf as his inspiration for Toys R Us's business model.

The tiny family bike shop on 18th Street in Northwest D.C. was no match for his ambitions, so Lazarus launched his first Toys R Us store in suburban Rockville. Unlike Macy's and Sears, which spent a lot of money to create Christmas windows and children's wonderlands, Toys R Us put no emphasis on aesthetics. Lazarus's priority was stocking the most toys, selling them for the lowest prices, and letting people pick out what they wanted as easily as possible. The store didn't even provide bags; customers could bring their own or carry their purchases in their arms.

The name of the game was volume. Prices were low and inventory was large, which meant Toys R Us could make a small profit on a thousand items rather than a larger profit on just a dozen. The marketing plan, meanwhile, was "no advertising, all word of mouth." The result of all these strategies combined, he explained, was that "everybody said you get real bargains."

By 1967, Lazarus had four stores, and the chain was attracting attention from larger companies. A buyout would make him wealthy and give his company more resources to expand, so he sold Toys R Us to Interstate Department Stores for $7.5 million, or $71.2 million in 2024 dollars. Though he was now richer than he ever dreamed of, he was not the early-retirement type: as a condition of the sale, he maintained almost complete control over Interstate's toy division. His initial annual salary was $60,000—far more than the $10,000 he had once aspired to make, but relatively low for someone in his position—but that was beside the point. Under the terms of the deal, he was also guaranteed 1 percent of Toys R Us's pretax profits. As revenue soared, he became one of the richest men in retail.

The infusion of cash from Interstate allowed Lazarus to dramatically expand the number of Toys R Us stores to fifty-one by 1974, making it the largest toy retailer in the country. As the company expanded, its influence allowed him to engage in some creative legal extortion. Major suppliers were required to debut new toys there, plus offer exclusive products and free advertising—or risk being blacklisted by the company, thus tanking their own finances.

Lazarus was ruthless. But he also took genuine delight in selling products that made people happy. Nobody *needed* most of the things Toys R Us stocked, but nor did he have to give anyone the hard sell. People *wanted* to spend some of their hard-earned cash on toys. They were over the moon about their nephew's second birthday or their third grader's perfect report card or the birth of their first grandchild. "It's a happy consumer as a rule," he once said, "as opposed to a consumer who goes into a car showroom, who's aggravated to start out with, he's going to have to negotiate. . . . It really works out to be a good business from that point of view."

As Toys R Us grew, though, the rest of Interstate's stores weren't faring nearly so well. The company went bankrupt in 1974, and Lazarus regained sole control of Toys R Us, which was described as "highly profitable." Four years later, with sales approaching $2 billion, he took the chain public, remaining the CEO and largest shareholder. He never considered selling again, preferring to rely on his own decision-making in order to maximize profits.

In the process, he drove department stores, once the only major player in the toy business, out almost entirely. Business school case studies now credit Lazarus with pioneering the "category killer," a single company that dominates one slice of the retail industry so effectively that no one else can compete.

———

BUT NOTHING LASTS FOREVER.

The first blow to Toys R Us, and the other category killers it inspired, came from Walmart, whose founder, Sam Walton, considered Lazarus an icon and credited Toys R Us for many lessons he learned about the business. (Lazarus actually sat on Walmart's board for eight years—against the advice of his lawyers, he said later.) The company had been around since 1968, but it expanded rapidly in the 1980s, and its low prices and one-stop shopping model allowed it to begin sucking away business from Toys R Us.

When Lazarus retired in 1994 at age seventy, Toys R Us was still growing, reaching a peak of 1,400 stores worldwide, but the free fall began soon afterward. Within six years, the company stock dropped more than 50 percent. In an attempt to turn things around, the board, on which Lazarus still held a seat, hired John Eyler away from FAO Schwarz, the company known for its luxury toys and the iconic scene of Tom Hanks playing the dancing piano in *Big*. When Eyler took over Toys R Us, Bloomberg wrote that he had gone "from the Ritz to the Motel 6 of toy retailers." "All of retail has become more theatrical," Eyler said. "It's about making it fun. What's fun about going to a warehouse?" Eyler planned to turn Toys R Us stores into well-designed destinations—the exact department store model Lazarus had rejected when he opened his first store in Rockville, the opposite of how he had turned his invention into a category killer.

Enter the Ferris wheel. In Eyler's first big move as CEO, with much fanfare, he paid $35 million to build an 101,000-square-foot flagship store in the middle of Times Square. It had a life-sized Candy Land section laid out like the board game, with a path kids could follow, buying candy as they went. It had a two-story Barbie Dreamhouse, complete with a working elevator. It had a two-story-tall T. rex that turned its head from side to side and roared, baring stunningly realistic-looking teeth. It had personal shoppers. And the centerpiece: a sixty-foot indoor Ferris wheel, visible from the street so as to lure in wheedling children and their weary parents. It was a toy wonderland, and the timing was awful: the store opened in November 2001, just as foot traffic in Times Square was at an all-time low after the September 11 terrorist attacks. The rent, meanwhile, started at roughly $12 million a year and rose quickly as the city recovered.

The second blow came from Amazon. Founded in 1994 as an online bookstore, it expanded into toys and electronics in 1999. The company's ascendance was so dramatic that, just a few years into the twenty-first century, the same companies once vilified for driving locally owned stores out of business—Best Buy, RadioShack, Staples, and Borders, to name a few—were fighting for their own lives.

Most retail leaders decided early on that their only chance of survival in the Amazon era was to develop their own robust e-commerce offerings. Not Toys R Us. A fierce fight was raging for market share in the toy business among Toys R Us, Amazon, and eToys, a hot late-'90s startup. Toys R Us executives were struggling to fulfill online orders, and its leaders pegged Amazon as the best positioned to dominate. Naïvely hoping for a symbiotic partnership, they approached their rival to propose what would become an infamous devil's bargain. Toys R Us would become Amazon's exclusive supplier of most toys, games, and baby supplies. Toysrus.com would redirect to Amazon. And Toys R Us would pay Amazon $50 million a year, plus a percentage of each sale, for the privilege of giving up its own sales platform. The contract would be good for ten years, an eternity in retail—and especially in e-commerce, a world changing so fast that no one could predict what would happen in the next six months, much less a decade later.

Unsurprisingly, Toys R Us got the short end of the stick. In 2003, Amazon sold $376 million worth of Toys R Us products, yet because of the terms of the arrangement, Toys R Us *lost* $18 million on those sales. The agreement did help kill off eToys in 2001—just four years after its buzzy launch—but the spoils were going to Amazon alone. For years after other specialist retailers had developed robust web presences, Toys R Us seemed content to let Amazon eat its lunch.

Then, during the 2003 holiday season, Walmart cut prices on the hottest toys, the very same strategy that Charles Lazarus used to turn Toys R Us into a behemoth. Walmart's scale, though, was orders of magnitude larger, making the company orders of magnitude more powerful than Lazarus's ever had been. That Christmas, Walmart discounted toys and games so far that some items actually cost the company money. But few shoppers were buying just that one item. The "loss leader" strategy led to record profits for Walmart—and helped seal Toys R Us's fate. The retailer limped along for another year, but it had become clear that Christmas 2004 would be its last as a public company.

It was equally clear that only a certain type of buyer would have any interest in acquiring it. Amazon and Walmart had no incentive to take over a chain they were already soundly defeating, and the other toy specialists were either out of business or on death's door. Toys R Us still controlled 17 percent of the toy market, but no one could see a future that didn't involve its slice of the pie continuing to shrink.

From the perspective of someone outside of Wall Street, one option might have been to scale back: close all but the most productive stores, develop a real web presence, and become a specialty retailer offering expertise and quality rather than the world's largest selection. But the people envisioning a smaller Toys R Us were not the people with a few billion dollars to spend. The people with the billions were "turnaround specialists," financial firms that promised to transform distressed assets back into huge public companies. The *Wall Street Journal* reported that all four contenders to buy the chain were partnerships that included a private equity firm: Apollo Global Capital, Cerberus Capital Management, Bain Capital, and KKR.

Notably, two of the four groups vying for Toys R Us also included a real estate firm: Bain was partnering with Vornado Realty Trust, and Cerberus with Kimco Realty Corporation. The *Journal* was unequivocal about the implication. "The inclusion of Vornado and Kimco," it wrote, "is indicative of how the buyers regard the potential investment—largely as a real-estate play rather than primarily as an opportunity to operate retail stores." In other words, selling off the stores' real estate would make far more money than selling toys ever could.

By that point, selling a portfolio company's real estate had become a key part of the private equity playbook, a way to guarantee healthy returns for investors even if the company itself wasn't flourishing. Toys R Us's core business was almost beside the point for Apollo, Cerberus, Bain, and KKR, and entirely irrelevant to Vornado and Kimco. Experts agreed that the chain would need a major overhaul to have any long-term future, but the private equity bidders didn't need to worry about that; selling real estate is a short-term plan, with only an upside for investors. And if—as common sense suggested—requiring Toys R Us to pay rent for the same plots of land it once owned weakened the business instead of turning it around, well, that was just the cost of maximizing shareholder value.

In the end, two of the four bidders joined forces to create the winning group. KKR teamed up with the Bain Capital–Vornado alliance to offer $6.6 billion, which the Toys R Us board accepted in March 2005.

News stories about the deal didn't go into much detail about the ramifications of the real estate strategy for the actual toy-selling arm of Toys R Us. They didn't mention the key term of the contract either. The majority of the purchase price was funded not by the firms themselves, nor by investors who entrusted those firms with their money, but by loans. KKR, Bain, and Vornado borrowed more than $5 billion to finance the acquisition. But, as in any leveraged buyout, they weren't the ones who would have to pay it back. Technically, they weren't the ones borrowing the money at all. The debt belonged to Toys R Us.

BY THE TIME LIZ ACCEPTED a job as an overnight stocker at the Juneau store in 2011, Toys R Us had been owned by private equity for six years. That hadn't been the firms' goal: ideally, private equity looks to turn a company around within a few years and either take it public or sell it again. But without a sharp improvement in sales, Toys R Us's $5 billion in debt made the company an unattractive target for anyone else.

Initially, Liz had no idea who owned her employer; rank-and-file workers rarely need to know which conglomerate ultimately controls the company whose name is on their paychecks. What mattered to her was that the company offered her the ability to advance, and to transfer easily among stores. In 2014, Henry was accepted into the pharmacy program at Pacific University, just outside Portland, Oregon. The Marins would be relocating that fall. The nearest Toys R Us was less than twenty miles away.

Liz's manager at the Toys R Us in Juneau invested in her career ambitions. He committed to teaching her how every part of the operation worked so she would be able to transfer to any department with an opening. So Liz learned how to run the registers and assemble car seats. She learned how to handle inventory for each section of the store. She worked shifts at Babies R Us, which was doing better financially than its sister store. By the time the Marins moved to Oregon, Liz said, "I knew *everything*. I could run a store by myself if I needed to." She immediately got a job at a Babies R Us store in Tigard, a suburb southwest of Portland. Within a year, she had been promoted to floor supervisor.

She had worked retail since she was seventeen, but Toys R Us felt different. The days could be grueling, especially on a $12-an-hour income, and she had her gripes with management, but she felt like she was providing a valuable service to customers, and like they thought so too. Her coworkers, meanwhile, became family. Liz met her best friend when she was assigned to help with the holiday rush at another Portland-area store. When Henry took a pharmacy internship in southern Oregon, she relocated to a store there. She and her colleagues even got Toys R Us tattoos. On her left shoulder, peering over the letters *TRU*, a small Geoffrey the Giraffe head peeks out from underneath the strap of her tank top.

She especially loved the role Toys R Us played in customers' lives. Once, a couple she had gotten to know rushed into her store. She had helped them set up a baby registry once before, but the woman had had a miscarriage. Now the woman told Liz that her doctor had said she was unlikely to be able to have a baby, so she and her husband had joined an adoption waiting list. They didn't know whether they would need a crib or clothes for a kindergartner—until they received a call asking if they could adopt a baby who would be born later that day. They were frantically looking for the basics. Liz dropped everything for two hours to help them, stacking boxes of diapers and fitting a car seat in their vehicle. When the woman apologized for the inconvenience, Liz responded, "Don't apologize to me. This is your life. If you need me, you need me."

A few days later, the couple returned to the store to introduce her to their new daughter. They had named her Liz.

TWO

ROGER

———————
———————

THE FIRST CRUCIAL LESSON ROGER GOSE LEARNED FROM RIVERTON,
Wyoming, was about the existence of black ice.

Roger had always loved the mountains, but mostly from afar. He
grew up in Texas, went to college and medical school in Texas, did his
residency in Texas, worked his first job in Texas. He knew Wyoming
was beautiful, loved the idea of it so much that he specifically went
looking for jobs there, but he was unprepared for a few aspects of the
lifestyle. For one thing, he had never lived in a rural place. For another,
he was a Democrat, and Wyoming is the reddest state in the union.
Then there was winter.

Roger arrived at Riverton's tiny airport from Dallas via Denver
one December night in 1977. He was there to interview for a job at the
primary care clinic in town, but he got the feeling that the locals were
trying to woo him more than vet him: then, as now, recruiting doctors
to practice rural medicine in places like Riverton was like convincing
Wall Street bankers to move to Waterloo.

When he got into town, he went to pick up a rental car. "Beware of
the black ice," said the guy checking him out.

Roger was baffled. "Geez, I really am in a foreign country," he
remembered thinking. "Most of the ice I've seen is pretty clear!"

As he told the story forty-five Wyoming winters later, Roger started
laughing so hard he could barely get the words out. That's a common
occurrence at the Gose home. Roger and his wife, Barbara (everyone

calls her Barbi), are constantly making each other giggle with stories they've happily repeated dozens, if not hundreds, of times. Still built like an athlete well into his eighties—tall and lanky, with wire-frame glasses and a full head of snow-white hair—he's fond of folksy portmanteaus like "I guarant-damn-tee you" and retains his Texas twang even after spending more than half his life in Riverton.

Roger was born in 1939 in Corpus Christi, a midsize but fast-growing city on the Gulf of Mexico where his father, Joseph, built a home for his family. The Goses moved around a lot: first to Wichita Falls, five hundred miles north near the Oklahoma border; then to Austin, where Joseph got his master's degree in education; and finally to San Antonio, where Joseph became the principal of a junior high school. Along the way, Roger's mother, Clara, had three more children: Sylvia, in 1943, who died in infancy; Frank, in 1944; and Martha, in 1949.

The Gose family never went without meals, but they were poor, the five of them crammed into a small house in run-down south San Antonio, fighting for time in the single bathroom. Weekends meant projects for Roger and Frank, like hauling boulders a quarter-mile in a homemade cart for twenty-five cents a load so their dad could build a retaining wall. Summers meant trips to Clara's parents' farm in the Rio Grande Valley to pick cotton—all day, every day, Roger dragging an ever-heavier sack behind him on hundred-degree afternoons.

Compared to all that, school was easy. Roger earned good grades, and he was popular enough to be elected student body president at Brackenridge High. But he felt most at home when he was running. He realized he was fast in junior high, when he reliably beat everyone in playground races. In 1958, his senior year of high school, he ran leadoff on a 440-yard relay team that set the national high school record at the state championships.

He was offered scholarships at Texas Christian University, in Fort Worth, and Pepperdine, in California, but since he was a little boy, he had only wanted to go to the University of Texas at Austin, the state's flagship university. As a sports-obsessed kid, he had rooted for UT in basketball and football. To this day, Roger's home is filled with UT

memorabilia, from large prints of photos taken at football games to a
LONGHORNS PARKING ONLY sign in the driveway to a brick from the old
medical school building. He often dresses in University of Texas swag:
on a freezing day in March, he was in a Longhorns pullover, a Longhorns
T-shirt underneath, Longhorns track pants, and Longhorns sneakers.

He wasn't recruited for track, but he was accepted to Plan II, the
university's prestigious honors program. Part of the appeal of attending
UT was that he thought someday he might like to attend its medical
school. From a young age, he had known he wanted to be a doctor. He
wanted to be like Uncle Austin.

Austin was Joseph Gose's older brother. He and his wife were more
affluent than Roger's side of the family, so trips to his house in Wichita
Falls—a ranching-turned-oil town—offered new levels of fun: piles
of Christmas presents, dove-hunting excursions, celebratory family
meals. Austin wasn't a disciplinarian like Joseph was. Spending time
with him felt like a respite. But most importantly, he was a doctor, and
being a doctor seemed like the best thing in the world.

Uncle Austin was a family medicine physician who did everything
from delivering babies to treating diseases of old age. He had a clinic
downtown, but he did a lot of house calls—scheduled and not. Even if
the family had just sat down to dinner, if a patient in need called, Uncle
Austin was out the door.

The first time Roger appreciated Uncle Austin's stature in the community was when he developed acute appendicitis at age five. In 1944,
removing an appendix was no small task, but with one phone call,
Austin had his nephew in the operating room of the best surgeon in
town. Whenever Roger told the story, even decades later, his voice still
sounded awed by his uncle's power to heal patients. "It was obvious
that he meant a lot to the community. I just totally idolized him," he
said. "In every way I wanted to be in that category."

Fulfilling that goal—and fighting those who didn't see it as
worthy—would come to shape Roger's entire life.

WHEN UNCLE AUSTIN WAS MAKING house calls in Wichita Falls, medicine was "a relatively weak, traditional profession of minor economic significance," in the words of sociologist Paul Starr, whose 1982 book, *The Social Transformation of American Medicine*, remains the definitive work on the business of health care. While his description might sound derogatory, the limitations offered plenty of advantages. Financially speaking, being a physician was as simple as running a grocery store: doctors provided services; patients paid agreed-upon fees. "The doctors escaped becoming victims of capitalism and became small capitalists instead," Starr wrote.

That same basic schema had governed American doctors since before the United States was its own country. After the College of Philadelphia (now the University of Pennsylvania) created the first medical school in the new world in 1765, doctors fanned out to communities across the colonies, treating patients with a mix of pharmaceuticals, leeches, and homemade concoctions. There was no widely accepted licensing system or board certification to validate physicians—anyone who claimed knowledge of medicine could hang a shingle and begin practicing. If a patient found their doctor's advice suspect or disliked his prices, they could simply visit a different one next time.

The idea that general physicians could only ever work for themselves was an unquestionable tenet well into the twentieth century. Either by themselves or with a tiny team of a nurse and a secretary, family practitioners set their own rates, booked their own appointments, billed their own patients. Roger remembers his uncle sometimes accepting gifts in lieu of payment, or simply going without his fee if a patient couldn't afford it. And still, his practice was thriving.

But that setup was becoming less and less sustainable for patients. As science and technology improved, medical care got better, but also much more expensive. In the first three decades of the 1900s, industries where workplace injuries were common, like manufacturing and mining, began offering basic on-site medical services. But for the majority of the population who didn't work in a factory, mine, lumberyard, or railway, medical expenses remained theirs alone. Doctors were divided on the idea of creating a broader insurance system: some favored it as a way to protect patients *and* their own profits, while others considered it perilously close to European socialism. "It is a dangerous device, invented in Germany, announced by the German Emperor from the throne the same year he started plotting and preparing to conquer the world," a group of physicians in California wrote in a pamphlet during World War I.

A major impetus for the eventual movement toward private insurance was the growth of hospitals as a core part of American medicine. Historically, hospitals had primarily been palliative care facilities for the ailing and elderly. Often run by religious or philanthropic organizations, their focus was caretaking, not curing. With the rise of industrialization, though, new urban hospitals were established as cathedrals of science: facilities with labs and advanced technologies and doctors working to *heal* people instead of merely tending to them. When the Baltimore banker Johns Hopkins left $7 million and thirteen acres of land with orders to create a university and hospital in his name in 1873, he revolutionized American medicine by intertwining research, education, and patient care.

For generations, physicians at these hospitals were generally private practitioners, not employees. "Admitting privileges" allowed licensed doctors to follow their patients into the hospital, which meant they didn't have to cede control to someone else. It also allowed them to continue to avoid having bosses; they simply split the cost of a patient's stay with the hospital. Institutions like hospitals were "but expansions of the equipment of the physician," the American Medical Association wrote in 1934. "No third party must be permitted to come between the patient and his physician in any medical relation."

Early in the twentieth century, courts in several states ruled that companies generally could not directly sell medical services because a company could not hold a medical license—an inversion of the "corporations are people" doctrine later established by several court cases in other industries—and that medicine should be free of commercial motivations. These legal prohibitions against the "corporate practice of medicine" eventually spread to thirty-three states. The

party line among doctors was that keeping third parties like corporations out of medicine was about doing what was best for the patient.
It just happened to also be the best thing for physicians' own bottom
lines.

But prohibiting commercial enterprises from practicing medicine
was not the same as keeping financial interests out of the field, especially as hospitals became mainstream. In 1910, roughly 56 percent of
hospitals were for-profit businesses. That created huge costs for those
unlucky enough to wind up seriously ill: while only about 6 percent
of Americans were hospitalized in 1929, their medical bills could total
10 percent of their annual income.

From the providers' side, caring for sick people turned out to be
a terrible way to make money. Some patients couldn't pay but needed
treatment anyway; others required therapies that cost more than a
doctor could realistically charge. Running a hospital successfully but
ethically seemed to require eliminating the need to profit. By the mid-
1940s, just 18 percent of hospitals remained commercial enterprises;
the rest were nonprofits.

The challenge of keeping hospitals from losing money was particularly grim in rural areas. As people moved from the country to
the city, doctors followed, knowing there was more money, and better
equipment, in urban areas. "Just think for a moment what it would
mean if you were cut off absolutely from all kinds of laboratory and
X-ray service, if you were cut off from all association with your
colleagues, from all assistance from specialists, and you were left to
practice everything—every specialty in surgery, medicine, gynecology,
obstetrics, and everything else," New York State health commissioner
Hermann Biggs told a medical society in 1920. "I doubt if there is any
one of us who would undertake this work."

Roger was the exception.

He was inspired to go into medicine by watching how Uncle
Austin ran his business and became a pillar of the community in the
process. But he also realized over time that he wanted to do one thing
differently. Austin practiced in a boomtown, becoming part of a group
of colleagues with access to all the most advanced medical technologies

of the era. Roger was the rare aspiring doctor who set out to do the work Hermann Biggs had scorned a few decades earlier. He wanted a life as a rural community doctor.

———

WHEN ROGER MET BARBARA BAKER at a University of Texas fraternity mixer, she wowed him with her intelligence and wit. His fraternity brothers coached him on how to ask her out, and the pair got serious fast. He quit the frat the next year, but never let go of Barbi; they celebrated their sixtieth wedding anniversary in July 2023. The home they share is filled with books—everything from midcentury philosophy to contemporary literary fiction—and they love to debate current events over the dinner table after reading every word of the day's *New York Times* and *Austin American-Statesman*. Roger feels strongly that attempting to understand the human condition beyond science makes for more attentive, more understanding physicians. There's another advantage too: "Nothing is more boring than going to a cocktail party with a bunch of doctors who can only talk about medicine," he likes to say.

In 1962, shortly after Roger graduated from UT, he and Barbi moved to Galveston, the narrow islands in the Gulf of Mexico just southeast of Houston. He enrolled in the University of Texas Medical Branch, then the state's flagship public medical school, while she took a job as a teacher in a small town nearby. Roger thought he would do his four years in Galveston and then set up shop practicing medicine somewhere in Texas.

The military had other plans. By his fourth year in medical school, doctors were being conscripted to go to Vietnam. If he agreed to spend three years in the service, he could earn a second-lieutenant salary during his final year of classes. Roger jumped at the chance. He thought a stint in the Air Force might help him figure out what he most wanted to do, and the Department of Defense would pay him $222.30 a week (about $2,300 in 2024 dollars). He did his first year of residency at Dallas Methodist Hospital, then was assigned to Westover Air Force Base in southwestern Massachusetts as a flight surgeon for the rest. By the time he was discharged in 1970, he had paid off all of his medical school loans.

Then he had to find a job. He hadn't thought much about leaving Texas—a brief flirtation with a dermatology program in Manhattan left him overwhelmed by the city's chaos and appalled by the cost of renting a tiny apartment. So when an offer came in from a small practice in Garland, a fast-growing city near Dallas, it sounded perfect. He became one of three doctors who rotated shifts on call and had admitting privileges at one of the town's two hospitals. He and Barbi bought a house where they planned to raise their two young boys. Within a couple of years, Roger was named chief of medicine at the hospital. By all accounts, he had made it.

But he wasn't happy. Working as a doctor in Garland came with a certain social scene: the men all golfed at the Dallas Athletic Club every Wednesday; their wives all played bridge. "It was very stereotypical," Roger recalled. "Looking ahead, I could see twenty or thirty years downstream a lifestyle and a practice I didn't know I'd be satisfied with." The most fun part of his life was his trips to Estes Park, Colorado, for medical conferences and training sessions. He and Barbi would drive up with the kids, hiking or camping along the way. Each trip, the lifelong Texans fell a little more in love with the American West.

Back then, physicians often found new jobs via listings in medical journals. One day in 1977, Roger came across one that stopped him. It was one sentence long. "Young, aggressive internist in Mountain West desirous of partner." Gary Smith, who called himself the first full-time primary care physician in Riverton, Wyoming, needed a coworker. Roger called, got Smith on the phone, and made plans to fly to Wyoming on his own dime. His friends in Garland thought he was out of his mind.

When he got to town, it felt like everyone who was anyone had turned out to meet him. Locals were thrilled by the idea that a young man would give up a cushy job in a wealthy area that offered amenities like golf courses and high-end restaurants. Riverton had none of that.

For a moment, Barbi was apprehensive—the potential for unhappy spouses is a challenge for any rural area looking to recruit doctors—but she loved the mountains as much as Roger did, and she didn't feel all that much at home in Garland either. A few days after landing back in Texas, Roger accepted the offer to be the second full-time primary care physician in Riverton.

———

RIVERTON SITS IN the Wind River Valley, nearly in the dead center of Wyoming, more than one hundred miles from any town with twenty thousand people or more. It is surrounded by the Wind River Reservation, which for thousands of years has been home to the Newe, the Indigenous tribe often called Shoshones. In 1878, the U.S. forcibly assigned the Nank'haanseine'nan, or Northern Arapaho—a tribe with whom the Eastern Shoshone had a history of clashes—to share the reservation, an arrangement that continues to this day.

Riverton's primary claim to fame came before its official existence, when "Mountain Man Rendezvous" events were held in the area in 1830 and 1838 as places for explorers, fur traders, Indigenous people, and others to exchange goods and celebrate. (Riverton later dubbed itself "Rendezvous City" and still celebrates the 1838 occasion every summer.) The town's population grew steadily thanks to discoveries of oil and uranium in the area, from 1,600 in 1930 to 8,000 by 1970.

As hospitals became a more central part of the American health care system in the first few decades of the twentieth century, even run-of-the-mill farming towns needed one. A nurse and homesteader named Henrietta Petersdorf opened Riverton Cottage Hospital in 1916, in a large white house that could host up to ten patients at once. But when Petersdorf died four years later, her hospital shuttered, leaving volunteers to take patients into their own homes.

By 1944, Riverton residents wanted their own professional, technologically advanced hospital to replace its system of converted houses. A committee composed of prominent local residents began investigating how to fund a county-owned hospital. They concluded that it would cost $200,000 (about $3.6 million in 2024 dollars) and proceeded to raise $110,000 from a Fremont County bond, $62,000 in a government grant, and the rest from donations. On November 26, 1950, Riverton's first formal hospital opened its doors.

Ten years later, Fremont County acquired an existing hospital in Lander, twenty-five miles southwest of Riverton, and appointed a five-member board to oversee both hospitals' operations and expenditures. To run the hospitals, the county signed a contract with Lutheran Hospitals and Homes Society, a nonprofit operator of rural hospitals based in Fargo, North Dakota. For the first time but not the last, the hospitals in Riverton and Lander would be jointly overseen, their fates intertwined.

Riverton's poverty rates run several points higher than the state average. Per capita income on the surrounding Wind River Reservation is less than $28,000 a year, compared to $77,000 in Wyoming as a whole. Lander has always been wealthier, in part thanks to a world-class rock-climbing scene that has made it a tourist destination. Its Main Street is dotted with multiple coffee shops, two craft breweries, and a cafe serving quinoa bowls and wasabi crab avocado toast. Riverton's Main Street, meanwhile, has a thrift store and pawnshops; most of the town's restaurants, which skew more toward chicken-fried steak than quinoa, are on the state highway that cuts through town, nestled among big-box stores and chain motels.

Lander is also, as any Riverton resident is quick to point out, smaller: about 7,600 people to Riverton's 10,900. Visitors get the sense that Rivertonians have a chip on their shoulder about their fancier neighbor, while Lander residents rarely think about the larger town up the road.

———

WHEN ROGER MOVED TO RIVERTON in 1978 as a thirty-eight-year-old physician, his job wasn't so different from what Uncle Austin's had been: work in the clinic, make house calls, care for his patients in the hospital when necessary, work on-call shifts in the emergency room.

It was a good life. He didn't make as much money as he would have by climbing the ladder in Garland, but plenty to live well and build a house outside of town with panoramic views of the Rockies. He and Barbi didn't even miss big-city amenities all that much. "We're hardly the middle of nowhere; we're the tenth-largest city in Wyoming," he said of his adopted hometown, not a trace of irony in his voice.

Beneath the surface, though, the system governing Roger's profession was shifting. Increasingly, med students didn't want to be general practitioners. Before World War II, roughly three-quarters of all doctors were generalists or part-time specialists. By 1966, the ratio had flipped almost completely: 69 percent were full-time specialists. At the same time, American hospitals were becoming a bigger part of the health care economy, so much so that private practices in small towns like Riverton were becoming an endangered species. Rather than primary care doctors following their patients, more and more hospitals were employing their own physicians—so-called hospitalists, whose entire job was working the wards, treating patients they had never met outside the hospital.

Most Americans aren't used to thinking of physicians as *workers*. They make too much money, have too much societal clout, aren't forced to fight for scraps like, say, factory or retail employees. But by the time Roger had established his career as a practicing doctor, most American physicians had bosses and were part of a nationwide network that included hospital administrators, boards of directors, pharmaceutical companies, insurers, governments, and shareholders. While Roger and a minority of his colleagues still ran their own practices, even they weren't truly independent.

Many rural hospitals, including Riverton Memorial, remained too small to employ a full staff of hospitalists, but the broader shifts in the system meant doctors like Roger were increasingly accountable to their local hospital. In 1979, Roger was elected president of the medical staff at Riverton Memorial, which gave him responsibility for the overall management of the hospital, including staffing, budgets, and contracts. So when the county's efforts to create the first for-profit hospitals in Wyoming spiraled into a federal court case, Roger was named as a defendant despite the fact that he wasn't even an employee.

In 1980, Riverton Memorial was in its fourth decade of operation, and it was plainly unsuited for modern medicine: "There was no way to isolate anyone, so you could have someone with contagious meningitis next to a complex myocardial infarction," or heart attack, Roger remembered. The hospital had been losing money for years, for which he blamed its operator, the nonprofit Lutheran Hospitals and Homes Society: the group had pumped huge amounts of resources into an open-heart surgery program that he saw as completely unnecessary for a rural hospital—complex cases were flown by air ambulance 120 miles to Casper—and then told doctors there was no money to improve the hospital's core functions. He was over it, and he wanted someone else to come in and fix things.

At a public meeting in January 1980, the Hospital Corporation of America (HCA), a for-profit hospital chain, offered to lease the Riverton and Lander hospitals from Fremont County for $500,000 total, or to buy them for "several million dollars," even though Lutheran Hospitals and Homes still held the license to operate both. Lutheran sued for $8.5 million in damages, plus a guarantee that the Riverton Memorial staff and county officials would stop courting or being courted by rival companies. After nine months of back-and-forth in the U.S. district court in Cheyenne, the case was settled, under confidential terms, and the suit was dismissed on August 13, 1981. The Fremont County Commissioners were free to sell their hospitals to other operators. They soon did exactly that, with HCA leasing Riverton Memorial for two years, then buying it outright for $2.6 million. Lander's hospital was sold to a smaller for-profit chain.

After years of mismanagement, the HCA deal looked like an ideal solution. But looking back, a line from one of Lutheran Hospitals and Homes Society's court filings sticks out as prescient: "Obviously, HCA has no interest in making a charitable contribution to Fremont County. . . . You may rest assured that HCA, as a profit-making venture, will not be willing to tax its other profitable operations simply for the privilege of doing business in Fremont County. That leaves only one source of revenue to pay those expenses: the patients who use the two units of the Fremont County Memorial Hospital!"

———

HCA WAS FOUNDED IN 1968 in Nashville by Kentucky Fried Chicken founder Jack Massey and father-son pair Thomas Frist Sr. and Jr. The trio wanted to build a huge—and hugely profitable—corporation, believing that high-quality health care could be provided at scale. That was a radically different vision of "the way healthcare was intended," as HCA puts it in its official company history, than that held by community doctors like Roger, who saw scale and profit margins as contradicting the point of medicine. But it was an increasingly popular philosophy: in 1982, Paul Starr called the final section of his book "The Coming of the Corporation."

HCA's rise was a tiny early sign of what would become a drastic change in the American economy in the late twentieth century, a complete transformation in how revenue was generated. Sociologist Greta R. Krippner calls this shift "financialization": companies began making their profits primarily through financial channels—interest, dividends, capital gains, and the like—rather than through the production of actual goods and services. It wasn't just the growth of investment banks and private equity firms: the ratio of investment income to cash flow at nonfinancial corporations, Krippner found in an influential 2005 paper, was as much as five times higher in the 1980s as in the '50s and '60s.

In other words, even companies that *were* selling goods and services began making much more of their money from everything else. The chief driver of a company's success was no longer supply and demand, but back-end maneuvers both invisible and incomprehensible to the company's employees, its customers, and often even its senior leaders. In health care, where demand was stronger than ever but providing services was less lucrative, this posed an opportunity for firms that specialized not in medicine, but in consolidation and conglomeratization.

Throughout the 1970s, hospital chains grew faster than the computer industry. Corporations had seemingly endless appetites for hospitals, and none were hungrier than HCA. Two years after its creation, HCA owned 23 hospitals, more than any single company. A decade later, the company owned more than 300.

Then, as now, Roger wasn't wild about the idea of hospitals being owned by for-profit corporations. All else being equal, he would have preferred to return to the days when doctors were independent operators and national conglomerates had no interest in health care. But he was also a realist. The Lutheran Hospitals and Homes Society had neglected Riverton, and that hurt his patients. And the county didn't have a tax rate high enough to build something new without outside help. Selling to one of the large for-profit companies looked like the only option to provide the high-quality care he believed his neighbors deserved.

From HCA's vantage, meanwhile, Riverton fit perfectly into their fast-growing portfolio. A key component of the company's strategy was acquiring rural facilities that had "failed to thrive" under nonprofit ownership, as the *Tennessean*, HCA's hometown newspaper, put it. That was exactly the situation Riverton found itself in.

It wasn't alone. In 1986, 46 percent of "community hospitals"—those not affiliated with a university or residency program—lay outside of metropolitan areas, but researchers found that 600 of the existing 2,700 were at risk of closure by 1990. The causes they identified all boiled down to money: rural residents didn't have enough of it, which meant the hospitals that served them were seen as financially inviable. Young people were moving out of town, leaving the hospitals to serve disproportionately older ones in need of more expensive care while relying disproportionately on Medicare payments, which were lower for rural hospitals than urban ones. Poverty rates were significantly higher in rural areas than elsewhere, while significantly fewer eligible rural residents received welfare or other safety-net benefits than urban or suburban ones, leaving them less money to pay out of pocket.

The idea that hospitals had an obligation to make money, no matter where they were located or what kind of populations they served, went without saying. That idea powered for-profit companies like HCA, but also nonprofit operators like Lutheran Hospitals and Homes Society, which were focused on expanding throughout rural America. HCA's founders may genuinely have believed that they were well situated to improve the care patients received, but they would never have entered the world of rural health care had they not believed they could wring more money out of hospitals like Riverton Memorial than their previous owners had.

But this mindset was not inevitable; it was a choice, and a distinctly late-twentieth-century one. The concept of a for-profit hospital largely did not exist until Richard Nixon's administration created health maintenance organizations (HMOs)—the basis of employer-sponsored health insurance—in 1971. Even Milton Friedman, the creator of shareholder value theory, had allowed that hospitals were a special case. Within a mere few years, though, this perspective began to look almost quaint.

Without involvement from a corporation like HCA, Riverton may well have been left with no hospital at all; rural facilities were closing regularly across the country. Riverton's hospital sits twenty-eight miles from Lander's, but few Rivertonians would agree that Lander counts as local, at least in the case of a medical emergency. The brutal combination of snow and wind leads to travel bans multiple times each winter; whiteout conditions make it remarkably dangerous. "People say, 'Oh, just drive to Lander,'" said Corte McGuffey, a Riverton native who moved home to raise his family after two decades away. "Well, there's times we can't."

HCA, though, didn't want to close Riverton's hospital. In fact, HCA wanted Riverton Memorial to be a top-tier community facility. After spending millions to buy it, the company invested millions more in building a new facility from scratch—one with a proper intensive care unit and real isolation rooms. Its administrators seemed to listen to doctors and give them what they needed. Riverton started to appear on lists ranking the best rural hospitals in the country. Though Roger had been hesitant about corporate involvement in hospitals, he got over his fear of HCA pretty quickly. To his mind, the company was "our savior."

FOR THE MAJORITY OF HIS career, Roger's mostly positive feelings about HCA didn't change. He never felt like a cog in a multinational machine even as the company grew dramatically. His life was about his patients; HCA kept things running so he could take care of them.

That's not to say things were perfect. Doctors would cycle in and out, sometimes accepting a job in town only to realize the reality of rural medicine wasn't for them or that their spouse was miserable in a town with little to do. (This was never a problem for Barbi, who seems practically allergic to sitting still even in her eighties: she taught history and women's studies at Central Wyoming College for decades, joined the local library board, and volunteered for just about every charitable cause in town.) That left Roger and his colleagues chronically short-staffed and overworked. And working in rural Wyoming meant fewer resources than he would have had if he had stayed at the hospital in Garland, Texas. "It was demanding, but I asked for it," he said. "Doctors are very good at bitching and moaning, but they're not very good at problem-solving. My attitude was, look, if you're not going to get in here and problem-solve, you give up your bitch rights."

HCA kept getting bigger, snapping up multiple hospitals when possible and picking off its rivals through acquisitions. In 1994, HCA merged with its top competitor, the Kentucky-based Columbia Healthcare Corporation, creating the largest health care company in the world. Owning more hospitals, the company said, would allow it to strike favorable deals with suppliers, offer more types of care across the network, and streamline central services. It still wasn't clear whether anyone could save America's floundering rural hospitals, but consensus said that financial efficiency through consolidation offered the best shot. That kind of language felt a world removed from Roger's life as a community doctor, but he was willing to give it a shot.

So Columbia/HCA became the poster child for a new model of financially efficient health care. It also became infamous for fraud. In March 1997, the FBI, the IRS, and the Department of Health and Human Services searched the company's offices in El Paso, Texas.

More than a dozen employees eventually filed federal whistleblower suits. The allegations included fraud of several varieties: deliberately inflating expenses, ordering huge numbers of unnecessary blood tests to bring in more federal money, striking illegal sweetheart deals with doctors in exchange for patient referrals. In 2003, a decade after the first whistleblowers came forward, the Justice Department settled with the company for $1.7 billion in fines, the largest health care fraud penalty in U.S. history.

Yet at no point did the scandal prompt a larger reckoning over how profits had become the driving force behind the American health care system, or what to do about it. When the Clinton administration tried to make a bid for universal health care, insurance lobbying groups told Americans that changing the system would cause prices to rise and quality of care to fall. Former HCA CEO Rick Scott, who would go on to serve as a U.S. senator, became a leading voice against health care reform. The shareholder value philosophy had taken over American medicine.

In 1997, HCA's rural hospitals were assigned to their own division, called LifePoint; two years later, as part of the overhaul prompted by the lawsuits, LifePoint Health became its own publicly traded company. Throughout the first six years of the twenty-first century, LifePoint went on a buying spree, acquiring thirty-seven hospitals. Most were similar to Riverton Memorial: small, rural, making less money than company executives believed they could. A company SEC filing from early 2007 used classic industry jargon to describe LifePoint's business strategy: buying other hospitals would "continue to provide efficiencies and enhance LifePoint's ability to compete effectively in complementary markets."

Most significant for Roger and Riverton was the second of those thirty-seven acquisitions. On July 1, 2000, LifePoint bought Lander Valley Medical Center, the hospital twenty-eight miles down the road from his own. After nearly two decades apart, Riverton's and Lander's hospitals would be part of the same parent company once again.

FOR YEARS AFTER RIVERTON MEMORIAL joined LifePoint, nothing changed. Roger continued treating patients in his clinic and in the hospital, watching his neighbors grow up under his care. Confident that his patients were in good hands, he retired from his practice in 2012 at age seventy-three. He and Barbi wanted to travel—both tennis fanatics, they've since been to Wimbledon, the Australian Open, and the French Open, among many other adventures—and spend time with their grandchildren. But he remained on the hospital's board, eager to continue to help Riverton Memorial any way he could.

As a board member, he supported one of the most consequential decisions in the history of the hospital. In 2014, LifePoint formally merged the hospitals in Lander and Riverton into one, which the company called SageWest. SageWest Riverton and SageWest Lander would still operate separately, but some of their central services would be combined. Roger was unconcerned: he'd had a good relationship with LifePoint as a doctor and board member, and he understood the financial pressures facing his for-profit hospital. Working more closely with Lander's hospital seemed like a good idea; it would allow each to spend less money on administrative costs. And even as LifePoint's stock price dropped, Riverton's hospital was profitable, he said.

Still, squeezing juice from the health care fruit was getting more difficult. Just as in the 1980s, the cost of care was rising while the number of admitted patients was falling. Now there was a new problem: changes to Medicare and Medicaid reimbursement policies were leading to less revenue. It was starting to look like making money from hospitals was going to require more creative solutions.

Private equity firms saw an opening. If patient care wasn't going to lead to profits, perhaps tricks of the trade could. Selling off hospitals' land and eliminating services and providers would go a long way. They could also take advantage of financial engineering maneuvers available to Wall Street firms but not to pure health care companies.

U.S. tax law helps private equity in several key ways. Like many types of corporations, private equity firms are based offshore, which allows their returns to compound tax-free. Interest payments on borrowed money, meanwhile, are tax-deductible. But most importantly, private equity profits are treated not like those of every other imaginable type of business, but as "carried interest," a structure unique to the finance industry.

The concept dates back to the Middle Ages, when ship captains tasked with moving goods across the Mediterranean faced threats of shipwreck, piracy, and mutiny. To incentivize safe transport, whoever was waiting for the cargo would offer an incentive: a stake in whatever profits came from the future sales—a literal interest in what the ship carried.

In modern times, carried interest has been treated not as regular income but as capital gains, which comes with preferential tax rates. Corporate and individual income taxes top out at 37 percent; capital gains are taxed at 20 percent. Presidents Obama, Trump, and Biden all promised to close the so-called carried interest loophole; none did. Victor Fleischer, a tax law professor at the University of California, Irvine, estimated that maintaining the loophole would cost the government $200 billion in lost tax revenue over ten years. As the *New Yorker* put it in 2012, "for an industry that's often held up as an exemplar of free-market capitalism, private equity is surprisingly dependent on government subsidies for its profits."

These tax breaks helped make private equity a major force in other industries in the 1990s and 2000s, but the industry remained a bit player in health care. HCA's success began to change that. Still reeling from its record fine for fraud and suffering from a declining stock price, the company put itself up for sale in 2006, looking for a buyer who could restore stability. That November, a group including KKR and Bain Capital bought it for $33 billion, replacing the 1989 RJR Nabisco acquisition as the largest leveraged buyout in history and dramatically expanding private equity's public profile.

It was a risky bet on a volatile industry, but it paid off. HCA returned to the public market in 2011, setting a record for the largest initial public offering of a private equity–owned company. The value of KKR and Bain Capital's investment more than tripled. The firms had figured out "how to get more revenue from private insurance companies, patients and Medicare by billing much more aggressively for its services than ever before . . . [and reducing] the cost of its medical staff, a move that sometimes led to conflicts with doctors and nurses over concerns about patient care," the *New York Times* reported.

After the HCA triumph, everyone in private equity wanted in on health care. In the four decades since the company was founded, financialization had become the primary engine of the American economy, and private equity had become one of the most powerful forces in American capitalism. But broader economic shifts meant that some of the industry's early targets, including manufacturing and retail, no longer seemed like good bets. Health care, though, would always be big business. The same changes that worried public health experts—including America's aging population and growing chronic-disease burden—presented an opportunity for investors focused on shareholder value. And HCA had shown just how lucrative the payouts could be.

The 2010 Affordable Care Act honed private equity's interest in hospitals even more. The law's passage meant far fewer uninsured Americans, which meant increased demand for hospital care, which meant an opportunity to make more money. Throughout the 2010s, health care was the hottest market for private equity.

And 2018 was the hottest year yet, with multiple multibillion-dollar acquisitions. Firms weren't just targeting the HCAs of the world, the ones that had already shed their rural hospitals in favor of wealthier urban and suburban ones. The third-largest deal that year was a chain of small-town hospitals whose stock price had been in free fall: on July 23, Apollo Global Management agreed to pay $5.6 billion for LifePoint Health.

THREE

NATALIA

BEFORE SHE MOVED HOME TO SOUTH TEXAS, NATALIA CONTRERAS kept two sticky notes tacked to the bathroom mirror of her rental apartment in Austin. Written in her own neat script in thick black marker, the three-by-three squares drew her attention every time she washed her hands or applied her makeup. "You have more power than you realize!" announced a fluorescent green note. Just below and to the right, a neon pink one carried a more specific message: "News organizations need people like you!"

As a kid, Natalia didn't dream of being a journalist, but looking back, she can see how it happened. She's thrilled to talk to new people for as long as they'll let her, the type of person who answers a question with a twenty-minute story peppered with expletives and colorful descriptions. She's endlessly curious about the world, about why everything from America's voting system to her favorite local Mexican restaurant works the way it does. With long straight black hair parted to the side, a Cindy Crawford–esque birthmark just beneath her mouth, and perfect eye makeup, she exudes glamour, but her wide smile makes her easy to talk to.

Natalia was born in 1989 in Tampico, a midsize city three hundred miles from the U.S. in the Mexican state of Tamaulipas. Her parents divorced before she was out of diapers, and she never had any siblings. As far back as she can remember, it was always just her and her mom, Luz, at home. Luz was a teacher, and to make ends meet, she worked multiple shifts: she would drop Natalia off at private school early in the morning, then continue on to her first job of the day. In the afternoon, Luz would teach at a second school, while Natalia would take a school van to her grandparents' house and stay there during her mom's afternoon and evening classes.

Every day, Natalia's grandfather read the afternoon newspaper as soon as it was delivered, and both grandparents watched the news on TV. Natalia wasn't especially interested in the coverage; it was always something "terrible, terrible, terrible," she remembered. Her cousins, who lived nearby, sometimes came over to play, but mostly she was on her own for hours, watching cartoons in the bedroom or talking to her friends on the phone until her mom picked her up at 8 or 9 p.m.

Natalia didn't like school much—she thinks in part because she had undiagnosed attention-deficit hyperactivity disorder. She realized later that she actually liked reading, but her school didn't assign novels, just boring textbooks. And she constantly got in trouble in class for talking. In elementary school, she remembered, a teacher said, "Natalia, I never see your face; I only see the back of your head." "And it was true!" Natalia said, laughing.

Saturday brought time with her mom. Natalia and Luz would pick a restaurant for breakfast. On the way, they would stop at a newsstand, where Luz—ever the teacher—would instruct Natalia to pick out something, *anything*, to read. As they ate, Luz would read the newspaper while Natalia flipped through a magazine about beauty or celebrity gossip. Then they'd go hang out at the beach or see a Julia Roberts rom-com dubbed into Spanish. When possible, they'd sneak into a second movie afterward; for years, Natalia had only seen the last scene of *Bridget Jones's Diary*, the one where Renée Zellweger sprints through the snow in her tiger-print underwear to find Colin Firth, then makes out with him in the street.

When Natalia was in middle school, her life flipped upside down. Through a friend, her mom met a man from Corpus Christi, a Gulf town in Texas. Within a few months Luz was making plans to move with Natalia to the U.S., a country Natalia had never even visited. She was in seventh grade, with a close-knit group of friends and crushes on boys. Moving 450 miles away, to a country whose primary language she didn't speak, felt unfathomable. But she was excited too. Her wealthier cousins had passports, and they frequently crossed the border to shop, go to Six Flags, and eat at Mr Gatti's—a place Natalia describes as "like Chuck E. Cheese, but better." She figured her school would look just like the one in *Saved by the Bell*, a show she loved. Plus, Selena was her favorite singer, and Corpus Christi was *Selena's hometown*.

When Natalia arrived in Texas at the beginning of eighth grade, her mom and new stepdad wanted her to go to Baker, a highly regarded middle school that also happened to be just down the street from their house. But Baker offered no resources for students who didn't speak English, and the counselor pointed out, correctly, that Natalia didn't. The counselor suggested she go to Martin, which was all the way across town, in a building that seemed dark and scary. She and Luz said no, she'd pick up English on her own as a Baker student.

School had never come easily to Natalia, even in her first language, but her new English teacher, Ms. Guerra, refused to let her skate by. One day, the teacher kept her after school to rework an assignment. They sat side by side in the library, the teacher explaining the work over and over until Natalia understood. Ms. Guerra also always made sure to tell people "Natalia is bilingual," never "she doesn't speak English." That made Natalia feel special, like speaking another language was a superpower instead of a disability.

There were a lot of Latino students at Baker, but Natalia learned the hard way that few of them spoke anything close to fluent Spanish. She'd try to talk to them and they'd look at her blankly; they'd try to talk to her and she'd do the same. But she was an extrovert, so she had no choice but to figure it out. One day, a girl asked to borrow Natalia's pencil. That taught her how to ask to borrow something, and it gave her an opening to befriend the girl. Another girl never seemed to say anything, which struck Natalia as strange because *she* literally always had something to say. She decided to find out why. It turned out the girl was just shy, but Natalia's investigation made them friends too. "At the time, all I could do was observe and try to figure out what was going on," Natalia said. She didn't realize it at the time, but later, it seemed obvious: she was teaching herself how to be a journalist.

Natalia realized as an adult that there was another reason she was destined for a life as a reporter: before she was born, both her parents had been journalists. They met in the newsroom of a newspaper called *El Heraldo*—Luz was a reporter for the society pages, Natalia's dad a cartoonist and illustrator. There were three newspapers in Tampico at the time, but *El Heraldo* was the most important, a progressive trailblazer with a storied history of advocating for workers and peasants and providing much of the best coverage of the Mexican Revolution.

In July 1981, eight years before Natalia was born, *El Heraldo*'s staff went on strike, demanding better wages and benefits. Low pay was a chronic problem for newspaper reporters in Mexico, and the journalists' union believed *El Heraldo* was making plenty of money that it should be sharing with its reporters, so they occupied the building, blocking its owners from entering. The owners refused to negotiate, and the workers were locked out of their jobs permanently. The newspaper never published again. So Luz became a teacher.

Back in Mexico, when Luz would drive by the abandoned, graffiti-covered *El Heraldo* building, she would tell her daughter stories about the strike. Natalia took note of a key detail: years later, long after Luz had left journalism behind, a judge ruled that the newspaper's owners owed every member of the union back pay. Luz won a decently sized payout. Natalia never forgot that story.

———

NATALIA HAD ALWAYS ENJOYED DRAWING and painting, so she thought she might try to become an artist like her biological father. During her senior year in high school, she joined the yearbook staff and developed an interest in photography. But she also discovered that she loved interviewing members of student clubs; after years of getting in trouble in school for talking instead of doing her work, she almost couldn't believe that now teachers *wanted* her to go ask her classmates questions.

After graduation, Natalia enrolled at Del Mar, the local community college in Corpus Christi. She knew she needed to sign up for intro English and math classes to be able to transfer to a four-year school, but she wasn't prepared when the registrar asked her what kind of degree she wanted to earn. She said she liked art and photography, but Luz, who had accompanied her to the appointment, pointed out that she also loved to write. The registrar offered a suggestion: "There's a newspaper here if you want to do that." Suddenly, that idea seemed perfect. She was directed to the journalism department, where she signed up for the intro-level class in news writing as well as the staff of the student newspaper, the *Foghorn News*.

Both the class and the newspaper were overseen by a professor named Robert Muilenburg, who taught Natalia how to report and how to structure a news article. But he also preached a more fundamental lesson: being a journalist, Muilenburg explained, is not just about talking to people, but about closely following current events. Natalia had never picked up on her family's habit of reading and watching the news every day, but now she wanted to know everything that was happening in the world. "If I didn't know it, I was like, 'Fuck, I feel stupid that I don't know.'" That's how she started reading the *Corpus Christi Caller-Times*. That's how she started to think, for the first time, about a career as a reporter.

═══════

IN 2008, THE YEAR NATALIA started at Del Mar, there was plenty of news to follow. The world was mired in the second year of the worst economic crisis since the Great Depression. Congress passed the historic bank bailout during her first semester. A month later, Barack Obama was elected president.

The newspaper industry was also in the midst of upheaval. Advertising revenue plummeted during the recession, nearly 30 percent across the industry in the first quarter of 2009. That led to layoffs in newsrooms across the country. In 2009, the *Baltimore Sun* laid off 61 employees, nearly a third of its newsroom; the parent company of *Time*, *Fortune*, and *Sports Illustrated* cut around 540, a year after cutting around 600. The *Los Angeles Times* laid off 300 and folded its state news section. In a single week in June 2008, roughly 900 people at nine newspapers were informed their jobs would disappear. Even the vaunted *New York Times* announced it would "trim" 100 jobs in 2008 and another 100 in 2009. Swaths of journalists a few years older than Natalia, the ones just starting their media careers, were driven out of the industry for good.

But the Great Recession didn't create newspapers' financial crisis. Media industry leaders had done that to themselves.

Long before the internet glimmered to life, even medium-sized towns were home to as many as half a dozen newspapers. Each charged as little as possible so they could boast they had the most readers— even if the low price of those subscriptions didn't cover the cost of getting the paper to people. The real money came from advertisers, and advertisers liked lots of subscribers.

Many economists and other experts, including those affiliated with the United Nations, consider journalism a "public good." In technical terms, that means it is both "nonexcludable" and "nonrivalrous": many people can access it at once, and consumers don't need to pay in order to benefit from it. In other words, news spreads. Even if you don't pay for the *New York Times*, for example, information from its biggest stories will be aggregated and reprinted in numerous free outlets, and discussed in coffee shops and around the dinner table, not kept secret from everyone who fails to subscribe.

Because public goods are expected to serve the public interest, they are often funded by taxes. In the United States and many other democracies that guarantee an independent press, journalism is a striking exception. While public television and radio are partially taxpayer-funded, the vast majority of American publications and broadcast outlets are owned by for-profit companies. Media is almost singular among public goods for how it must grapple with competing notions of value: worth to the community versus worth to profit-minded executives.

That anomaly has always made journalists vulnerable to owners looking to maximize shareholder value. But for most of U.S. history, their goals were more or less aligned. As Warren Buffett, who once owned more than two dozen newspapers, put it, they were the "ultimate bulletproof franchise": everybody read their local newspaper in part because it had ads for every local business, and it had every ad because everybody read it. For much of the twentieth century, running a profitable newspaper barely required any strategy, Buffett said—the perfect place to stash an "idiot nephew" in need of a cushy job.

In the early 1900s, there were newspapers for every type of person: morning versus evening delivery, conservative versus liberal editorial pages, sensationalist versus straight-down-the-middle sensibilities, stories and ads targeting factory workers versus bankers and lawyers. In the first decade of her journalism career, Natalia would work at three papers—the *Caller-Times*, the *Indianapolis Star*, and the *Austin American-Statesman*—all of which once had competition in their hometowns. By 1999, when the evening *Indianapolis News* stopped publishing, none of them did. That made those three newsrooms typical. By the start of the twenty-first century, just 1.4 percent of U.S. cities had multiple local newspapers.

That shift proved lucrative for newspaper owners in the short term. Suddenly each surviving newsroom had sole control over its market. Between 1975 and 1990, ad rates jumped 253 percent, nearly twice as much as inflation. As recently as the early 2000s, this rapid growth created fears that newspapers could grow *too* powerful. When the *Denver Post* and *Rocky Mountain News* agreed to centralize their printing and commercial operations in 2001—while continuing to operate separate newsrooms, preserving Denver's status as the rare two-newspaper town for another eight years—then–attorney general Janet Reno had to approve an exemption to antimonopoly regulations.

Looking back, the idea that two newspapers sharing a printing press could violate antitrust laws is laughably quaint. The following decade showed that the concept of a newspaper holding a monopoly was a castle in the sky. In rapid succession, Craigslist took over the classified ads market; print advertising revenue fell off a cliff; readers became accustomed to getting journalism free online and stopped paying for print subscriptions; local TV news stations expanded their web coverage to go head-to-head with daily papers; Google and Facebook gained control over outlets' readership and local ad markets; owners began cutting back on true local news in favor of cheaper syndicated coverage; and the advent of ad-targeting technology undercut the prices publications could charge. The vast majority of American newspapers might have been the only one in their respective towns, but they didn't hold monopolies either as news purveyors or places to buy ads.

Traditional journalism business models were becoming difficult to sustain, in large part because executives were unable to catch up to, or keep up with, the changing world. Publishers failed to anticipate the downturn in the ad market, failed to adapt to the rise of the internet, failed to protect themselves against social media devouring their market, failed to develop a strategy for online subscriptions. They failed to take advantage of their status as one of the few types of court-endorsed monopolies. Long before Natalia dreamed of a career in journalism—long before she was born—newspaper executives' blind spots were creating the conditions that would usher private equity firms through the doors.

BY THE TIME SHE BEGAN reporting stories for the *Foghorn News* in late 2008, Natalia knew the media industry was in trouble. Her professors talked about the financial challenges newspapers were experiencing, and the dwindling number of jobs. But Natalia had discovered she loved reporting more than anything she had ever done, and she couldn't imagine doing anything else. She wasn't going to be talked out of a career in journalism.

She was also committed to improving her skills, no matter how much hard work it took. Muilenburg, the newspaper advisor, was legendarily tough on his student journalists. He rarely doled out compliments, only criticism. But she thrived on the feedback: "He didn't just say 'this is terrible,'" she remembered later, "always 'this is terrible, *because* . . .'" She would write down what he said, resolving to do better next time. She never forgot what happened when she filed one of her first stories, for which she had taken her own photos. "Did you get their names?" Muilenburg asked of the people in the picture. Sheepishly, she admitted she didn't. "We're not going to be able to use it now!" he told her. "Next time get everyone's names!" She never made that mistake again.

By her second semester on campus, Natalia was promoted to managing editor, which came with a small stipend. That spring, the staff went to the annual conference of the Texas Community College Journalism Association, which would crown one student its Journalist of the Year. The title was prestigious in its own right, but more importantly, it came with a guaranteed summer internship. Natalia was nominated for the award in the spring of 2009. She desperately wanted that spot in a professional newsroom.

A girl from Amarillo, in the extreme north of the state, won the title. But something surprising happened: the judges had been impressed by Natalia, so impressed that they awarded her an internship too. The summer after her first year at Del Mar, Natalia went to work for the *Corpus Christi Caller-Times*, her hometown paper.

She knew the pressure was on. She had one more year of community college, during which she would have to apply to four-year schools. So when she got to the newsroom, she resolved to outwork everyone. "I was always fucking on time. If they told me, 'Go here, go there, do this,' I was like, 'Yes, yes, yes.'" She wrote breaking news, obituaries, crime stories, event previews, profiles of local residents. When she filed a bad draft, she memorized what the editor told her about how to make it better, and she fixed it the next time.

One day, Natalia was assigned to cover a Bob Dylan concert, for an article and for the paper's fledgling social media presence. *Just tweet what songs he's playing*, an editor instructed. The problem was, she had barely heard of Bob Dylan—even a decade and a half later, telling the story, she struggled to come up with his name—and didn't know a single one of his songs. So she found a guy in the crowd, clearly a Dylan superfan, and stood next to him all night. Every time a new song started, he told her what it was, and she would put it on the paper's Twitter account from her BlackBerry Pearl. "It was very much an intern moment, but I did the assignment," she said, laughing. She loved working at a real newspaper.

In 2009, the *Caller-Times* still had more than a hundred people on staff between writers, editors, designers, copy editors, and photographers. There was a features department, a bustling sports desk, even a couple of reporters covering local real estate. The paper was owned by the E.W. Scripps Company, which had bought it and four other midsize papers from a San Antonio–based firm in 1997. Scripps wasn't a big player in newspapers; in 2004, before the worst of the industry's challenges began, it only served about 1.5 million readers, spread among twenty-two newsrooms. But it *was* a highly profitable company. In 2004, its profit margin was 35 percent, compared to 20 percent at the *New York Times* and around 10 percent at the typical Fortune 500 company. By 2008, the year before Natalia arrived at the *Caller-Times*, revenue had plummeted at Scripps (and every other newspaper chain), but the company's profit margin was still a healthy 14 percent.

To many people, 14 percent profits in an industry trying to adapt to seismic change would be a cause for celebration. But to the corporations that owned an ever-growing number of American newspapers, the acolytes of the Milton Friedman gospel, 14 percent was a crisis. Just as Natalia was starting her journalism career, the executives who controlled the industry were working to reinvent how daily newspapers operated—at the expense of an almost unfathomable number of journalists.

———

DURING HER SECOND YEAR AT Del Mar, Natalia was accepted to the journalism program at the University of Texas at Arlington to complete her bachelor's degree. The school was just outside of Dallas, more than six hours from Corpus Christi. It would be her first time living away from home.

As soon as she got to campus, she applied to join the staff of the *Shorthorn*, the university's award-winning daily student newspaper. The staff of major college dailies skew toward the obsessive and cultish, boasting about pulling all-nighters in the newsroom and treating coverage of picayune scandals as if they're the Pentagon Papers. Budding student journalists tend to react one of two ways: either they dive headfirst into the depths of the mania, never emerging until graduation day, or they feel totally alienated and quit as soon as they can.

Natalia joined the *Shorthorn* thinking she was the first kind of person. She quickly realized she had been wrong. The *Foghorn News* had been a weekly publication; even when she was managing editor, journalism didn't dominate her *entire* existence, and hanging out in the newsroom involved as much shooting the shit as actually putting the paper together. At UTA, though, working full-time—or more—on the paper was the norm. "I was living my life for the first time, and these people were acting like they worked at the *Washington Post*," she said. "It was like, 'Come on, y'all, this is not even real life.'" Suddenly, the girl who had been known at Del Mar as the most reliable person in the newsroom was blowing deadlines and half-assing stories. During her first semester, she still wrote more articles than anyone else on staff, earning the title "Byline Champ," but she disappeared after winter break.

She had never been a disciplined student, but back in Corpus Christi, her mom had kept her on track, enforcing curfews and minimum GPAs. Now she was living on her own, drinking heavily, and thrilled by her newfound freedom. She started partying regularly and going to class seldomly. Some mornings, she and her boyfriend would wake up and go immediately to Applebee's, the only bar they knew of that opened that early. By the time she and the guy broke up at the end of her first year, she was failing so many classes she knew there was no chance of returning to school the next year.

When her mom found out that Natalia wasn't going to earn a degree, she was furious. Luz told her she had better get a job, because she sure wasn't going to get any help with living expenses anymore. Natalia, who had come home when the semester ended, yelled at her, calling her overbearing. She wasn't going to stay in Corpus Christi after that, so she threw all her stuff in her car and drove back to Arlington. She didn't have a plan for what she would do when she got there. She didn't even say goodbye. The memory still made her weep more than a decade later. She knew her mom was right. "I fucked up school. I felt really dumb," she said.

Natalia found an immigration law firm in Dallas that was looking for a bilingual administrative assistant, which allowed her to pay $300 a month in rent for an apartment she shared with a former classmate. Her old editors from the *Caller-Times* were still kicking her freelance work, mostly writing event previews for the entertainment section. But she worried that with no college degree and few recent clips, she would never be able to get a full-time job in journalism.

Then she hit a new low. Some friends had been hanging out at the pool in someone's apartment complex all day, drinking case upon case of beer. By the evening, the booze had run out. Natalia, who was, in her words, "so fucked up," decided to drive to the store to re-up.

She didn't even make it out of the parking lot before hitting another car. The crash drew the attention of a guy in an apartment nearby; he called the cops. By the time they arrived, Natalia had pulled back into a parking spot, but her keys were still in the ignition, which was enough to get her charged with drunk driving. Still wearing a swimsuit and skimpy cover-up, she was handcuffed and booked into the city jail. As she sobered up in a holding cell, she developed a raging hangover—and an even more painful sense of shame and fear. Natalia made no excuses for what she did; if that guy hadn't called the cops, she volunteered, she may very well have killed someone.

Despite a blood alcohol level twice the legal limit, Natalia still remembers essentially every detail of her night in a holding cell: the woman having a drug-induced manic episode, the one who was in for unpaid parking tickets, the ones who lifted her up so she could affix a piece of cardboard with toothpaste on the corners to the ceiling, blocking a vent that made the space freezing cold. She remembers when her mom, sobbing on the phone, told her she didn't have the money to bail her out. Natalia had to spend an extra night in jail until a friend put up the cash.

Her mom did call Natalia's employer to tell them her daughter wouldn't be into work that day because of an "emergency," even though

Natalia had instructed her to tell them the truth. She was afraid she'd get fired, but she was also a journalist at heart, committed to facts above all else. Besides, she was a green-card holder who worked at an immigration law firm—she needed their help. So on her first day back, she walked into her boss's office, told him what had happened, and said she needed a lawyer but couldn't afford to pay. He didn't fire her, and agreed to assign someone to represent her. She accepted a plea deal for two years' probation, plus community service and a suspension of her driver's license.

Natalia estimated she was paying half her monthly salary from the law firm for court supervision fees and the Breathalyzer she was required to have installed in her car when she got her license back. (While it was suspended, her mom temporarily moved to the Dallas area to take her to and from work; without that sacrifice, she has no idea how she would have been able to keep her job.) She had stopped drinking cold turkey, but at one point she missed a required periodic breath test because her grandmother's funeral ran long, which meant she had to pay for an ankle monitor too. She never doubted she deserved the punishment. She was simply curious about how the system worked and why, about who wins and who loses when things are set up a certain way. Her reporter's instincts were buzzing.

IN JULY 2014, AS SOON as she finished probation, Natalia moved back home to Corpus Christi, back into her childhood bedroom. Now twenty-five, she wasn't sure anyone would hire her with a criminal record. She picked up some shifts filing papers for a local oil company and got an interview for a full-time job at a regional office for Subway. She thought her mom would be happy. Instead, Luz was baffled. "You can do better!" she told her daughter. "Why aren't you calling the *Caller-Times*?"

That question transformed the course of Natalia's life. It had been five years since her internship; she had no idea whether the editors would even remember her. But she called. A former editor told her the paper needed someone to fill in for the news clerk while she was on leave; the temporary job was hers if she wanted it. She typed up the events calendar and obituaries and took reader calls—which "suuuuuuuuucked," she said; someone was always mad about *something*. But she was back in the newsroom, which was all she had wanted.

In the five years she had been gone, the *Caller-Times* had cut its staff by half. Revenue across E.W. Scripps's newspapers was dropping, in large part because of the declining ad market. (Employment and classified ads, the two sectors most imperiled by the ubiquity of the internet, declined 17.5 percent and 11.3 percent at Scripps newspapers in the second quarter of 2013 alone.) The conventional wisdom was that newspapers might not survive the digital age, but were persevering in their heroic quest to tell the truth. The fact that many journalists couldn't survive on the wages they were paid—the median entry-level salary for graduates of undergraduate journalism programs was $32,000 in 2013—wasn't their employers' fault, they were told, but rather the inevitable outcome of choosing such a mission-based career path. *We're all in this together*, newspaper owners routinely told their workers. *We're doing the best we can.*

The truth was more complicated: those newspaper owners were making out just fine; only the workers were suffering. Overall revenue from Scripps's fourteen newspapers did drop about 3.5 percent in 2014, the year Natalia returned to the *Caller-Times*, but *profit* remained steady: $28 million, the same as in 2013 and 7 percent higher than in 2012. It wasn't the 30 percent profit margins of a decade earlier, but it hardly indicated a mortally wounded industry either. In Scripps's 2013 annual report to the Securities and Exchange Commission (SEC), filed three months before Natalia went to work for the company, executives made clear how they were growing profits in the newspaper division: "During the past five years, we have reduced our workforce from 4,100 employees to approximately 2,300."

For Scripps, though, $28 million in profits wasn't nearly enough. The company's fourteen television stations were making almost four times as much profit, and dumping the newspaper assets would allow Scripps to acquire new stations without worrying about federal regulations that prohibit one corporation from controlling multiple major outlets in a given region. So, in the summer of 2014, Scripps announced it would merge with a company called Journal Communications, the publisher of Milwaukee's daily newspaper, then spin the newspapers off into their own company so as not to weigh down the strong TV division. In a press release, the company's CEO said the move would create an "industry-leading" local television company and a "financially flexible" newspaper company. When it came down to it, Scripps was first and foremost a corporation focused on shareholder value.

Industry observers viewed the Scripps–Journal Communications spinoff as a worrisome sign for local journalism. "The persistent financial demands of Wall Street have trumped the informational needs of Main Street," media critic David Carr wrote. Most newspapers "are being cut loose after all the low-hanging fruit, like valuable digital properties, have been plucked.

"More ominous," Carr wrote, "most of the print and magazine assets have already been cut to the bone in terms of staffing. Reducing costs has been the only reliable source of profits as overall revenue has declined. Not much is left to trim."

In the short term, though, the turmoil was the reason Natalia was able to restart her journalism career. The news clerk she was filling in for briefly came back from leave but decided to retire, which meant Natalia got to keep the job. Then the editors needed someone to pick up Sunday reporting shifts because they were so short-staffed, so she volunteered. Then, in the fall of 2014, the paper needed to replace a full-time breaking news reporter.

Putting her hand up for that opportunity was scary. Applying required a background check, and no one knew about her DWI conviction. So she bucked herself up and went to tell the hiring editor, one of the few other Latinas in the newsroom. The woman reacted nonchalantly.

"You're done with probation?" she asked.

"Yes," Natalia responded.

"And it was a misdemeanor, not a felony?"

"Yes."

"Okay, that's fine," the editor said.

Natalia got the job. At twenty-five, she had become a real news-paper reporter, just as she had dreamed about.

———

SIX MONTHS INTO NATALIA'S NEW job, a maneuver many, many levels above her pay grade changed the trajectory of her career.

In April 2015, eight months after E.W. Scripps agreed to merge with Journal Communications, the renamed Journal Media Group officially acquired fourteen local newspapers, including the *Caller-Times*. The move was part of a trend: "In just over a week, three of the biggest players in American newspapers—Gannett, Tribune Company and E.W. Scripps, companies built on print franchises that expanded into television—dumped those properties like yesterday's news in a series of spinoffs," Carr wrote.

The scale of the Gannett Company breakup, which came seven days after the Scripps–Journal Communications deal, was far larger. Like Scripps, Gannett started as a newspaper company: in the early 1900s, Frank Gannett was the co-owner of the *Elmira Gazette* in Upstate New York. Then he went on a buying spree, acquiring newspapers across the region—and often merging one-time rivals to ensure control over advertising rates in a given town. *Time* magazine dubbed him "The Great Hyphenator." Over the second half of the twentieth century, the Gannett Company added a series of TV stations to its portfolio, just as Scripps was doing. By the beginning of the twenty-first century, TV revenue at both companies was dramatically outperforming the original newspaper business.

When Gannett announced that it would split its print and broad-cast divisions, the newspapers kept the Gannett name. The TV com-pany, which had been renamed Tegna Inc., held on to most everything else of any value. Tegna even got the most profitable digital assets: Cars.com and CareerBuilder.com, two of the sites that had risen from the ashes of newspapers' once-lucrative classified advertising business.

In interviews with reporters the day the deal was announced, Gannett CEO Gracia Martore sought to assure doubters that the newspaper company was set up for success. The new Gannett would assume no debt, which would leave its leaders free to acquire other papers. In a quote that belongs in a corporate buzzwords hall of fame, she told the *New York Times* that "we can now do smart, accretive acquisitions of community newspapers in an unlevered company where they can create tremendous synergies." (Despite the use of "we," Martore was in fact going to run the TV business, leaving Gannett in the hands of a deputy.)

After the deal closed, at the end of June 2015, Gannett didn't wait very long before executing its first major accretive acquisition to create tremendous synergies. That October, the company announced plans to buy Journal Media Group, the Scripps spinoff that owned the *Caller-Times*, for $280 million. None of the Journal Media newspapers were particularly lucrative targets on their own, but the deal created a company with newspapers in 106 cities and towns across the U.S. In a press release announcing the purchase, Gannett's CEO made the larger plan clear: "This transaction is an excellent first step in the industry consolidation strategy we have communicated to our shareholders."

Consolidation had been Gannett's goal for decades, as journalist and critic Ben Bagdikian laid out in his seminal 1983 book, *The Media Monopoly*. Bagdikian identified twenty-three corporations that together controlled more than 50 percent of the media business (including newspapers, magazines, television, books, and movies). He took a special interest in Gannett, then the largest newspaper chain in the country: "It is neither the best nor the worst. But Gannett Company, Inc. is an outstanding contemporary performer of the ancient rite of creating self-serving myths, of committing acts of greed and exploitation but describing them through its own machinery as heroic epics."

Gannett executives boasted about how they stayed out of newsrooms, leaving control over each paper's journalism to its editor. That seems to have been largely true, but the reasons for that philosophy were arguably less noble than the company claimed: seen through another lens, its deliberate oblivion to what its newsrooms were producing looks more like apathy to journalism writ large.

Increasing profits could mean raising ad rates, boosting subscriber numbers, and launching new products, but that was rarely enough in the eyes of media executives. The real key to growth, financially speaking, was cutting staff. Between 1966 and 1980, Bagdikian found—a time when Gannett newspapers were routinely increasing profits by 30, 50, or even 100 percent every quarter—the average newsroom size dropped from 45 to 26, while average circulation remained steady. Unsurprisingly, the pressure to juice profits resulted in decreased journalistic quality: multiple studies in the 1970s and '80s concluded that chain-owned papers published fewer news stories than independent ones. Many began relying more on syndicated national news to replace the local stories they no longer had enough staff to cover.

Well before private equity was in the local media game, Gannett was creating firms' playbooks for them: ruthlessly consolidate, centralize as much as possible, boost shareholder value at all costs—even when the cost was the journalism, the company's ostensible raison d'être. "The highest levels of world finance have become intertwined with the highest levels of mass media ownership," Bagdikian wrote, describing the state of affairs but also forecasting the next half century of change in the industry, "with the result of tighter control over the systems on which most of the public depends for its news and information."

By the time Gannett acquired the *Caller-Times* and its sister Journal Media née Scripps publications, the evolution from locally owned newspapers to investment firms controlling the entire industry was nearly complete.

FOUR

LOREN

PUBLIC HOUSING WAS NOT WHERE LOREN DEPINA WANTED TO BE. But as long as she was there, she was going to make the best of it—no matter who she had to piss off along the way.

At the end of 2019, Loren and her husband, Rashad, were both laid off, which got them and their sons, Jaxon and Cameron, evicted from their apartment in Alexandria, Virginia. They moved into a cheap motel long enough to figure something else out, but with no salaries, another apartment wasn't an option. They could have asked Loren's dad, a successful businessman, for help, but she was too ashamed to admit they were homeless. Instead, they applied for a spot in a government-subsidized building on Princess Street in the city's Old Town neighborhood.

When pandemic lockdowns began a few months later, Loren made improving her family's living situation her full-time job. A group of guys was selling drugs out of her building—not even neighbors, dudes from all the way across town—and she wasn't going to stand for it. So she marched straight up to them and asked, "Why the fuck are y'all doing this shit *here*?" The guys acknowledged they didn't live there, but insisted it was their territory. "My cousins are all gangbangers," she told them, "and they never leave their community to go to someone else's. Go do this shit in your own hood."

Her attempts at persuasion didn't work. So instead she called Alexandria police every day, for six months, until the guys finally got sick of being harassed by cops and found somewhere else to deal.

To this day, she said four years later, no one sells drugs from that building.

Then something surprising happened. Her one-woman stand drew the attention of the housing authority's CEO, who invited her in for a chat. She showed up with a full agenda and a notebook full of ideas— "Daddy says opportunity is only going to come once, and it's up to you what you do with it," she recited, one of many lessons her father drilled into her. By the time she left the CEO's office, she had been appointed the chair of a brand-new safety committee representing public housing tenants across the entire city. Suddenly she was meeting with the police chief, the mayor, and the city council to talk about residents' concerns. She had always had ideas for how to improve the world around her, but now powerful people actually wanted to hear them.

Simultaneously, a separate crisis was pulling her into advocacy work at her children's elementary school. Cameron was in kindergarten, attending Zoom school while she supervised and Rashad went to work at his new job as an information technology specialist. One morning she was brushing her teeth when she heard an adult woman's voice yelling over the computer speakers, so she rushed out and demanded to know what was going on. It turned out that the teacher was talking to the students about George Floyd—a lesson plan that had been approved by the school district—when a white mom came on-screen, furious that her child was learning about police brutality. The mother complained to the principal, who instructed the teacher not to talk about Floyd or related topics—at a school where more than half the students were Black.

Loren had always been engaged in her kids' education, but not particularly involved in school governance. The incident with the white mom, though, lit a fire under her. At a parent–teacher association meeting soon afterward, she stood up and delivered an impassioned speech, arguing that the school's willingness to capitulate was just a symptom of a racist culture: the gifted and talented program was overwhelmingly white. The PTA itself was overwhelmingly white, and wasn't making any effort to get Black families involved. Though the principal was Black, he acted like he didn't have time to talk to parents about their concerns. Nobody, it seemed, was doing anything to engage the mostly poor, mostly Black people who made up the school community.

A few weeks later, Loren was voted onto the PTA board. Her first official action was a door-knocking campaign to personally invite parents—especially those from public housing—to the next meeting. Sixty-seven people showed up, far more than anyone could remember ever attending. She knew that the school was an inconvenient location for people in many neighborhoods, so she pushed the group to rotate among various community centers, which led to even more parents getting involved. She saw that things were improving, and they were improving because she spoke up.

Loren had always been a loudmouth and a busybody, a person who says what's on her mind no matter the consequences. She doesn't lack the capacity for fear—she's terrified going over bridges, especially old ones—but whatever gene makes everyone else shy away from un-comfortable interactions with powerful people didn't make it into her body. But the confrontation with the drug dealers and the fight with the school had transformed her from a person with an occasionally self-destructive need to call out injustice into a real activist with nearly every Alexandria official on speed dial.

Before long, her months of volunteering evolved into full-time employment as an organizer, a job she didn't even know existed be-fore a guy she knew through the public housing safety committee told her he was putting her up for a role at VOICE, a nonprofit that works in communities across Northern Virginia. She'd be focusing on issues affecting low-income and middle-class people, including after-school programs and affordable-housing initiatives. After years of taking whatever job would pay the bills, she had stumbled into something resembling a calling.

After several months of building their savings back up, Loren's job also gave her family the financial security to leave public housing after four years. She looked at apartment rental listings across town, but one place, next to Interstate 395 in Alexandria's West End neighborhood, stuck out. The 1960s-era complex was the size of a small city, with five buildings and 2,346 apartments, plus swimming pools, a dry cleaner, a bank, a 7-Eleven, and a commuter bus hub. It was called Southern Towers.

⸻

UNTIL 2008 OR SO, LARGE investors like private equity firms didn't have much interest in housing. Private equity requires scale, and buying individual houses or apartment buildings by the thousands made for a tedious way to get there. Commercial real estate, on the other hand, came with scale built in, which meant it began attracting private equity attention in the 1990s.

One of the early trendsetters in the field was the result of a fluke encounter between a couple of Israeli military veterans and a wealthy finance executive. Shaul Kuba and Avi Shemesh were childhood friends who ended up in the same brigade of the Israel Defense Forces, then left Israel in search of bigger things. They traveled to the United States and settled in the Israeli community in Los Angeles, taking on landscaping and contracting work. They also began flipping houses. In 1994, they got a lucky break. As the story goes, the pair often showed up at houses in wealthy neighborhoods to pitch them gardening services. One day they happened to call on Richard Ressler.

Ressler was around the same age as Kuba and Shemesh, but he was already finance-world royalty. Like his older brother Tony, he made his career at Drexel Burnham Lambert, the investment bank that, in the words of *Barbarians at the Gate* authors Bryan Burrough and John Helyar, "transformed the [leveraged buyout] industry from a Volkswagen Beetle into a monstrous drag racer belching smoke and fire." Ressler had been at Drexel when an SEC investigation into insider trading and securities fraud began, one that would eventually lead to the company's collapse. The infamous case also resulted in a prison sentence for executive Michael Milken, who had become known as the "junk bond king" for his use of risky debt to finance leveraged buyouts.

But the scandal didn't taint Drexel's reputation as the prime breeding ground for private equity executives. After leaving the firm,

Richard Ressler started what became a small but successful investment firm called Orchard Capital. At the same time, Tony was teaming up with three other former Drexel executives to create Apollo Global Management, which would soon become a private equity colossus.

By 1994, Richard wanted to get on the private equity train too. He was impressed by the moxie of the two Israelis who had shown up at his house, and as he talked to them, he decided they were destined for bigger things than landscaping. So, shortly after Ressler met Kuba and Shemesh, the trio went into business together, launching a Los Angeles–based private equity firm focused on real estate. Ressler and Shemesh would handle operations and fundraising; Kuba would take charge of developing properties. They called their company CIM Group; to this day, employees maintain that the acronym "does not stand for anything in particular."

In the early days, the group's projects were limited to Southern California; local trade publications noted when CIM bought a few buildings or a few parcels of land, which it often leased to national chain stores. In 1999, the Los Angeles Times reported on the company's innovative business strategy: spotting urban districts just starting to become trendy, then buying as much of the area as possible to capitalize on the coming spike in rents. CIM had recently bought "about $40 million worth of humdrum properties in Hollywood, including an outdated office building and a failed shopping mall," in hopes of reviving the moribund Hollywood Boulevard, the Times noted, and it was playing a major role in developing areas like San Diego's Gaslamp Quarter and Santa Monica's Third Street Promenade. Crucially, those projects were also eligible for significant amounts of public funding via grants, low-interest loans, and tax breaks from municipalities eager to encourage development in neglected neighborhoods.

For the first six years of its existence, CIM remained fairly small, with $35 million in assets. The company had a strategy for expanding its business, though. It ran through the California Public Employees' Retirement System, or CalPERS.

Pensions are a key source of money for any major private equity firm: 60 percent of all private equity capital comes from public pension investments, according to a 2024 study. State organizations like CalPERS, the richest public pension fund in the United States, invest the money promised to teachers, firefighters, police officers, and other public workers after they retire, aiming to grow the pool enough to cover all future retirees. Many funds don't come close to this goal—CalPERS is currently short more than $150 billion—which makes them hungry for the better-than-average returns that private equity promises. The accuracy of those promises, though, is controversial. While a 2022 report from the industry's main lobbying group found that median returns after ten years were higher from private equity than from any other type of investment, an SEC "Risk Alert" that same year warned of firms misleading clients about their performance.

CalPERS's size makes it a particularly desirable source of funds for any private equity firm looking to grow, and in 2000, CIM Group broke through. The firm had hired Alfred Villalobos, a former CalPERS board member and deputy mayor of Los Angeles, to persuade the pension fund to invest $250 million in exchange for a predicted 20 percent return (and $9.6 million for Villalobos for his work as the middleman). Initially, CalPERS's board balked, voting down CIM's attempt to win the investment without undergoing a standard staff review. Three months later, and despite objections from the staff that led four senior employees to quit, the board voted to invest $125 million with CIM. After Villalobos's involvement became a conflict-of-interest scandal, CIM fired him and agreed to stop using third-party agents; Villalobos was later indicted for allegedly bribing CalPERS's CEO in exchange for investments into Apollo Global Management. All the while, CalPERS kept investing in CIM, pouring nearly $1.9 billion into the firm over the course of a decade. While the firm remained headquartered in Los Angeles, its portfolio expanded across the entire country.

CIM bought Chicago's iconic Tribune Tower from Tribune Media and converted it from a newsroom into luxury condos. It bought Jack London Square, a historic waterfront area in Oakland, California, named after the *Call of the Wild* author, and added luxury apartments, a luxury hotel, and high-end restaurants. It developed Manhattan's 432 Park Avenue into one of the tallest and most expensive residential buildings in the world, then was sued by the building's condo board for $125 million in damages after an outside engineering firm found some 1,500 construction and design defects. It opened offices in Atlanta, Chicago, Dallas, London, New York, Orlando, Phoenix, and Tokyo. It also became a go-to partner for the Trump family, bailing out the floundering Trump SoHo hotel and apartment building and partnering with Jared Kushner on at least half a dozen projects.

Often, CIM developments followed the same formula that had worked so well in the company's first few years: buy into what the company calls "thriving and transitional urban communities" and give them a glow-up, recruiting as many high-paying commercial and residential tenants as possible. Neighborhood groups have long accused the company of driving up housing prices and accelerating gentrification. In CIM's hometown of Los Angeles, Kuba oversaw the transformation of West Adams from a working-class Black and Latino neighborhood into an area where, as Bloomberg put it, "white millennials who work in booming Culver City sip matcha drinks and walk their labradoodles on the boulevard, even at night, babbling obliviously on AirPods."

========

LONG BEFORE SHE BECAME A professional organizer working on affordable housing issues, long before she was struggling to afford a place of her own, Loren was used to fighting white people who didn't think she belonged.

She knows she intimidates people, as Black women who speak their minds often do. She was always the tallest kid in school—she's now just south of six feet—and the more passionate she gets about something, the louder she talks. She's not one for dressing up and *never* wears makeup; her long straight hair is usually up in a no-nonsense bun contained by a cotton scrunchie, drawing attention to whichever of her collection of large graphic earrings she's picked out that day. Her wardrobe skews toward leggings and T-shirts, many of them with political statements or provocative messages: "Black Lives Matter,"

"Thou Shalt Not Try Me," "I Wish a Karen Would." "When I'm being an asshole, there's definitely a message there," she said. "People are going to get it, or not."

Loren's parents, Victor and Maria DePina, immigrated to Boston from Cape Verde in 1975, the year their native country won independence from Portugal. Five years later, Maria gave birth to Loren, the first DePina born in the U.S. Maria had left school after fourth grade, but Victor earned an engineering degree from Wentworth Institute of Technology in Boston. The DePinas spent more than a decade in the Dorchester neighborhood, an epicenter of Cape Verdean life in America, settling into a comfortable middle-class existence. The family spoke Kriolu, or Cape Verdean Creole, at home, but made sure their daughter spoke Portuguese as well as English. Many of Loren's friends were Latino, so she picked up Spanish too; as an adult she's fluent in all four languages.

When Loren was eight, her father got a job at Narragansett Electric, the biggest power company in Rhode Island, and moved his family to Providence. Even though they were less than fifty miles from Boston, it felt like a different world: many fewer Cape Verdeans, many more racist white people. The family wasn't religious, but she was sent to Catholic school. She hated it—hated all the rules, hated the strict teachers, *hated* mandatory Mass.

As the only Black girl at school, she also faced discrimination she had never encountered in Dorchester. One girl would always bully her in the bathroom, but school staff brushed her off when she complained. Her parents told her to do what she needed to do to protect herself, so finally she beat the girl up, the first of many times she'd get physical in school.

A few years later, on the first day of eighth grade, she refused to sit next to a girl whose last name was Pina. Her surname, "DePina," can mean "from Pina" or "of the Pina family," a construction Cape Verde's Portuguese settlers often used to name the people they enslaved from mainland Africa. "She's a slave owner," she told the teacher. "Her people owned slaves. They actually owned my family."

The teacher pushed back, trying to teach a lesson about speaking respectfully to one's classmates. Loren was having none of it. "It's facts, and let me explain to you why it's facts," she said.

The teacher moved her to a new seat.

Sitting on a worn brown leather couch in her living room decades later, occasionally punching her palm to punctuate her thoughts, she marveled that there was ever any controversy over her demand. "I struggle, heavily, when people who have been colonized have a desire to go kick it with their colonizers," she said, the pitch of her voice rising with disbelief. "I'm just not built that way."

When he left Cape Verde, Victor DePina vowed to earn enough money to bring the rest of the family, including his seven siblings and their many offspring, over the Atlantic to join him, which he did. Everyone settled in the Boston area, which meant that for the first eight years of her life, Loren was always surrounded by aunts, uncles, cousins, and people who weren't directly related but were family all the same. She's one of thirty-nine cousins on her dad's side, and even though she's the first to volunteer that she doesn't *like* them all, she always loved being part of the DePina brood. She still had plenty of friends after they moved away, but between the mean white girls at school and the distance from the rest of her family, living in Providence made her lonely.

Looking back, though, she also saw that getting away from the extended family was a big part of the reason Victor and Maria moved to Rhode Island. When she was six, a male cousin started molesting her, and kept going for two years, until investigators from the state's Department of Children and Families approached her mom in the pediatrician's waiting room. Another child had come forward, and the authorities wanted to know if the man had abused Loren too. She said that he had, for years. Her parents had never known. "Why didn't you tell me this was happening?" her mom asked over and over. She remembers thinking she really wished she had.

After the family relocated to Providence, Loren made a promise to herself that she would never again remain quiet about injustice.

At times she thinks her experience—being abused, and being questioned about why she didn't report the abuse—is what made her different from other people. "We've all had different walks of life, and I don't wish my walk on anyone else," she said, wiping away tears. "But because of my walk, I'm a force to be reckoned with."

By the time she graduated from La Salle Academy, a small Catholic high school, she was ready to flee New England altogether. She wanted to be around more people who looked like her but to whom she wasn't related; fewer than 5 percent of Rhode Island residents were Black the year she graduated from high school. She also needed someplace bigger, someplace her larger-than-life personality wouldn't stick out so much.

Her mom, who had divorced her dad during Loren's freshman year at La Salle, had strong opinions about what should come next: matriculate at a Catholic college—ideally Providence College, just across the street from La Salle—then attend either law or medical school. Maria hadn't made it past elementary school, and she wanted her daughter to get as much education as possible.

That wasn't going to happen. While Loren was always among the smartest kids in class, her tendency to chafe against the rules—and to talk back to teachers and other authority figures—made her largely uninterested in school. And as a committed atheist, she sure as hell wasn't going to sign up for four more years of Catholic school on top of the twelve she had already done. She was ready to build a life on her own.

Shortly after graduation, she visited an aunt who was living in the Washington, D.C., area. She loved the energy immediately. "Everywhere I turned, people looked like me, and they were all winning," she said. She went home to Rhode Island, and though she had neither a job nor a place to live in D.C., she told her parents she was moving, packed her things, and left. She settled in Alexandria, a diverse town of 160,000 people seven miles south of downtown.

IF NOT FOR THE GLOBAL financial crisis and the Great Recession, residential real estate might have remained a niche market for the private equity industry. Instead, it became one of the hottest fields for investment.

The economic crash in the fall of 2008—prompted in part by 10 million foreclosures against homeowners who'd been awarded much larger loans than they could afford to pay back—upended America's housing landscape. Home prices fell by more than 30 percent over the next few years, but the recession meant that fewer people could afford to buy. That combination created the perfect opening for institutional investors on the hunt for profits wherever they could find them.

All private equity functions essentially like house flipping: a firm buys a property, spruces it up, and sells it for a profit. In most industries, though, there's at least a small amount of gambling involved—while there is little financial risk to the firm itself, it's never clear that the bet will result in a huge payout. But when private equity firms get involved in *actual* house flipping, there's far less danger: because the value of real estate generally appreciates over time, even small investments can result in outsize returns. And whereas the exceptions to that "generally" can bankrupt individual families, firms worth billions of dollars can easily stomach the occasional loss, knowing that bigger wins are just down the road.

Once the scale on which private equity operates is factored in, the value proposition is even simpler. If adding quartz countertops and replacing carpet with wood planks leads to a $15,000 profit from a house flip, why not do it in 100 or 1,000 or 10,000 homes? If you own enough of a neighborhood's housing stock to single-handedly raise market-rate prices, why not jack up rents? If consolidation and occasionally neglecting needed repairs saves money, why not share one maintenance worker between three buildings and postpone replacing those old radiators? You don't need to be a strategic genius to make money in real estate; you simply need to have enough cash to invest in the first place. And luckily for private equity firms, the federal government makes it easy to get the cash.

Fannie Mae and Freddie Mac are publicly traded private companies, but they are also "government-sponsored enterprises," a category of business created by Congress to make loans more available and affordable. (Since the two companies nearly went under during the 2008 crisis, they also have been subject to a government conservatorship through the Federal Housing Finance Agency.) Fannie and Freddie buy mortgages from private lenders, package them, and then resell them to investors in bundles known as mortgage-backed securities. The profits the companies make from selling these bundles go into the pot of money available for home loans. That, then, allows the companies to lower interest rates and make homeownership more accessible. The origins of the companies date back to the New Deal, part of a plan to help ordinary Americans buy homes.

Private equity firms are hardly the "ordinary Americans" the New Dealers had in mind. Yet those firms are the recipients of a large and growing number of Fannie and Freddie loans. A 2022 analysis found that private equity accounted for 85 percent of Freddie Mac's twenty largest apartment complex deals. In at least one year, private equity firms got more than 10 percent of the agencies' total deal volume. In 2017, private equity firm Greystar—the largest apartment management company in the world, with nearly 730,000 individual homes in 2023—set a record for the largest single borrower deal in Freddie Mac history, at nearly $1.8 billion. The availability of these low-interest loans has meant that ever since the recession, private equity firms have snapped up individual homes by the thousands.

Fannie and Freddie loans offer one huge advantage over the typical sources of cash for leveraged buyouts: they only require paying back the loan amount, with its subsidized interest rate, rather than a percentage of all profits. The private equity company pockets the rest of the returns. Combined with the classic private equity 2-and-20 fee structure and the ease of increasing rents, deals that have high percentages of Fannie or Freddie financing are essentially all upside.

And while federal law requires Fannie and Freddie to finance affordable rentals for low-income families, it doesn't require much in the way of protecting them. Landlords are free to raise rents as much as they can under local laws, and the Federal Housing Finance Agency doesn't regulate rent increases after the completion of a deal. Because raising prices is a standard part of the private equity playbook, the result is government-supported consolidation of the housing market. By 2021, private equity firms were backing half the country's largest landlords.

———

IT'S NOT JUST APARTMENT BUILDINGS: private equity is now a major player in every segment of the rental housing economy. In 2011, no single company owned more than 1,000 single-family houses; a decade later, at least 32 did. In 2022, institutional investors—a category that includes private equity firms and hedge funds as well as real estate investment trusts—owned 3.8 percent of all single-family homes.

That's a tiny fraction of the overall housing supply, but zooming in on a handful of cities shows a much larger impact. Some 72,000 homes in Atlanta are owned by institutional investors; two of them own more than 10,000 houses each. One researcher found that investors' home-buying activity in the region single-handedly caused homeownership rates among Black residents to drop by 4.2 percent. Homeownership has long been considered the cornerstone of the American Dream, the most achievable path for middle-class people to build generational wealth. But in Atlanta and other cities across the country, institutional investors have slammed the door of opportunity shut on scores of aspiring homeowners.

In manufactured homes (colloquially known as mobile homes), meanwhile, private equity's influence is even bigger—and the residents even more vulnerable to abuse. More than 20 million Americans live in mobile homes, making them the largest source of unsubsidized affordable housing in the country. Many mobile home residents own their home, but they still must pay monthly rent for the lot it sits on. And for most people, the homes are "mobile" only in theory: they often sit on a concrete foundation, which means moving one can cost anywhere from $5,000 to $10,000, a sum out of reach for the lion's share of the people living in them.

So if a private equity company hikes lot rent beyond what its residents can pay, many will have no choice but to sell. If a resident falls too far behind on payments, they can be evicted from the park, which means walking away from the home they own. That, in turn, legally makes the home abandoned property, freeing the park's owner to assume control, sell or rent it, and pocket the proceeds.

This recipe has made mobile homes irresistible to many private equity firms, including Apollo Global Management, Blackstone, Carlyle Group, Stockbridge Capital, and, more recently, Alden Global Capital, the most infamous newspaper owner in the country. Twenty-three percent of all mobile home park purchases in 2019 and 2020 were made by large investors. In 2017 and 2018, that number was 13 percent. Park owners have described the opportunity in eye-poppingly crass terms. Most infamously, Frank Rolfe, the co-owner of a large chain of mobile home parks, once compared his business to a "Waffle House where everyone is chained to the booths."

Between apartments, single-family houses, and mobile homes, private equity firms now own millions of individual homes across the U.S. The industry's money and political clout, meanwhile, gives them outsize power to raise rents, lobby against regulation, and put homeownership out of reach of more people. Blackstone, which is both the world's largest private equity firm and the nation's largest landlord, is explicit about how America's affordable-housing crisis benefits its shareholders: "a structural shortage of housing has resulted in pricing power for rental housing assets," it wrote in a 2023 letter touting its growing investor returns. The firm has also poured millions of dollars into fighting ballot measures designed to expand rent-control protection in California. In 2019, a United Nations committee labeled Blackstone's involvement in the housing industry a human rights concern, writing in a letter to CEO Stephen Schwarzman that the firm was "having deleterious effects on the right to housing" through buying up houses and apartment buildings and opposing regulation.

CIM Group had built its own apartment buildings as part of its developments ever since the company launched in 1994. During the 2010s, though, it joined the trend of acquiring existing housing. Not all of the buildings the firm bought were for wealthy computer programmers like in West Adams or billionaires like at 432 Park. Occasionally CIM also purchased a single large and unglamorous apartment complex that was home to working-class people. In those cases, the appeal seemed to have been largely about scale: investing a relatively small amount of money in aesthetic upgrades would allow the firm to raise rents for hundreds or thousands of apartment dwellers at once. In the early 2020s, CIM purchased or copurchased 710 units in Denver, 1,012 in Phoenix, and 301 in Washington, D.C.

The firm also bought 2,346 units in Alexandria, Virginia, acquiring a sprawling 1960s-era complex. In 2020, CIM paid $506 million for the five buildings known as Southern Towers, the largest residential deal ever completed in the region. Sixty-eight percent of the total purchase price, $346 million, was financed by a Freddie Mac loan with a 2.2 percent interest rate.

———

AS FAR AS LOREN'S FATHER, Victor, was concerned, he had already given her everything she needed to be successful in the world; she just had to figure out how to apply it. "There are people with six degrees who can't do what you can do; you can dance circles around them," she remembered him telling her.

A Victor DePina education did include many lessons his daughter never got in school. He would hold up a hundred-dollar bill and tell her "this is your only best friend." He had seen how his own father, like many traditional African men, taught his sons to build successful careers and his daughters to marry men with successful careers. He was going to raise his daughters to be self-sufficient. The details would be up to them.

When Victor was promoted to a supervisory role at Narragansett Electric, a white underling told him he planned to be promoted above him, because he didn't care to report to a Black man. Victor smiled and nodded. Eventually the white man did get promoted—the very same week Victor put in his resignation notice: he was starting his own shipping company, importing cars and other American goods to Cape Verde. By the time Loren reached adulthood, her father was a wealthy man.

Finding a career path didn't come easily to Loren, though. She could barely remember all the jobs she worked to make ends meet: running the front desk at Jiffy Lube, wrangling unruly children at Sears Portrait Studio, dealing with rental cars at Hertz, selling cell phones at AT&T, sorting medical records at a dermatologist's office. When she got sick of a company's bullshit, or the company got sick of her attitude, she would move on. The common thread in all her jobs was customer service: she can talk to anyone, and is an expert at making people feel heard.

The common thread in all her *firings* was that she was a pain in the ass for her bosses. The dermatologist fired her for allegedly bullying a new employee, which she denies; she said they wanted her gone because she exposed a different employee for embezzling funds. AT&T fired her for raising a stink about labor violations; among other tiny demonstrations, she printed a copy of the relevant laws, laminated it, and placed it on her supervisor's desk. To settle her wrongful termination case, she said, they paid her unemployment for a full two years.

In 2005, when Loren was twenty-five, Victor summoned his four adult children to his office. "That's how we knew we were in trouble, that he was calling us all in together," she said. When they arrived, he pulled out a folder with four sheets of paper. Each page had one of their names on top, followed by an estimate of the total amount he had spent on them over the course of their lives. Loren's figure wasn't nearly as high as her brother's, but the exact cost wasn't the point. None of them had graduated from college; none had real careers. He demanded they all shape up. Loren, he announced, would be enrolling in college at the New England Institute of Technology, where a two-year program in health care management would give her what he said was a recession-proof career.

She followed his orders and earned her degree in 2007, but it didn't change much. She worked in some hospitals and clinics, but none of the jobs stuck for all that long. She wasn't particularly invested in health care management. She was also staying out late every night, drinking too much, hooking up with guys who were bad news. She cycled through terrible apartments, occasionally getting evicted when she couldn't pay rent. In 2010, she got pregnant. Things with Rashad, the father, had only ever been very casual, but when she forwarded him the results of the paternity test, he called her crying, saying he'd always wanted a son.

Rashad is the opposite of Loren in many ways. He is quiet and reserved, rarely one to make a fuss. She hates effusive displays of emotion; he's a believer in saying how he feels. A few months after Jaxon was born, he told her he loved her. He also told her he wanted to move in together, wanted to give Jaxon a life with two parents at home. She wasn't so sure about that, but she said they could try it out. They've been together ever since. Their second son, Cameron, was born in 2014. A few years after that, Loren finally agreed to marry Rashad.

When Loren talks about Jaxon and Cameron, her demeanor turns solemn; it's clear how much she loves them, but equally obvious how much responsibility she feels for raising two Black men in America. Jaxon was six feet tall by his thirteenth birthday; even though his toothy grin and round cheeks make him look more like a cherubic child than a grown man, she's hyperaware that many people don't see past his height and skin color. She's hell-bent on doing everything she can to protect him and his brother.

Her regimen for keeping them safe includes strict etiquette rules—they never meet a stranger without offering a firm handshake and uncommonly focused eye contact—and an insistence on making the honor roll. "What's not an option?" she asks them daily. "Failure!" they respond dutifully yet enthusiastically. She takes her cues on child-rearing from Victor, who exclusively refers to the boys as Mr. J and Mr. C to teach them they are worthy of respect.

Even when Loren, Rashad, and their kids wound up briefly homeless, she did whatever she could to avoid her kids realizing their family was in financial trouble. Jax and Cam had to know they were safe, that they were loved, that they were going to achieve great things. That's why she had to run the drug dealers out of their building on Princess

Street. That's why she had to fight the white parents who wouldn't let Cameron's kindergarten class learn about George Floyd. That's why she had to get them into a better living situation as quickly as possible.

After four years in public housing, moving into Southern Towers felt like a dream. The complex was across the street from Rashad's office and just down the road from both boys' schools. The kids could walk to the 7-Eleven, the playground, and the swimming pools without ever leaving the property. The apartment itself was bright and spacious, with a large living room, a balcony, a washing machine, and three bedrooms, which meant Jaxon and Cameron wouldn't have to share anymore. Not only had they made it out of "the projects," they had landed the type of home where Loren had always dreamed they would live.

PART II

DURING

FIVE

LIZ

IT WAS ONLY THANKS TO TWO PRIVATE EQUITY GIANTS THAT THERE was a Toys R Us for Liz to work for at all. Or at least that's the story the giants told.

After KKR, Bain Capital, and Vornado Realty Trust spent $5 billion of other people's money to buy the company, revenue held steady into the next decade. If Toys R Us was no longer a category killer, it at least appeared to be a functional specialty retailer, one with enough market share and name recognition to last. When Liz started working at the company in 2012, seven years after its leveraged buyout, she was impressed by how well things ran, and heartened that the stores always seemed to be busy.

For the first several years of Toys R Us's private equity era, in fact, its continued survival was considered such a triumph for the private equity model that an industry lobbying group promoted the company as its poster child. When *PBS NewsHour* ran a mildly critical segment about private equity's growing dominance in 2010, the CEO of the Private Equity Council reacted with outrage in a letter: "You don't report that Toys R Us was saved from likely bankruptcy by PE owners, that it has more employees working for it than it did before it was acquired, and that it is on the verge of returning to the public equity market."

Private equity executives have always sold themselves as brash swashbucklers, eager to be the hero when no one else is brave enough to shoulder the risk. Think of *Wall Street*, the 1987 film that dramatized the forefathers of modern private equity. Michael Douglas's character, Gordon Gekko—he of the famous "greed, for lack of a better word, is good" speech—is the villain, while Charlie Sheen's Bud Fox is the good-hearted protagonist who winds up in prison because he fell under Gekko's spell. But Fox is only marginally less craven, always pushing his boss to take risky bets that he's sure will make them money while also saving the acquired company. In one pivotal scene, Fox tells his father that he will never understand his son's career because "you never had the guts to go out into the world and stake your own claim." Without Fox, the only one willing to jeopardize his own fortune and future for the good of Teldar Paper, yet another American institution would disappear. This is the theory underlying the entire industry: private equity firms and their executives have a greater incentive to improve a company's performance than salaried managers at a public company do, because the firm has skin in the game.

As it turns out, though, not much skin. Even aside from the loans that fund the majority of any private equity deal, most of the rest of the money comes from a firm's "limited partners"—the pensions, university endowments, and other external investors who keep their money in private equity funds. Three percent of the average private equity deal is funded by general partners, meaning the firms themselves, according to a 2024 report. At large firms, it is not uncommon for that number to be 1 percent; if a firm buys a company for $1 billion, it may be putting up just $10 million of its own funds. Blackstone was valued at $208 billion as of late 2024, with $1 trillion of assets under management. Losing $10 million makes no difference.

And because of private equity's trademark 2-and-20 structure—in which the firm takes 2 percent of the investors' money, plus 20 percent of all profits beyond a set threshold—and other assorted fees and dividends, making *some* money is all but guaranteed. An oft-cited 2009 paper by economists Andrew Metrick and Ayako Yasuda found that roughly two-thirds of a private equity firm's total revenues come from fixed costs rather than from actual company profits. Former private equity executive Jeffrey C. Hooke found that, in 2019, the state of Maryland was spending roughly the same amount of money on pri-

vate equity management fees as it was on its entire budget for higher
education financial aid, nearly half a billion dollars. No matter whether
the company succeeds or fails, the firm comes out ahead.

=====

THE ORIGIN STORY OF KOHLBERG Kravis Roberts & Company (com-
monly known as KKR), one of the three partners in the Toys R Us
deal, fits neatly into the narrative of swaggering daredevils willing
to go where no one else will. Jerome Kohlberg, Henry Kravis, and
George Roberts were all successful partners at Bear Stearns, the once-
legendary investment bank that would later collapse as part of the 2008
financial crisis. Kohlberg had joined the company in 1955 and gone on
to oversee its corporate finance department. Kravis and Roberts, first
cousins a generation younger, began working for Kohlberg in the late
1960s, and the three turned leveraged buyouts into a big business for
"the Bear," as the firm was known. When their ambitions exceeded the
overall company strategy, they walked. Then, in 1976, using money
they raised from a small group of friendly investors, they started their
own, eponymous company.

Just over a decade later, KKR had created a steady stream of
multibillion-dollar leveraged buyouts—most famously the acquisition
of RJR Nabisco, which came to exemplify corporate greed and essentially created the modern private equity industry. In fact, Kravis and
Roberts became so aggressive toward company takeovers—as *Fortune*
put it in 1988, they felt the company had "outgrown niceties"—that
Kohlberg, the senior member of the trio, left the firm. Kravis kept a
framed Machiavelli quote in his private conference room: "There is
nothing more difficult to take in hand, more perilous to conduct, or
more uncertain in its outcome, than to take the lead in introducing a
new order of things."

KKR's partner in the Toys R Us acquisition, Bain Capital, was part
of the wave of leveraged buyout specialists created in the decade after
KKR's launch. In 1984, Bill Bain decided to spin off a new division from

his eponymous management consulting company that would invest in and acquire companies instead of just telling them how to spend their money. To head up the project, he approached a rising star at Bain & Company, thirty-six-year-old Mitt Romney.

Romney wasn't sold. He was unconvinced a move from consulting to the comparatively speculative world of finance would pay off for his grander aspirations. So Bill Bain agreed to make Bain Capital its own firm, with Romney as CEO. He also made Romney a promise: take the job, and then if things don't work out, you can come right back to Bain & Company, under a cover story about how you were too invaluable to the management consulting business to stay away any longer. "All the risk and investment was basically on my side," Bill Bain said later. "I was clearly putting my neck on the line and the company on the line."

Early on, Bain Capital was much more conservative than many of its competitors, but sticking to traditional investment deals wasn't making enough money for Romney's tastes. So he decided to turn his attention from startup investments to private equity. That meant less risk to Bain because most of the money would come from loans instead of the company's own coffers; within a few years, his firm was making more than 50 percent annual returns. Those results earned him millions of dollars—and a reputation as a profiteer willing to lay off thousands of people and ship scores of jobs overseas, which would come to haunt him on the campaign trail during his run for president in 2012.

A few years after Romney formally stepped down in 2002 (keeping shares in the company funds), Bain Capital pulled off one of the most infamous business maneuvers in the history of American retail, making more than $100 million off the ashes of a once-venerable chain: KB Toys, once Toys R Us's primary competitor.

━━

WHEN LIZ STARTED HER CAREER at Toys R Us in 2012, she was impressed. She had been working in retail for fifteen years, her entire adult life, mostly at superstores Fred Meyer and Costco. She was used to meager pay, unpredictable schedules, and navigating mayhem when things went wrong—point-of-sale systems going down during peak shopping hours, coworkers calling in sick, managers getting vindictive. She knew how to survive chaos; she had been doing it since she was a kid. But now there just wasn't that much to survive. It wasn't that nothing ever broke at Toys R Us, but there always seemed to be a plan when it did.

Once, when Liz was still just a temporary employee, a couple came in. The man was difficult, dismissing her suggestions and asking absurd questions. That wasn't uncommon, but there was something suspicious about this man; *his* absurd questions seemed too specific for a run-of-the-mill clueless jerk. "Do you work for the company?" Liz asked cautiously. He confessed he was the regional manager, and he was there testing her skills. Right in front of his wife, Liz told him that going undercover was a terrible way to treat people. It was demeaning; it was a waste of both of their time. "If you don't hire this girl permanently, you're going to the doghouse," the manager's wife told him. He did. He also stopped secretly testing employees.

Liz started at a wage of $9.25 an hour as an overnight stocker during the Christmas season. Pretty quickly, the bosses noticed that she never seemed to slow down, that she soaked up new information like a sponge. So they offered her a full-time job at $14 an hour. She turned them down—her husband, Henry, was still working two jobs, and the couple had three kids, Daniyel just an infant. She couldn't find a daycare in Juneau that cost less than $1,000 a month. So Toys R Us kept her on part-time hours and gave her a raise anyway. The company also got her out of the stockroom and onto the floor.

When the Marin family moved to Oregon in 2014 so Henry could start pharmacy school, she finally took that full-time job. For the first time in her adult life, she had employer-sponsored health insurance.

Most importantly, and most uncommonly, Toys R Us gave Liz control over her schedule. Most retail chains use scheduling software to adjust employees' hours based on constantly shifting data like customer demand and inventory arrivals. That means many workers don't know whether they have a shift until the day, or even an hour, before it's supposed to start. In Liz's experience, Toys R Us store managers stuck to the schedules they set, making changes only when they were truly in a bind. Liz could plan around school pickups, doctors' appointments, and Henry's college schedule. When the Marins moved to Portland, she stopped working evening hours so the family could be together when Henry was done with class.

Liz felt like her life was more stable than it had been at any point in her thirty-five years, like all that advice about pulling herself up by her bootstraps and making her own destiny had finally paid off. Because she felt valued at Toys R Us, she worked hard, made herself indispensable. She stepped up when she saw a need; she volunteered to train new employees. In a matter of months, she knew how the store worked better than the managers did, so everyone treated her like their favorite boss. Fourteen dollars an hour—about $30,000 a year—wasn't much to support a family of five in Portland, but she was an expert budgeter. And the family's dependence on her salary was temporary; within four years, Henry would be making six figures as a pharmacist. She started to think Toys R Us was the kind of place she could work for her entire career.

═══

BY THE TIME LIZ GOT her job, though, Toys R Us was teetering more than rank-and-file employees—let alone company outsiders—could see.

Including contributions from limited partners, KKR, Bain Capital, and Vornado each paid roughly $430 million of the $6.6 billion it cost to acquire the chain; the other 80 percent was financed by loans from investment banks. That arrangement turned Toys R Us into a fundamentally different type of company, making it far less likely to survive.

Public companies generally maintain a ratio of about 30 percent debt to 70 percent equity, which includes cash, real estate holdings, inventory, and investments. If they take on much more debt than that, they're likely to run into problems with board members and other shareholders. When a private equity fund acquires a company, though, the ratio flips: 70 percent debt and 30 percent equity on average, scholars Eileen Appelbaum and Rosemary Batt have found.

Just before the company was acquired, about 70 percent of Toys R Us's assets were in equity and 30 percent—$1.86 billion—in debt. By the time the deal was completed and the $5 billion in loans had been signed for, Toys R Us had 78 percent debt and 22 percent equity.

On one level, it's baffling that "turnaround specialists" like those at KKR and Bain Capital would load their own portfolio company down with so much debt. Spending more money on interest payments leaves less for operations, increasing the risk of failure. But such elementary math only applies when the parent firm's interests align with those of the company it owns. Private equity firms themselves don't borrow money to fund their acquisitions. Rather, they have the company they are acquiring do it on their behalf. When KKR, Bain, and Vornado borrowed money to buy Toys R Us, they did it in Toys R Us's name, not their own. Even though the firms owned the company, even though their executives took out the loans, they would not be legally responsible for paying that $5 billion back.

For the first few years after the deal, Toys R Us's revenues ranged from $11 billion to just under $14 billion, with about 3 percent earnings after business expenses. But now it was having to pay interest expenses of more than $400 million per year, according to SEC filings. In other words, in any given year, between 80 and 120 percent of earnings were going straight to interest payments. That meant less money spent on improving stores, updating the company's strategy, or even paying down the loan's principal. "If they didn't have the debt, they would be making $500 to $600 million a year in profit," an industry analyst said later.

The Toys R Us deal also included one more element that kept the risk off the private equity firms' books: the company's real estate holdings. This was where the third partner came in. Vornado Realty Trust is not a private equity company, but a landlord that pays dividends to its shareholders. Vornado couldn't have cared less about selling toys. What it did care about was the huge potential profit from Toys R Us's 700-plus physical stores across the U.S.

Historically, Toys R Us owned almost all of its own real estate, which helped establish the company's reputation as a well-run, fiscally conservative operation. Rather than paying rent to a mall owner or commercial real estate firm on every store, every month, the Toys R Us of Lazarus's day preferred to buy as many store locations as possible outright, spreading the cost out over the life of the mortgage while the value of the properties increased.

When KKR, Bain, and Vornado bought the company, they up-ended that strategy via what is known as a sale-leaseback agreement. Within a few months of the acquisition, much of Toys R Us's real estate was sold to two newly created property companies, or "PropCos," controlled by Vornado. Now, in addition to its loan payments, Toys R Us also had to pay rent on the very same properties it had once owned. This left even less money for strengthening the business.

For KKR, Bain, and Vornado, meanwhile, selling the properties allowed them to recoup part of their initial investment up front, then continue earning more through monthly rent payments from their own portfolio company. Their interests were exactly opposed to those of Toys R Us, the company whose success they were supposed to be working toward. Charging higher rents meant more money for the firms—and yet more crushing expenses for the company they'd bought.

It is true that without involvement from private equity, Toys R Us likely would have eventually shrunk to a tiny fraction of its glory days. But it is also true that the company was much healthier financially before it was acquired than afterward. Anyone who put in the effort to look beneath the surface of Toys R Us's purported success post-acquisition would have noticed red flags almost immediately. From the very beginning of its life under private equity, the company was drowning in debt payments that made it close to impossible for it to survive long-term.

The Toys R Us saga also illustrates exceedingly clearly—perhaps more clearly than any other single private equity deal—how little private equity gambles when it steps in to "save the day." Contrary to the story they told about themselves, there was no substantive risk to the firms that acquired Toys R Us. Each was on the hook for under half a billion dollars, a drop in the respective buckets of companies with billions of dollars in assets. And when their management fees were combined with the revenue from selling off the company's real estate, plus dividends, performance bonuses, and tax loopholes, the risk of losing even that much wasn't particularly high.

The only threat was to the existence of Toys R Us—to an American institution, and to the 33,000 people who worked there. They were the people without the safety net of hundreds of other investments. They were the people scraping to make ends meet on near-poverty wages in twenty-first-century America. They were the only people involved who depended on Toys R Us for their survival.

———

WHEN THE REGIONAL MANAGER ALLOWED Liz to pick which Portland-area store she would work at, she could tell many were understaffed: no one offered to help her; she saw piles of toys in need of reshelving. She had worked too long in retail to blame the employees; she could tell they weren't getting enough help. Liz didn't want to work in a store like that. This job was going to be supporting her family for four years while Henry was in pharmacy school. She could not afford for anything to go wrong.

The Babies R Us in Tigard, a middle-class suburb of 55,000 people southwest of Portland, felt different. As soon as she walked in, pushing her infant son, Daniyel, in a stroller, an employee greeted her and asked if she needed help. When she said she was headed to the furniture department, the employee radioed to a colleague in that section, asking him to keep an eye out for Liz and her son. She felt taken care of—just what she wanted for her own customers.

Liz didn't know it at the time, but it wasn't accidental that the Babies R Us experience was more luxe than that of its sister store. In 1996, Toys R Us launched the spinoff to focus on cribs, car seats, strollers, baby clothes—coincidentally, the same market that Charles Lazarus had initially targeted when he started National Baby Shop in the 1940s before expanding it into Toys R Us. By the mid-2000s, Babies R Us—BRU to people inside the company—had been the bright spot

among the company's struggles for years. When Toys R Us went up for
sale, BRU was responsible for three-quarters of its parent company's
profits, even though there were less than a third as many BRU stores
as TRU ones. During the sale process, executives pitched the idea
of spinning BRU into a separate company to wall it off from TRU's
sliding revenue. KKR, Bain, and Vornado didn't do that, though they
did convert several underperforming Toys R Us stores into Babies R Us
locations.

Liz was the dream Babies R Us employee. She learned how to install
car seats to comply with state law, and talked her customers through
the process so thoroughly that even first-time parents walked away
confident about their new purchase. BRU's competitive advantage—
the chance to get advice from a trained specialist—was just what Liz
offered. She became a customer favorite; people she had helped prepare
for their first child would ask for her by name when they were about
to have their second. One of her favorite parts of the job was helping
people set up their registries. She never tried to upsell customers, but
she wouldn't let them forget anything either. She was raising three
kids on $14 an hour; she knew what parents on a budget needed and
what they could skip.

The work was great; her customers were great. The problem was
that the company was growing weaker every year. Babies R Us had
held off the threat from Amazon and Walmart longer than Toys R Us,
but by the mid-2010s, many people had lost their taste for going to a
store and talking to a real person, even when it came to specialty goods.
Once the company's saving grace, BRU's profit margins started slipping
too. Annual Toys R Us SEC filings stopped highlighting BRU in the
"opportunities for growth" section.

For store employees, the most notable change was that when
someone left their job, executives increasingly wouldn't replace them.
For as long as employees at the Tigard Babies R Us could remember,
one person oversaw the gear department while another ran clothes
and toys. Those two roles were combined into one job. And there had
always been one point person for "boy" toys and another for "girl" toys.

Those were folded together too. Liz was worried, but she didn't want to rock the boat. "I probably should have started doing more digging," she said later. "But you know, we're just retail employees. We do what we're told."

By 2016, Liz was doing what used to be two people's jobs. She was in charge of training all customer-facing employees, while simultaneously handling human resources for the store. Then she was asked to take on a third role, overseeing pricing and signing. She couldn't say no—she was just a retail employee, doing what she was told—but now there weren't enough hours in a day to get all the work done. Liz constantly felt guilty that she wasn't checking in on her colleagues as much as she wanted to, making sure they were okay and didn't need help.

Her work training new employees took the biggest hit. To her chagrin, many of them were now just watching the Toys R Us video curriculum and learning the rest as they went, instead of getting the full onboarding experience she took pride in providing. This also meant that when customers had complicated questions or problems, she often had to step in to cover for an undertrained colleague. That sucked up even more of her time. All the while, her wage never budged from $14 an hour. And even though she often ended up staying late, she was only paid for forty hours a week. But she was stuck. Few other retail chains were thriving either, and she certainly couldn't afford to go back to part-time hours. Her family's livelihood depended on Toys R Us.

———

TOYS R US HAD IDENTIFIED the biggest threats to its business well before private equity entered the picture. Its last annual report as a public company, in early 2005, identified brick-and-mortar competition like Walmart and Target as well as "Internet and catalog businesses" as among its principal challenges. The competitive landscape was exactly the reason Toys R Us was an attractive target for private equity: only the specialists at KKR and Bain could pull off such an ambitious turn-around and "realize the full potential" of the brand, in the words of a KKR director quoted in the press release.

But if two of America's largest private equity firms genuinely intended to save Toys R Us, their strategy was baffling.

Everyone who worked for the company—plus a healthy number of people who only shopped there—could see how the business needed to improve. Toys R Us didn't seem to be taking obvious steps to keep up with the times and sell more toys: launching a real web presence, modernizing stores, adding in-person services Amazon couldn't provide. Liz was just one worker, low on the chain, with no access to the executives at headquarters in New Jersey, but she could plainly see that stores needed more employees and better organization to be able to compete.

Plenty of issues predated the private equity acquisition. Among the most obvious was that Toys R Us's famous warehouse atmosphere—so innovative when Charles Lazarus introduced it in the late 1940s—had begun to feel dated and chaotic. Lazarus put *everything* on display in long rows so his customers would be overwhelmed by a feeling of abundance and know they never needed to go anywhere else. But that was before the internet. Even a 50,000-square-foot store—huge by retail standards, pretty standard for Toys R Us—could only hold a tiny fraction of the inventory of an Amazon warehouse. By 2021, those averaged *800,000* square feet.

But while the retail industry was confronting an existential crisis brought on by Amazon, it doesn't appear that Toys R Us's private equity owners ever tried particularly hard to forge a new path. By way of alternate reality, consider online pet supply retailer Chewy.com. Chewy made its name by adding abundance to specialty, offering any brand of cat food, birdcages, and dog toys a person could dream of. Crucially, though, it also didn't stray from its lane. That strategy allowed the company to promise the type of expertise Amazon could never offer, plus customer service that became the envy of the retail industry. Toys R Us could have taken that path, building massive warehouses of its own and using its exclusive relationships with toy manufacturers to beat Amazon on price and selection online.

Toys R Us's decision to outsource its e-commerce operation to Amazon half a decade before KKR, Bain Capital, and Vornado entered the picture helped sabotage its chances of becoming a thriving web retailer. Then things went from bad to worse. As part of founder Jeff Bezos's quest to make Amazon "the everything store," the company started breaching its exclusivity contracts, which meant selling competitor toys. A judge later found that in its quest for world domination, Amazon had openly broken the fundamental terms of the contract.

Toys R Us sued, and ultimately won, but the damage was done. The only penalty to Amazon was the termination of the contract, with zero dollars in compensation. After six years of losing money to Amazon, Toys R Us failed to recoup a dime. (Amazon did eventually pay $1 million.) Bezos's strategy of controlling every third-party seller across the world may have violated a contract or two, but it also gave the company a huge advantage in toys and almost every other retail sector.

Now it was 2006, and Toys R Us was starting from scratch online. That put it approximately an eon behind its competitors. Many executives would have treated the moment as *the* critical juncture for the future of Toys R Us, leaning as aggressively as possible into internet sales in a last-chance bid to modernize the company. But the company's new overseers from KKR, Bain, and Vornado seemed shockingly nonchalant about the need to make digital sales a core part of the business. While toysrus.com did launch its own, fairly primitive sales site that year, the lack of a major marketing push or an effort to make the user experience best-in-class left it feeling like an afterthought. Liz felt like she couldn't reliably refer customers to the website, because they weren't likely to find much she couldn't sell them in the store.

Another way to evolve, then, would have been to become the anti-Amazon, creating a curated experience and turning its stores into destinations like Target or Sephora. That's what John Eyler had in mind when he joined Toys R Us from luxury retailer FAO Schwarz, what he tried to achieve with the ill-fated Times Square Ferris wheel.

After the private equity takeover in 2005, Eyler left, walking out with a $65 million golden parachute, but Toys R Us's new bosses flirted with continuing his extravagant vision. In 2009, the company bought FAO Schwarz itself, for an undisclosed price, in hopes of dominating the high-end market. On multiple occasions over the years, one CEO or another would announce a plan to revamp the chain's stores to make them feel less like warehouses and more like entertainment palaces that happened to sell toys, but the plans never seemed to go anywhere. In the six years she worked at the company, Liz didn't see any significant improvements to the store experience. Instead, things got worse and worse. The famed Toys R Us Buyer Protection Plan was replaced by a more generic, less generous warranty program; suppliers were constantly in flux. The idea of, say, properly training employees—which, she was sure, would mean they'd sell more products and thus make more money—weighed heavily on her mind. But no one from corporate seemed to care.

Two researchers later found that while Toys R Us did make some investments after KKR, Bain, and Vornado took over, the lion's share of that money went to trying to optimize the supply chain in an attempt to save money on operating costs. The cash that was left after covering management fees and interest payments wasn't going toward upgrading the in-store experience or creating an online revenue stream, but to modernizing inventory systems in the service of "lean operations"—in other words, employing fewer people.

This is standard private equity practice: maximizing profit means cutting costs, and wages are expensive. More than 1.3 million Americans lost jobs in retail and related industries between 2009 and 2019 as a direct result of private equity acquisitions. Overall, the retail sector added more than 1 million jobs over that period.

It's certainly possible that Toys R Us would have failed no matter who owned it. Amazon was a merciless competitor, and plenty of legacy retailers buckled under the pressure. Surviving required extreme creativity and the capital to try new approaches.

KKR, Bain, and Vornado brought neither. Looking back, it's not difficult to diagnose the root cause of Toys R Us's failure to evolve. The $5 billion in debt that financed the acquisition grew more crushing every year. At times, more than 100 percent of the company's earnings were going toward interest payments, without even making a dent in the principal. The company wasn't taking any strategic risks because it could not afford to pay for them. Its owners also didn't particularly need to make Toys R Us a success; it didn't affect their management fees.

One turning point came in 2009, the same year as the FAO Schwarz acquisition. The bill for $725 million in debt came due, and the company didn't have the money. The solution? KKR, Bain, and Vornado took out more loans to pay off the original ones, like an online-shopping addict applying for a new credit card to cover the bill for the old one.

The following year brought a new plan to keep up with the mounting debt: go public, selling $800 million in shares. But after testing the waters, Toys R Us pushed back its public offering—conditions didn't look favorable for a company with more than three-quarters of its assets in debt.

By 2012, the company's prospects on the open market didn't appear to have improved, and yet more money was due to lenders, so Toys R Us's owners took out another $225 million loan. Talks of an initial public offering evaporated. For another five years, the retailer hobbled along, occasionally proposing new strategies in SEC filings and press releases, then coming up short financially when it came time to execute them.

Toys R Us's private equity owners had initially taken out $5.3 billion in loans to finance their purchase of the company. Twelve years later, their total debt had shrunk. Now they owed a mere $5.2 billion.

―――――

TOYS R US WENT UNDER gradually, then suddenly. From Liz's point of view, the chain wasn't thriving, exactly, but things seemed stable.

Her Babies R Us store in Tigard was a high performer, regularly beating sales goals and earning strong reviews from customers and regional managers. Surely, she figured, that would protect her and her coworkers even if other parts of the company weren't doing as well.

In 2017, Liz said, Toys R Us took everyone in management to Disney World. "Everyone" meant regional and district managers, but also the manager of every store across the country—hundreds of people in all. The company covered airfare, hotel stays, food, drinks, and entertainment for everyone. Organizers handed out swag, including plush knit Toys R Us sweaters. Swanky corporate retreats were common in finance and other white-collar industries, but Liz had never heard of retail managers receiving such treatment.

Yet when her boss came back from the trip, he was demoralized. "We're not giving our employees decent raises because they're telling us not to," she remembered him saying. "You guys are working your butts off for this company, making all this money, and they're wasting money on handmade sweaters and Disney World."

It seemed strange to Liz too. Practically every request her team made—for more staff, store improvements, anything—was rejected by corporate as too expensive. How could sending hundreds of people to Disney World be in the budget?

That year, Toys R Us owed $1.2 billion in loan payments; the next year, another $668 million. And it had no way to pay: lenders were sick of riding the Toys R Us merry-go-round. There would be no miracle deal or new set of loans. To make things worse, many suppliers began demanding payment before shipping merchandise to stores so they weren't at risk of getting stiffed. By September, stock-up time for the holiday rush, there wasn't nearly enough money in the coffers to buy an entire Christmas's worth of toys *and* pay off the loans. On September 18, a few months after the Disney World trip, Toys R Us filed for Chapter 11 bankruptcy protection, which helped secure a new $3.1 billion loan to finance a total company overhaul.

The entire point of bankruptcy proceedings is to give a company the financial breathing room required to find a path to success; it's much easier (and cheaper) to close up shop than to restructure if its bosses don't see a way forward. This can lead to comically overstated optimism on the part of leaders of bankrupt companies. "It's the dawn of a new day for the company," Toys R Us CEO Dave Brandon said when the filing was announced, as if he were promoting a glorious expansion rather than a last-ditch effort to save the American institution he oversaw. "It's the opportunity to do things we've wanted to do for a long time but haven't been able to."

Companies acquired by private equity firms are much more likely to go bankrupt than their peers, research shows: 20 percent of them enter bankruptcy proceedings within ten years, compared to 2 percent of other companies. This is an all-but-inevitable outcome of the high debt loads involved in leveraged buyouts; if market forces or increased competitive pressure causes a downturn in revenue, loan payments can easily become overwhelming.

While declaring bankruptcy is not the same as going under, more than half of companies that file for Chapter 11 end up going out of business, and retail chains are even less likely to emerge from bankruptcy. Meanwhile, studies have found that companies owned by private equity firms are more likely to liquidate than independent, public, or venture capital–backed companies after bankruptcy. Chapter 11 proceedings theoretically help a company get out from under debt, but the mountain becomes exponentially steeper as the amount of debt increases. Ten of the fourteen largest retail bankruptcies between 2012 and 2019 were at companies owned by private equity firms. Private equity–owned chains that went under in the 2010s include RadioShack, Claire's, Payless ShoeSource, Kmart, Sears, Gymboree, Charlotte Russe, A&P, Fresh & Easy, Shopko, Winn-Dixie, Fairway, Sports Authority, Mervyn's, Linens 'N Things, and dozens of others. When a business has $400 million in interest payments a year and a few hundred million a year in profits, mere restructuring is unlikely to save it.

After he announced the bankruptcy, Brandon and his executive team reassured Toys R Us employees and customers that everything would work out just fine. For a few months, Liz mostly believed him.

Lower-performing stores were facing staff cuts or closures, but her store continued doing well on every metric, and management told the team the metrics were what mattered.

By the start of 2018, though, Liz was getting nervous. It was impossible to tune out the bad news about Toys R Us, whose ongoing bankruptcy saga was being widely covered in the media. Her husband was a few months from graduation. His starting salary as a pharmacist would be more than twice what Liz was making, but until then, feeding the couple's three children was up to her. Stress kept her up at night.

One day, she called her manager. "Am I going to have a job through the end of my husband going to college? What's going on?" she asked.

"I don't know what you mean. They're telling us everything's fine."

"Are you *sure*? Are you not telling us something? I'm asking you as a friend, not just as my boss. You know my situation. I cannot be without a job."

"At our manager meeting, they told us we shouldn't worry. It's no big deal. You are in a high-volume store."

By this point, though, Toys R Us was almost entirely out of cash. Just making it to the 2018 Christmas season would require $250 million the company didn't have, and Brandon's plan to close 180 low-volume stores hadn't convinced investors to send yet more money. KKR, Bain, and Vornado proposed keeping the company alive on a smaller scale, but the lenders, who by now controlled a significant percentage of the company, outvoted them, deciding it would be more profitable to liquidate.

On March 10, Liz's boss called her first thing in the morning to ask her to come in early to cover his shift: corporate had announced a mandatory managers' meeting. That wasn't unusual; no one panicked. When the store manager emerged, though, he looked baffled. All they had been told was that an announcement would happen sometime that afternoon, nothing about what exactly would be announced. So they waited.

Later that day, one of Liz's regular customers, who was pregnant, rushed into the store. Liz had been helping the woman stock up on supplies, but she had also coached her through a case of gestational diabetes so severe that it caused fainting spells. Liz had had gestational diabetes too, so she advised the woman to keep a diary of everything she ate and her corresponding sugar levels so that she could identify what was making her sick. The woman discovered that fruit was the chief culprit. She stopped eating fruit, and stopped passing out.

On this day, the woman was crying as she approached Liz. "Liz, what am I going to do without you?" she sobbed. "Where are you going to work? I need you! I cannot survive this without you!"

"What are you talking about?" Liz blurted, and the customer realized with horror that she had just become the bearer of very, very bad news. She pulled up an article on her phone. Toys R Us, a titan of American retail for six decades, the favorite store of generations of children, the company about whom the term "category killer" was invented, was going out of business. All 735 U.S. stores would be shuttered, all 33,000 employees laid off. Liz was a top performer at a top-performing store, but it wasn't enough to protect her job in the face of $5.2 billion in debt.

It took another three hours for Liz and her colleagues to receive the official email announcement from their bosses.

———

U.S. BANKRUPTCY LAW IS CLEAR on the order in which creditors must be paid back with whatever money remains when a company closes shop. Loans secured by collateral, like the billions Toys R Us's owners took out in the company's name, come first, which gives lenders the peace of mind necessary to continue pouring cash into private equity firms. Taxes are another top priority. Suppliers like toy makers rank low on the list, even if the bankrupt company has already sold goods without paying for them. Employee severance ranks even lower.

Shortly after the company announced it was going out of business, Liz learned that she and the 33,000 Toys R Us employees across the country would lose their jobs—it wasn't clear when—and wouldn't receive a dime. It didn't matter that Toys R Us employee contracts specified that laid-off employees would be paid severance. At some point in the next few months, the $14-an-hour job on which Liz had supported a family for four years would simply vanish.

The injury was bad enough. But then came the insult. While the company was at death's door, Brandon was awarding a final bonus to each of the company's top executives: 75 percent of their base salary. For Brandon himself, that meant $2.8 million on top of his $3.7 million annual pay. The bonuses were paid out three days before the company's failure was announced, which meant the $16 million total expenditure wasn't subject to the bankruptcy order of operations. The estimated $348 million Toys R Us spent on lawyers, consultants, and bankers to orchestrate the seven-month restructuring effort between the bankruptcy and liquidation was safe too.

But what of the private equity firms, the ones who ostensibly took on more than a billion dollars' worth of risk in an effort to save a beloved American company? Losing $430 million is not entirely trivial even for a company as big as KKR (it managed $100 billion in assets at the time of the bankruptcy, about five times what it had when it acquired Toys R Us in 2005). Headlines bemoaned the $1.3 billion loss for KKR, Bain, and Vornado, fretting over what such a colossal failure would mean for the future of the private equity industry.

Except: *the firms didn't lose money.* Using SEC filings, journalist Dan Primack calculated that both Bain and KKR made more than they spent on the Toys R Us deal. Each had paid $430 million for their share of the company, but the vast majority of that money came from its limited partners, like pension funds and endowments. At the time of the Toys R Us acquisition, Bain general partners were required to commit 10 percent to a purchase, which meant around $43 million. Because these partners were the ones "doing the work" to manage the company, they also collected their industry-standard 2 percent fee each year, plus additional management and consulting fees. For Bain, that meant a total of $61 million in fees over the twelve years they co-owned Toys R Us, $18 million more than they paid. And that doesn't include the fees and interest they earned each time Toys R Us refinanced its debt.

Of course, a firm's management fees pay the salaries of the employees who work on a given deal, so it would be unfair to count that $18-plus million as pure profit. A Bain source told Primack that the firm's staff put in about 72,000 total hours working on Toys R Us, about 115 hours a week. But partners and associates at a place like Bain or KKR aren't really at risk of losing their jobs if a single deal is less lucrative than expected. After all, the firm is at no risk of failure. Bain general partners were managing about $27 billion in 2005, 627 times the amount they spent on Toys R Us.

KKR also profited from Toys R Us's demise—even without counting the 20 percent share private equity owners take from each year's profits. By design, it is nearly impossible to say which years the general partners at KKR took a profit share from Toys R Us, or how much they collected, but the general partners likely made out fine even in the company's worst years: their money came from management fees and other fixed costs. In the case of Toys R Us, like in most leveraged buyouts, the ultimate fate of the portfolio company wasn't the most important thing. Private equity firms make their money anyway. The only risk is that they will make a few million instead of tens of billions off a given deal.

———

THE STAKES FOR LIZ AND her 33,000 colleagues—the ones on hourly salaries that started at minimum wage—were much higher. Compounding the employees' stress was ambiguity about exactly *when* the stores would close. Henry was scheduled to graduate from pharmacy school in May, but he wouldn't be able to work until he passed his licensing exam, which would take at least an additional few weeks. Liz started taking on as much overtime as she could bear, adding as many $21-an-hour shifts as she could to stockpile for a future with three children and no income. She was barely seeing her kids— her workdays began to stretch from 4 a.m. to 10 p.m.—but it was better than being unable to feed them.

Working at Toys R Us was like keeping a terminal patient on life support, not knowing whether the dying process would take hours, days, or weeks. The feeling of dread was nearly unbearable. At one point, Liz was sure her entire family would end up homeless, but her landlord agreed to use their security deposit to cover a month's rent. She was grateful for his generosity, but then she immediately started worrying about the next month. On top of all that, she was doing whatever she could to help her colleagues find new jobs. Over and over, she covered for someone when they got an interview during work hours, then covered for their workload when they left and weren't replaced.

Liz got lucky. Her store was in the last wave of closings, on June 29, 2018. Henry passed his exam on the first try, which meant his first day as a salaried pharmacist was June 30, 2018. Their kids wouldn't be homeless. Even without the severance she was promised when she started at the company six years earlier, the Marin family would survive the fall of Toys R Us mostly unscathed.

Many of her friends weren't so fortunate. Liz had become close with a store supervisor in North Carolina named Annmarie Reinhart Smith, who had worked for Toys R Us for twenty-nine years. Annmarie looked for months without finding a job; several hiring managers told her tacitly or explicitly that they weren't interested in hiring people who were nearing sixty. She had never written a resume or applied for a job on the internet, so Liz talked her through every step of the process. If Toys R Us wasn't going to take care of its workers, they would have to take care of each other.

SIX

ROGER

SIX YEARS AFTER HE RETIRED AS A PRACTICING DOCTOR, ROGER WAS
more involved than ever in running Riverton's hospital. As a board
member, he had a hand in every aspect of the administrative work.
He didn't love management, not like he loved caring for patients, but
he believed he had an obligation to serve the place where he had spent
most of his career.

When Roger talks about his work, he slides easily into the realm of
the philosophical, talking about medicine as a true calling—not from
God per se, but from some force in the universe. Especially in his
eighties, he is reflective about what his career has meant. "I knew from
age ten or eleven that I wanted to be like Uncle Austin, and from then I
had blinders on—this is where I'm going," he said, his bright blue eyes
gazing toward the mountains behind his house outside of Riverton
as he worked out his thoughts. "You can argue that you shut a lot of
doors when you do that, and I think that's a fair statement. It would
be hard for me to imagine, however, that I could have done anything
with my life—now that I'm pretty late in the fourth quarter of it—
in which I could have made as much of a difference as I have out here
in rural Wyoming."

Occasionally, his deep love for his community, his colleagues, and
the way he's spent his life brings him to tears. "We all came here for
the right reasons, and I am extremely proud of that," he said of the in-
ternists who chose a career in Riverton over an easier, better-paid job,
like the one he had early in his career at the fancy suburban hospital

in Garland, Texas. Then he began to weep. "You want to leave a place better than you found it. For a long time, I really did feel that way."

But that was before Riverton Memorial Hospital became SageWest Health Care, before one of the biggest rural hospital chains in the country saw it as a distressed asset in need of saving through a ruthless search for efficiencies. That was before two hospitals collapsed into one, with basic services split between facilities twenty-eight miles apart. That was before executives at Apollo Global Management, the private equity firm whose office looms above the Plaza hotel in midtown Manhattan, began calling the shots for a hospital in a small Wyoming town none of them had likely ever visited. That was before Roger realized that in the private equity world, hospitals were just another widget, a tool to make money and nothing more.

———

WHEN LIFEPOINT FIRST FORMALLY MERGED the hospitals in Riverton and Lander under the SageWest banner, Roger was told the move would save patients money they didn't have. To his understanding, Riverton and Lander would both offer basic services, while specialists would be based at one or the other. A patient could have their appendix out, deliver a baby, or be treated for a heart attack at either location; to see an orthopedist or an oncologist, someone in Riverton would drive the twenty-eight miles to Lander or vice versa.

By the time of the SageWest merger in 2014, this kind of resource sharing had become popular among both for-profit and nonprofit hospitals. Finding "efficiencies" by combining nonmedical departments like IT, billing, and legal, the theory went, would allow hospitals to cut the cost of actual care. And while a Rivertonian might have to drive to Lander for his orthopedics appointment, he would pay less, and see a doctor who had access to his full medical history and who worked closely with his other providers. It would be a win-win for patients, doctors, and companies. The federal government generally waved away antitrust concerns—what could be better for customers than saving money by coordinating services across facilities? The normal laws of economics, like the one about how competition benefits consumers, didn't seem to apply.

It was a compelling theory—and, a decade later, it's clear that it was indisputably, entirely wrong. In 2018, researchers at the University of California, Berkeley, found that the price of an average hospital stay in twenty-five metropolitan areas across California increased between 11 percent and 54 percent over the course of three years in which mergers were common. The average price for a hospital admission increased 113 percent at the state's largest multi-hospital systems between 2004 and 2013. In another extreme example, the health care system affiliated with Yale University bought out the only other hospital in its hometown of New Haven, then expanded across the state until many Connecticut residents had no other choice but to go to a Yale facility for their care. In the New Haven area, the price of a hospital stay was already three times higher than in other parts of the state; after the great roll-up, prices went up another 25 percent in two years.

The commission in charge of advising Congress on Medicare concluded in 2020 that the "preponderance of the research suggests that hospital consolidation leads to higher prices." It turned out that normal laws of economics, like the one about how competition benefits consumers, apply to hospitals too. By the time those studies found that hospital consolidation was in fact harming patients, though, it was too late to undo all the deals.

In 2021, President Biden's administration took an interest in promoting competition in the health care industry, blocking several proposed mergers over antitrust concerns and calling on federal agencies to find ways to promote competition. Biden's executive order pointed directly to the threat rural hospitals were facing, citing a report that found that more than a hundred of them had closed since 2013. In some cases, a 2023 study found, being taken over by a larger system allowed rural hospitals to keep operating when they would have otherwise closed. The downside was that patients generally wound up paying more for care because of the lack of competition. In addition, the researchers wrote, mergers may "also drain resources from the local community."

By then, the nation's ten largest health care systems already controlled nearly a quarter of the hospital market.

————

AS A SAGEWEST BOARD MEMBER, Roger didn't immediately see changes that worried him after the Riverton and Lander hospitals merged in 2014. LifePoint had promised that the new arrangement wouldn't lead to staff cuts except in administrative roles, and at first it didn't. According to Centers for Medicare and Medicaid Services data, Riverton Memorial Hospital had 195 people on staff in 2013, the last full year before the merger, while Lander Regional Medical Center employed 178. In 2015, the first full year afterward, the two combined employed 331, just 11 percent fewer.

The first sign of trouble came in 2016. Hiring doctors and nurses had always been challenging in places like Riverton; not that many doctors wanted Roger's life. So when a staffing crunch hit, SageWest CEO Alan Daugherty announced in July that Riverton would temporarily suspend obstetrics services; patients would have to travel to Lander to deliver a baby or get a prenatal checkup. Daugherty didn't say how long "temporarily" was going to last. Roger was concerned, but not panicked. He trusted Daugherty, and Daugherty said this was a short-term solution.

Nine months later, the Riverton obstetrics department remained closed. In April 2017, SageWest management told Rivertonians it would be eight more weeks—ten at the most. Eight weeks passed, then ten, then several times that, and still people couldn't deliver babies at SageWest Riverton. Questions about when the department would reopen went unanswered. Nearly two years after the closure, Daugherty dropped the other shoe: the temporary solution was in fact permanent. The days of delivering a baby in Riverton were over. "There's no way I can do it on a cost-effective basis," he told the Fremont County Commissioners in June 2018.

Making money off a small-town maternity ward is extremely challenging. More than half of all births in rural areas are covered by Medicaid, compared to 42 percent overall. Medicaid reimburses at a lower rate than private insurance, paying an average of $6,500 per delivery compared to an average of $15,000 from private insurers. At hospitals with neonatal intensive care units and other advanced technologies that command higher prices, healthy deliveries can be a loss leader without threatening the bottom line. Rural community hospitals like Riverton's, though, don't have any of that, nor enough "normal" births to cover the department's fixed costs.

But accepting that some maternity wards don't make enough money to survive requires accepting the premise that an individual maternity ward must justify its own existence financially. In the long run, they probably do. A study in Louisiana found that living in a "maternity care desert" meant a higher risk not just of death during childbirth, but in the first year afterward, which comes with all sorts of increased costs. But what if it didn't? What if being pregnant and uninsured or on Medicaid and living in a community without an obstetrician only meant that you and your baby were more likely to die or experience extreme complications *during* delivery? What if only hospitals in places with a disproportionate number of privately insured patients can afford to have obstetricians on staff? Fewer than half of rural hospitals now have obstetrics departments, and that number drops further every year. As financial firms have swallowed up a growing swath of the American health care industry, maternity care has become a privilege that a growing number of people cannot access.

Today, SageWest Lander employs just one full-time board-certified obstetrician, plus one nurse-midwife and one family medicine doctor who lists obstetrics as an area of focus. Rivertonians can still drive twenty-eight miles to deliver a baby—assuming there are no complications that require a specialist, assuming wind and snow haven't made Wyoming Highway 789 impassable. But it's not clear how long Lander will be an option at all. During his term as CEO, Daugherty would not commit to maintaining its obstetrics department long-term. John Whiteside, SageWest's current CEO, did not return multiple calls and emails.

Many people don't trust SageWest anymore anyway. When Roger's neighbor Lauren got pregnant, she made plans to deliver fifty-five miles away in Thermopolis, a town of just 2,700 people whose hospital has nonetheless chosen to maintain a maternity ward. When she went into labor during a blizzard, her husband drove her through the Wind River Canyon, a treacherously winding road in the best of circumstances. If the smallest thing had gone wrong, she likely would have been loaded onto a medevac helicopter to Casper. Nothing did, luckily.

Years later, Roger remained stunned as to how things got so bad. He had always been realistic about the limitations of rural hospitals, but it never occurred to him that delivering a baby—among the most routine procedures in any hospital—would be counted among them. "Casper has advanced specialty care, cardiovascular surgery, things we can't and shouldn't do in a town of ten thousand people," he said. "Our goal was always primary and secondary care: family practice, pediatrics, OB, general surgery, and orthopedics. That's what we should do. And for a long time, we did it well."

——

THE MONTH AFTER SAGEWEST ANNOUNCED the permanent closure of Riverton's maternity ward, LifePoint announced it had agreed to a buyout from Apollo Global Management. LifePoint would merge with a smaller Apollo portfolio company called RCCH HealthCare Partners, creating a chain of eighty-four "non-urban" hospitals across thirty states operating under the LifePoint name. The deal was framed as a direct response to the financial challenges at rural hospitals: LifePoint CEO Bill Carpenter promised that it would generate "new opportunities for growth and partnerships that will help us navigate the changing healthcare industry dynamics."

The acquisition wasn't widely covered outside the financial press, despite the fact that, at $5.6 billion, it was one of the biggest private equity deals in the health care industry that year. LifePoint operated seventy-one rural hospitals no one outside of small towns had ever heard of—hardly the stuff of mainstream headlines. Yet the deal was part of a tremendously consequential shift. Private equity was becoming dominant in every sector of the health care industry. The number of private equity acquisitions in health care more than doubled between 2008 and 2017, according to industry database Pitchbook. Among health care *providers*, like hospitals and doctors' practices, the growth was even more dramatic: more than 2.5 times over the same nine-year period. In 2018, the year LifePoint was bought out, private equity firms spent more than $100 billion on health care businesses. Less than two decades earlier, that number was less than $5 billion.

By the late 2010s, private equity was losing interest in industries that had been disrupted by advancements in technology, like retail and manufacturing. Health care, though, was as stable as businesses get. People need doctors no matter the economic conditions. Plus, America's population was aging, which meant more demand for hospitals and specialists. Total spending on health care in the U.S. was rising every year, reaching $4.3 trillion in 2021, around 18 percent of the U.S. gross domestic product. The year Apollo bought LifePoint, four private equity health care deals topped $4 billion. The largest, KKR's buyout of staffing agency Envision Healthcare, cost $9.9 billion.

Apollo itself didn't put up much of the money to buy LifePoint: a staggering $4.975 billion, or 89 percent, of the purchase price was made up of loans. LifePoint already had $2.9 billion in debt and minority interest. Now the new company would owe just under $8 billion, plus interest—almost exactly the combined annual revenue of the old LifePoint and RCCH.

In Riverton, the need to make money from health care was nothing new—the hospital had been owned by for-profit companies for nearly four decades. But the wave of consolidation combined with the Apollo acquisition turned up the heat. Merely making a profit was no longer enough; now the goal was to *maximize* shareholder value. Looking back, Roger concluded that actual medical care played no role in the deal. "These are people for whom health care is just one aspect of what they're engaged in, and what they're engaged in is to make money as fast as they can," he said. "I've got to believe they don't give a damn about the discharge of health care in Riverton, Wyoming. They only give a damn about making money."

========

THE MOST OBVIOUS WAY TO make money off rural health care was to charge higher-than-average prices—which SageWest did, dramatically so. In 2019, the year after Apollo bought LifePoint, researchers examined the gap between Medicare reimbursement prices (which are set by the federal government) and prices paid by private insurers (which are set by hospital owners) between 2015 and 2017. They found that on average, Wyoming hospitals charged insurance companies 302 percent more than Medicare, the second-highest disparity among the twenty-five states in the study. When the researchers examined hospital data for fourteen individual Wyoming facilities, they found that SageWest charged the highest relative prices. Data from 2020 shows that SageWest maintained the largest price disparity of any general hospital in the state after the Apollo acquisition.

In January 2019, the hospitals' billing practices attracted scrutiny for the first time anyone could remember. The Eastern Shoshone tribe—which shares the Wind River Reservation with the Northern Arapahoes, bordering the town of Riverton—accused SageWest of bilking its members' health plan. According to the Eastern Shoshones' business council, an audit showed that the hospital was making a 700 percent profit margin from medical care for tribal members, and that 20 percent of charges on patients' bills contained errors in the company's favor. In one case, the audit found, the tribe was charged more than $120,000 for $12,700 worth of treatments for one patient. An administrator from a company that helped the tribe manage its insurance plan told a local newspaper that among the hundreds of plans the company oversaw, SageWest's bills were uniquely egregious, a trend that began after the Apollo acquisition. (SageWest denied overcharging tribal members, saying the Eastern Shoshones in fact received a substantial discount compared to other patients.)

Simultaneously, LifePoint was also cutting costs. By 2022, the last year for which Centers for Medicare and Medicaid Services data is available, SageWest employed 227 people across its two campuses, nearly 40 percent fewer than before the Riverton-Lander merger. According to Roger, the number of physicians based in Riverton had dwindled from twenty-something to just seven.

A few weeks after the Eastern Shoshones accused SageWest of overcharging members, the company eliminated its inpatient mental health unit, known as PineRidge, which left Fremont County without a single residential facility for mental health and substance abuse treatment. Roughly 7 out of 10 patients at PineRidge were Eastern Shoshone tribal members, the tribe said. Now the nearest place for Wind River Reservation residents to get inpatient treatment was more than a hundred miles away. "Our goal is to work with SageWest, but no one at SageWest or any of the Apollo affiliates ever bothered to come discuss this urgent matter with tribal leaders to help mitigate the damage," the vice president of the tribe's business council said.

SageWest CEO Alan Daugherty blamed the closure on new federal accreditation requirements, which would have required increased staffing and physical renovations. SageWest needed to make money for Apollo, and spending money to improve mental health care wasn't an option.

Although PineRidge had operated out of Lander, Rivertonians couldn't help but notice that the majority of the cost savings were focused on their home hospital. After Riverton's maternity ward disappeared, orthopedic surgery moved to Lander too. Residents began to report that even routine procedures usually performed by nonspecialist surgeons were being diverted twenty-eight miles away.

Apollo and other private equity firms were also applying lessons from other industries to health care. As had become common in retail several years earlier, firms that owned hospital chains were charging hospitals rent for the same land they once owned. This strategy, known as "sale-leaseback," has become key to private equity profits because real estate has value independent from the business itself.

Under a sale-leaseback agreement, a private equity firm divides a portfolio company into two parts: one for the company's core business, and one for its real estate holdings. The firm then sells off the real estate assets to the highest bidder, pocketing the profits, and signs lease agreements on behalf of the company to remain in its head-quarters. That gives the company a new, and costly, monthly expense, and leaves it with less money to improve its operations. Suddenly the company shoulders a greater risk of failure, while the private equity firm gets a little extra insulation from the need to make a profitable exit. Sale-leasebacks have proved particularly lucrative in industries like retail and health care, which generally require many individual parcels of land, as well as in the media business, where local newspapers once owned huge offices on prime downtown real estate.

In November 2019, LifePoint sold ten of its physical hospital facilities, including both Riverton's and Lander's, for $700 million to an Alabama-based real estate investment firm with the impressively generic name Medical Properties Trust. SageWest's press release responding to press coverage of the sale framed it as an opportunity: "It is a financial strategy that allows providers to focus more of their resources on clinical care and the services they provide their communities."

The statement didn't explain exactly how giving up the hospital's most valuable asset would allow providers to focus more of their re-sources on clinical care. For Apollo, though, the benefits were clear: the $700 million went straight to the firm, mostly in the form of a dividend for shareholders. Medical Properties Trust, a publicly traded company that became one of the nation's largest owners of hospital real estate by partnering with major private equity players, got guaran-teed rent payments and a favorable tax package: real estate investment trusts pay zero corporate taxes if they invest enough of their assets and pay out enough of their earnings as dividends.

Those earnings, of course, came from the small rural hospitals across the country. SageWest Riverton and Lander began paying at least $6.5 million a year for the land on which their hospitals sat.

Two years after the $700 million Medical Properties Trust deal, Apollo made its next, even more profitable move. In June 2021, one of the firm's funds sold LifePoint to another for $2.6 billion, essentially transferring control from one group of Apollo investors to another.

It initially seemed like an in-the-weeds move of little importance to people who weren't directly involved. But a month later, Bloomberg reported the true significance: Apollo had made $1.6 billion by selling its portfolio company to itself.

At that point, Apollo had only invested $975 million of its own money in LifePoint; the rest of the original $5.6 billion purchase price had come from loans and limited partners. Yet the $1.6 billion in proceeds from the 2021 sale went to Apollo directly, according to a quarterly report. Soon after, LifePoint spun off SageWest and seventy-eight other hospitals into a new company, still controlled by LifePoint, called ScionHealth. Individual rural hospitals owned by LifePoint were still in serious danger of closure, but their parent company was now officially well over a billion dollars in the black.

———

WHEN RIVERTON LOST ITS MATERNITY ward for good and Apollo bought LifePoint, Roger kept his outrage quiet. He had worked for the hospital longer than anyone, he reasoned; surely its owners would listen to him behind the scenes. At one point, he remembered, Bill Carpenter, LifePoint's CEO, told him that SageWest doctors trusted him, saw him as a leader. At the time, he accepted the compliment. But he was starting to worry that in fact Carpenter had used him.

Six weeks after Apollo acquired LifePoint, Roger sent a letter to Carpenter outlining his frustrations with the company's management. The tone was largely straightforward, reciting the chronology of the Riverton hospital's decline. But here and there, his feeling of desperation peeked through. "Is it any wonder that there is a definite climate of fear in the Riverton hospital, when workers see one service after another shunted to Lander, one colleague after another either transferred to Lander, terminated, or leaving because of job insecurity?" he wrote. "I trusted in our relationship. I want to trust you and believe you can help this town regain the hospital it once had. I am appealing to you, Bill."

Carpenter never responded.

The first person to raise a *public* stink was Vivian Watkins. This surprised no one. Vivian had lived in Riverton since 1985, almost as long as Roger, and was now in her early seventies. As the former head of commercial lending for U.S. Bank's fourteen branches across Wyoming—and the kind of person who can't leave the grocery store without stopping four times to ask about someone's kids or their neighborhood drama—Vivian knows everyone in town. She cuts a recognizable figure: her gray hair sticks straight out from her head like a halo; her laugh booms across restaurants. She loves Riverton like a member of her own family. After retiring from the bank, she did a stint as the state's economic development director; after retiring from that role, she volunteered for seemingly every cause. If you need to know what's happening in Riverton, you go straight to Vivian.

Among all her many passion projects, though, Vivian has a particular investment in the town's hospital. Her son Kale runs IT there; her daughter Shawnda was a nurse there before she died in 2013. "We were spoiled in that you could walk into Riverton Memorial Hospital and unless you were having a massive coronary or a massive stroke, you got taken care of right there. We had the personnel, the doctors, the specialists," she said over plates of biscuits and gravy at the Trailhead, a popular diner in town. So as the institution declined, she knew she had to get involved.

One evening, she gathered a handful of locals and laid out the situation. She told them she did not want to see her beloved community lose its hospital, and she was sure that's where things were heading—if not a total closure, a stripping of services to the point that it might as well be closed. "We can accept what we have, as LifePoint keeps telling us we must," she told them. "But if we do not accept it, what do we need to do?"

She knew she couldn't take on LifePoint, much less one of the biggest private equity firms in the world, alone. So soon after the meeting, Vivian recruited a handful of neighbors to the cause. One of her first calls was to Roger. She had known him for decades, and there was no one in town more trusted on medical matters. And Roger knew that there was no one in town better at organizing than Vivian. He signed on as a charter member of her group, which named itself Save Our Riverton Hospital.

One of their first moves was sending a letter to Daugherty. Vivian, Roger, and seven other residents traced the history of the hospital and their concerns about the current state of affairs. They didn't ask for anything specific beyond the opportunity to discuss the issues, but they made it clear they weren't going anywhere: "If access to medical care is a basic essential for a community, we believe that we must fight to keep essential hospital services," they wrote. "To do that, we must make our case public, and we must take it to our community, our City Council, our County Commission, our state legislators, our federal congressional delegation, the Governor and other state officials, LifePoint corporate management, and the media."

Neither Daugherty nor anyone from LifePoint or Apollo replied to the letter. Perhaps they thought the group was bluffing about their commitment, or about their ability to reach all these powerful people and make them listen to the woes of a small-town hospital. If so, they underestimated two key facts.

One is that Vivian Watkins does not quit, *ever*. Another is that Wyoming is so small that it can feel like all 576,000 residents know each other. In most states, the governor is generally out of reach to ordinary citizens. In Wyoming, if you didn't go to high school with him or work with his niece, you probably know someone who did. Daugherty had lived in Wyoming for less than two years at the time of the Save Our Riverton Hospital launch; LifePoint leaders had never spent much time there. Apollo executives barely knew it existed, as far as local residents could tell. The Riverton group may have been vastly outmatched in terms of resources, but they had advantages money couldn't buy.

No one from SageWest, LifePoint, or Apollo accepted the group's invitation to a town hall at Central Wyoming College. One person who did attend was a reporter from the state's largest newspaper, the *Casper Star-Tribune*. In the days after the meeting, the paper ran a long story about the campaign, with a large photo of Roger addressing the group. The reporter included a quote from the town's seniormost physician: "If we acquiesce to people we know have been deceiving us for four years, we'll never achieve anything. This city deserves better." Many of the attendees wanted to know to whom they should make out checks. Soon Save Our Riverton Hospital had a mailing list and a Facebook page and was taking out ads in local media.

A week and a half after that first town hall and a month after the group formed, Daugherty finally responded to their complaints in an open letter published by County 10, a local news site. SageWest was operating in a "tough healthcare environment," he wrote, which necessitated difficult conversations about cuts. He also said the company was "aggressively recruiting" doctors and nurses to work in Riverton, including general surgeons. And while he was clear that obstetrics was never coming back, he promised to restart the hospital's cardiovascular program and launch a new telehealth option. "I first want to address this idea that SageWest Riverton is at risk of closing—that the hospital needs to be 'saved,'" Daugherty wrote. "This could not be further from the truth."

———

DAUGHERTY WAS BEING FORTHCOMING ABOUT one thing: there was no risk of Riverton's hospital shutting down entirely. Centers for Medicare and Medicaid Services reports show that SageWest nearly doubled its operating margin between 2013—just before it combined the two hospitals—and 2019, its first full year under private equity ownership. At a time when dozens of rural hospitals were closing, LifePoint and Apollo had figured out how to make one profitable.

But LifePoint's philosophy about how to "save" hospitals was diametrically opposed to that of the Save Our Riverton Hospital crew. The exact private equity strategies that made money for hospitals like SageWest—consolidating and outsourcing whenever possible, increasing costs to patients and insurers, cutting staff and entire departments—were the ones making patient care worse. From

LifePoint's headquarters in Brentwood, Tennessee, or Apollo's offices in Manhattan, eliminating the maternity ward in a tiny town in central Wyoming represented a clear win. From the perspective of a pregnant patient in that tiny town, or that of a doctor who had spent forty years delivering babies there, it was a tragedy.

Academic research over the past five years has attempted to make sense of what private equity's growing dominance in health care means for hospitals, nursing homes, mental health treatment facilities, and other service providers. In 2020, a study of 204 hospitals owned by private equity firms and 532 with other ownership structures found that those acquired by private equity grew net income, charged patients more per day, and increased the ratio of what they charged to what they paid. Effects on patient outcomes, though, were murkier: quality scores for heart attack care appeared to improve by 3.3 percent—but the increase was only significant at hospitals operated by HCA, the largest player in the industry, which was partially owned by Bain Capital and KKR. At non-HCA private equity–owned hospitals, quality scores for heart failure treatment decreased; no other factors related to treatment were statistically significant.

In other words, you'd certainly pay more if your local hospital got acquired by a private equity firm; whether you'd get better or worse care was unclear. "We have to decide whether the goal of a healthcare system is to increase profits, because private equity firms are selecting those parts of healthcare where they can see a profit," said Barbara McAneny, the president of the American Medical Association, in 2018. "The consolidation of various parts of the healthcare industry has been shown to increase prices and decrease choice, and if you're lucky, quality stays about the same."

Then, in late 2023, a landmark study from a team of scholars from Harvard and the University of Chicago finally presented at least a partial answer to the question of whether hospital care improved or declined under private equity ownership. The article found that in the three years after a private equity acquisition, the rate of serious preventable medical complications increased significantly. Patients were more likely to fall in the hospital, more likely to experience bed-sores, more likely to acquire infections at the site of a surgical incision. Arguably the most damning finding was that the number of central line infections, which often result from improper insertion or cleaning, rose 38 percent. Though the study didn't delve into the reasons for the increases, the implication was clear: focusing on short-term profits was leading to cost cutting that could be dangerous for patients.

Quality of care measures, though, only take into account types of care that a hospital actually provides. And since LifePoint bought the hospitals in Riverton and Lander, the primary trend has been offering fewer services. Data from the Wyoming Department of Health shows that the number of air ambulance flights from Fremont County to hospitals elsewhere in the state skyrocketed after the Lander-Riverton merger, from 155 in 2014 to 937 in 2019. According to the state health department, nearly one-quarter of all air ambulance flights transporting Medicaid patients were originating from Fremont County, home to just 12 percent of Wyoming's Medicaid patients. LifePoint and Apollo leaders had promised to invest more resources in SageWest, but the numbers didn't lie: more than six times as many people were unable to get the care they needed in their home communities.

In at least one case, the cost cutting directly resulted in a patient's death. In November 2020, a psychiatric patient was at SageWest Lander awaiting transfer to the Wyoming Behavioral Institute in Casper. Since the closure of the PineRidge mental health unit nearly two years earlier, SageWest had had no way of segregating people experiencing severe mental health episodes from other patients: no rooms with doors that locked, no security guards with specialized training. According to a state report, the man ran into the room of an elderly female patient and began gouging out her eyes with his fingers. He managed to entirely remove her right eye from its socket and pull out the optic nerve. He also caused severe damage to her left eye before hospital staff were able to restrain him. The woman died two weeks later; an autopsy listed the cause of death as homicide.

A federal inspection the week after the attack revealed major problems at SageWest, including inadequately trained staff, insufficient supervision of psychiatric patients, and a failure to administer recommended medications. The daughters of the woman who was killed filed a wrongful death lawsuit asking for monetary damages from SageWest. "It had been known for more than a year that SageWest Healthcare (Lander) had grossly insufficient supervision and monitoring of its psychiatric patients," the plaintiffs wrote in the suit. "In spite of repeated complaints, [the hospital] (and its officers, directors, and employees) failed to spend the money required to assure patients' safety."

The horrific nature of the Lander attack made it a statewide news story. Roger, though, wasn't shocked something awful had happened; he had been warning of the potential for years. His trust in SageWest and LifePoint had dried up long ago. He didn't believe for a second that "aggressive recruiting" was going to bring back the services Riverton had lost. By then he had seen the PowerPoint.

Back in 2014, executives at SageWest and LifePoint had developed a slide deck that was meant to be kept confidential. Then, one night in late 2018, a nurse found the file on a hospital server and shared it with a young ER doctor, who passed it along to Roger. The presentation outlined SageWest's plan for the combined hospital, and it directly contradicted what Roger had been told at the time, when he was on the board, talking regularly with LifePoint executives.

The eighteen slides said that SageWest would eliminate all but one pathologist position, consolidate its two radiology departments and anesthesia groups, and combine "some surgical services." The second-to-last page said that Riverton would become "a community focused outpatient center," while Lander would be upgraded to accommodate an influx of patients coming from Riverton. That was exactly what Daugherty had promised Roger would never happen.

The most damning page of the document was about obstetrics. "Consolidate OB to the Lander campus by Q4 2016/Q1 2017 after necessary improvements and remodel to existing structure," an executive had written. In other words, for those two long years when SageWest was promising to reopen Riverton's maternity ward, the company intended to do no such thing. In fact, it had planned two years before that to eliminate OB for good.

Roger had trusted LifePoint leadership, had publicly vouched that they had the best intentions for the hospital where he had spent nearly his entire career. Now it was clear that scores of people had lied to him for years. He was livid. Maybe, he began to think, saving Riverton's hospital wasn't the right goal. Maybe what Riverton needed was something else entirely.

SEVEN

NATALIA

BY THE TIME NATALIA RETURNED TO THE *CORPUS CHRISTI CALLER-Times* after five years away, the staff had shrunk dramatically. Still, the place vibrated with energy. She grew close with a few other young reporters, including one who had been hired at the same time she was. As a breaking news and general assignment reporter, she was covering a ribbon cutting one day and a murder the next, which could feel a little disorienting, but she could tell her skills were improving quickly.

One day she came back from a crime scene, frustrated that she hadn't been able to get very much information out of the cops. She asked the managing editor how to write the article. "Well, what did the place look like? Was anyone there?" the editor prompted. From then on, Natalia made sure to carefully notice every detail when on assignment. When Natalia ended up with three stories on the front page the next day, that same editor also told her to make sure to save the paper because it was an accomplishment to be proud of. They were all just quick news blurbs, not groundbreaking investigations, but an editor calling it out made Natalia feel valued.

She was finally on the right path: doing work she loved in a city she loved, developing her skills as a reporter and writer, and spending valuable time with her mom and stepdad. About a year after she moved back to town, she also started a new relationship.

It started with professional advice. When she had applied for the *Caller-Times* job, she was worried about whether her DWI conviction would stand in her way. So she asked Robert Muilenburg, her old journalism advisor from Del Mar College, what she should do. "Just be honest," he said, which she did. After she was hired, she started seeking his counsel on how to advance her career, and other stuff too. Initially, Robert was in a relationship, and she *swears* she never thought of him romantically anyway. But things happen. He broke up with the girlfriend, and she started running into him at bars. Then he asked her to lunch. Her friends told her that meant he *liked* her, though she wasn't convinced. But she started to think she *liked* him too. Things moved slowly at first—Natalia was nervous about doing anything that might mess with her professional goals—but the connection was undeniable.

Robert quickly became Natalia's chief advocate, encouraging her to pursue bigger and better opportunities, helping her navigate dilemmas in her reporting and in the newsroom. When a job as the entertainment writer for the *Caller-Times* opened up in 2017, she knew she'd be perfect for it. Robert helped her craft her application materials to make her best case. She got the job.

She was intent on making sure her arts and culture coverage appealed to people like her: Latinos, millennials, people who were very different from the average newspaper subscriber in the late 2010s. She wrote about new businesses launched by young Mexican Americans that were revitalizing the downtown area's long-gone nightlife. She reported a series on new restaurants around town (always including the disclaimer "she does not claim to be a culinary expert—and can't cook to save her life"). Her stories brimmed with voice, with spunk, more like recommendations from someone's coolest friend than stodgy newspaper write-ups.

Working with a handful of colleagues, Natalia focused on how to make the *Caller-Times* a digital-first publication, instead of a print newspaper that threw its stories online as an afterthought. She knew her friends weren't picking up a daily paper, and they also weren't flocking to caller.com. Inspired by NPR's wildly popular *Tiny Desk Concerts*, she worked with a venue in town to get bands into the newsroom to perform on Facebook Live during lunchtime, when people were likely to be scrolling their phones. There was no stage, no background; viewers could see Natalia's colleagues typing away behind the performers. People loved it.

She was also one of the few journalists in the newsroom who took a real interest in topics like search engine optimization and video, which had long been the backbone of web-first publications, but which newspapers had been woefully slow to adopt. She became the digital trainer for new reporters, helped develop the staff's best practices for publishing video, and was frequently called in to optimize someone else's story for the web—while also writing multiple stories a week. As a reporter, and with under three years of experience, not a particularly senior one, she was making $32,000 a year. That was a significant step up from what she was paid during her first days at the paper—$14,000 as a news clerk, $20,000 as a breaking-news reporter—but it was only enough to survive on because she was still living with her parents.

Like so many journalists who entered the industry when profits were declining and newspapers were pleading poverty, Natalia absorbed the message that she should be grateful for whatever she got. The narrative was that her employer couldn't afford to pay her any more; she didn't have reason to question it. Even after the *Caller-Times* was taken over by Gannett, a much larger and more powerful media company, "it didn't even occur to me to ask my colleagues how much they were making, or to ask for a raise," she said. "I just wanted to be in."

———

A MASTHEAD FROM THE END of 2017 lists fourteen news reporters at the *Caller-Times*, a lot smaller than what Natalia remembers from when she started in 2014. The Corpus Christi newsroom was hardly alone in downsizing through attrition, buyouts, or layoffs: Gannett was looking to trim costs by whatever means necessary across its more than a hundred newspapers. Other corporate-owned chains were cutting even more.

GateHouse Media also started as a chain of small and medium newspapers, the majority of them in towns that many Americans had never heard of: places like Metamora, Illinois; Taunton, Massachusetts; and Devils Lake, North Dakota. GateHouse was never known as a company that published best-in-class journalism. It was, however, a leader in one major respect: it was the first major newspaper chain to be owned by a private equity firm.

In fact, unusually, GateHouse spent its entire existence under private equity ownership. The company (first known as Liberty Group Publishing) was created from a $322 million leveraged buyout of 166 community newspapers, previously owned by a Canadian-based chain, in 1998. The buyer was Los Angeles private equity firm Leonard Green & Partners, one of the earliest practitioners of leveraged buyouts. The mastermind of the deal, though, was a hotshot young attorney from Chicago named Kenneth Serota, whom Leonard Green installed as Liberty's CEO.

Serota brought big plans to dominate the local newspaper game through consolidation. "They are very, very good cash-flow engines," Serota said in 1999, in a quote that took less than five years to age exceptionally poorly. "These are generally low-tech operations, insulated from media competition—no local TV station, maybe one radio station. Through consolidation, we make changes that benefit advertisers." Under Serota's leadership, Liberty went on a buying spree, making local owners offers too lucrative to refuse in a quest to scoop up as many papers as possible.

As at every media company, Liberty Group newspapers were under tremendous pressure to grow profits. But the situation was even more extreme than at Gannett and other chains because of the debt Leonard Green had taken on to finance the deal. Just $60 million of the $322 million used to purchase Liberty came from the firm itself; the other 80 percent was funded by loans. Every time Liberty bought a new paper, it added to its debt. Even when times were good, Leonard Green had taken out so many loans to finance purchases of new newspapers that by 2005, Liberty owed $350 million. Earnings jumped 30 percent through the first three quarters of that year, but debt payments consumed all of the increase, plus $3 million more.

Serota and his overseers at Leonard Green never claimed to care about newspapers beyond their ability to generate cash. So when they saw an opportunity for a profitable exit, they jumped. For $530 million, 41 percent more than they had paid for it six years earlier, Leonard Green sold Liberty to another private equity firm, New York–based Fortress Investment Group, in 2005. With three hundred papers, it was now the second-largest newspaper owner in the country, behind Gannett. Fortress renamed the company GateHouse; Serota walked away. The size of his payout was never reported.

GateHouse never had the name recognition or cultural cachet of Gannett. It dealt almost exclusively in small-town newspapers and lacked a flagship product like Gannett's *USA Today*. Yet it's clear now that GateHouse was the much more important company for the future of the industry. It set the trend for the financialization of American media. Newspapers across the country—hobbled not only by the collapse of the ad market but by their own failure to adapt to the digital era—were now looking less like cash-flow engines and more like anachronisms. GateHouse became the leader in laying off staff, consolidating once-independent papers, selling others for a song, and, if profits weren't growing, shuttering the only source of news in a community. Whereas Gannett had started as a *newspaper* company—one with a single-minded focus on local journalism—GateHouse was never anything more than a cog in a private equity machine designed to maximize shareholder value.

While it was easy to blame larger trends in the media industry for the endless newsroom layoffs, private equity strategies were just as much to blame. GateHouse was following a well-established playbook: cutting costs is a quicker path to boosting profits than the tedious work of improving a business's strategy. And cutting costs often means cutting jobs—private equity–owned companies shrink their staff size significantly, according to multiple studies.

After one such study was published, industry leaders hailed it as good news about private equity's role in the economy. In a letter criticizing the *Financial Times'* summary of the research, Drew Maloney, the CEO of the industry's lobbying group, pointed out that the authors also found that leveraged buyouts increased worker productivity by

7.5 percent. "This means that workers at private equity–backed businesses became more efficient for every hour they worked. This affirms
that private equity managers add value and improve businesses over
the long term through their expertise and hands-on work," he wrote.
Maloney did not include the finding that while those workers were
becoming more productive, their average earnings dropped as much
as 6 percent.

Local journalists are paid to report on their home community, but
that isn't a maximally efficient business model. To private equity executives, a whole newsroom serving a region of just a few million people
is an unrealized opportunity. If you have no particular interest in local
news—and if a publication is covering a community you're not a part
of and may never have set foot in—it's irrelevant whether the newspaper makes money by reporting stories or by being sold off for parts.
When GateHouse came for Gannett, it had already won the game.

⸻

IN 2018, NATALIA MOVED AWAY from her adopted hometown for the
second time.

She was happy at the *Caller-Times*, happy living with her mom and
stepdad and helping out around the house, happy in her friendships
with coworkers and old classmates. She was happy in her relationship
with Robert, whose job teaching at the community college kept him
tied to Corpus Christi. What she really wanted, she told her editor,
was a chance to formalize her role as a leader on new initiatives. She
wanted to become an editor herself. Her boss was encouraging, saying
everyone in management wanted her to rise through the ranks too.
But there were no jobs. She'd have to wait.

Her editor did send her to leadership training, an opportunity
Gannett offered to employees of all its newspapers. He also paid her
way to the annual Online News Association conference, where digi-
tally minded journalists gathered to network and swap insights into
the changing industry. People seemed impressed with the concert
series and other digital projects she had pioneered in Corpus Christi,

which felt good. One of the people she talked to was so impressed that he passed along her name to an editor at the *Indianapolis Star*, a much larger Gannett paper.

When she received an email asking if she would be interested in covering business development in Hamilton County, a fast-growing suburban area just north of Indianapolis, she thought it was meant for someone else. She had never been to Indiana. She wasn't a business reporter. But it turned out the *Star* editor *was* interested in her, in her passion for covering shops and restaurants opened by immigrants and people of color—and in the fact that she was fluent in two languages.

The idea of leaving home felt strange. But it was time to try something new. "At the *Caller-Times*, I wasn't learning anymore," she said. Even though the new job offered her $10,000 more a year, her mom was worried about how she would cover rent, student loans, *and* the payment for a new car she desperately needed. A former colleague who had left Corpus Christi for a job in Michigan warned that, unlike Texas, most states have income tax, so the raise wouldn't actually mean $10,000 more in her pocket. But Natalia had grown up since her disastrous stint in Arlington. She was almost thirty, and she never missed a payment on her bills. She knew she was ready.

When Natalia arrived at the *Star*, fifty-six journalists bustled around the newsroom. This was exciting; she had left behind a newsroom with just fourteen reporters. To the *Star*'s old-timers, though, fifty-six felt tiny: just five years earlier, the newsroom had been home to ninety-eight. Still, the *Star* was among the most distinguished local newspapers in the country, with two Pulitzer Prizes and a slew of other awards. Just two years earlier, the paper had uncovered what became one of the biggest stories in the country: the decades of sexual abuse against elite gymnasts by their team doctor, Larry Nassar.

The *Star* stood out in one other key way: it was home to one of the oldest journalist unions in the country.

In 1933, socialist *New York World-Telegram* columnist Heywood Broun made a radical proposal: journalists needed to unionize. Until then, labor unions had largely been for factory workers and other folks doing manual labor—not, reporters thought, for intellectuals like them. But journalists were overworked and underpaid, and Broun argued that their owners and publishers would never change that voluntarily. His column called upon reporters to "take a more practical view of their working conditions and organize against the rapacity of publishers."

The American Newspaper Guild—"guild" to avoid those blue-collar connotations of "union"—was born. Within several months, the organization held bargaining power at several newspapers, representing seven thousand workers. In 1937, they were joined by the staff of the *Indianapolis Star*, whose first contract guaranteed them overtime pay for the first time. The Indianapolis NewsGuild has operated ever since.

Like 84 percent of American journalists, Natalia wasn't in a union at the *Caller-Times*. She had never talked to anyone about what they were getting paid; there was no structure set up for them to do so, no minimum salaries or requirements that management must negotiate with workers.

Someone came by Natalia's desk to ask her to join the Indianapolis NewsGuild during her first week at the *Star*, she remembered, but she forgot about it, and no one followed up for quite a while. (The paper was an "open shop," which meant she benefited from union protections even without paying dues.) The enrollment form languished on her desk—until one day, months into her tenure, all the union members showed up to work in their NewsGuild T-shirts. "I was like, fuck, I want to be friends with them! So I joined," she said.

The Guild contract was hardly a paragon for workers across the industry. Minimum salaries for reporters were set at $615 a week, less than $32,000 a year. News assistants, the position Natalia had started in at the *Caller-Times*, were guaranteed just over $25,000 a year. An employee who was laid off would get just one week of severance pay for every year they had worked at the newspaper. The union hadn't even won a cost-of-living increase from its 2014 contract; Gannett had developed a reputation for fighting hard against pay bumps in union negotiations to preserve their bottom line.

By 2018, the goal at Gannett's corporate headquarters in McLean,

Virginia, seemed to be to cut the staff of each of its newspapers to the bone—and then keep cutting. Thanks to the withering ad market and the dwindling number of subscribers, revenue was in free fall, and nobody in leadership seemed to know how to turn it around. The only solution, to the owners' minds, was to keep making each newsroom cheaper to run through layoffs and attrition. That meant less news—researchers found that coverage of local politics dropped by more than 56 percent between 1999 and 2017—which meant fewer reasons for people to subscribe. Each quarter, when subscriber revenue dropped, Gannett would simply lay off more people, starting the cycle anew. In late 2018, a few months after Natalia arrived, six *Star* employees took buyouts. Just a few weeks later, three more were laid off, including the paper's most popular columnist.

Within her first year at the *Star*, Natalia got a raise, to $48,000 a year. She was thrilled to be making more than she ever had, but she was still tens of thousands of dollars in debt from student loans and old credit cards, and she wasn't sure how she'd ever pay it off. Then she learned through the union that several colleagues—people with the same job and similar levels of experience—were making $14,000 more than she was. Meanwhile, rumors were flying about how Gannett was going to merge with another huge newspaper company. When the union president asked Natalia to join the committee in charge of bargaining the Indianapolis NewsGuild's next contract, she couldn't say yes fast enough.

———

IN JANUARY 2019, THE *WALL STREET JOURNAL* published a scoop on the media beat: MNG Enterprises Inc., better known as Digital First Media, had offered more than $1.3 billion to buy Gannett.

Digital First was the owner of once-venerable papers like the *Denver Post* and the *Orange County Register,* among roughly two hundred others. But despite its size, it wasn't a widely known brand. The name that really mattered in the proposed deal wasn't noted until more than halfway through the *Journal* article: that of the company's majority owner, Alden Global Capital LLC, a New York firm with a particular interest in the newspaper business.

Alden set up shop in 2007, but the firm wasn't its founder's first foray into squeezing profits from flailing businesses. In 1985, former Bear Stearns partner Randall Smith created R. D. Smith & Company, a stock trading firm specializing in the assets of distressed companies. In 1991, the *New York Times* reported on Smith's penchant for gaming the system: the company, "whose office near Wall Street fittingly overlooks the Trinity Church graveyard, is profiting from other people's misery by trading the stock and debt of troubled companies." In the 1990s, a large painting of a vulture hung in the lobby of Smith's office.

Between 2010 and 2012, Alden scooped up the Journal Register Company, with two dozen newspapers across the country, and MediaNews Group, another major chain. Suddenly two of the three largest newspaper owners in the country, GateHouse and Alden, were private equity firms, and no one seemed to know much about the latter. "So who is Randall Smith and what does he want with all these newspapers?" a columnist for the Poynter Institute wrote in 2011. "The man behind a rising tide of private equity newspaper company investments and takeovers has kept from the public eye even the barest information about himself and his companies."

Then, as now, Smith and his protégé and business partner Heath Freeman almost never gave interviews. No one from Alden returns phone calls or emails; the entirety of the company's website is a logo, a stock image of sunlight streaming through redwood trees, and the sentence "Alden Global Capital is an investment manager based in West Palm Beach, FL."

Yet, at first, industry observers were hopeful about Alden; the Poynter Institute column called its interest in newspapers "flattering." The print ad market had been declining for years, and no one had cracked the code of getting people to pay for local news online. It wasn't clear why *anyone* would want to buy newspapers; perhaps Smith and Freeman would become the benevolent overlords journalism so desperately needed.

Instead, Alden immediately began slashing the staffs of newspapers across the country. Throughout the 2010s, the firm laid off or bought out even more journalists than Gannett or GateHouse, crippling award-winning outlets as well as the only source of information in many rural communities. In 2018, journalists at Denver's daily newspaper revolted against their owner, printing a series of editorials and columns describing the brutal cuts Alden had inflicted and pleading for a new owner to "step up and save the *Denver Post*." Atop the page, a photograph showed 142 journalists celebrating a Pulitzer win in 2013. When a viewer slid a scroll bar to the left, the three-quarters of *Post* journalists who had quit or been laid off in the five years since vanished from the image. The protest brought Alden's vampiric cost-cutting to the attention of a mainstream audience, creating a universally recognized villain for all of the job losses that had racked the media industry.

When Alden made its $1.3 billion offer for Gannett in February 2019, Gannett's board unanimously rejected it. In his statement on the matter, the board chair claimed a moral high ground the company hadn't exactly earned, saying Alden was responsible for destroying local newspapers. He didn't mention that less than two weeks earlier, Gannett itself had laid off another round of journalists, or that many of its papers were half the size they had been just a few years earlier. He left out that the *Indianapolis Star* had employed 285 people in its newsroom when Gannett acquired it in 2000, and by 2019 there were around 70.

After Gannett rejected Alden's overtures, the firm took a new approach, attempting to win a smaller number of board seats and increase its influence over the company's strategic decisions. That failed too. So Alden gave up, saying the saga had created "a win for an entrenched Gannett board that has been unwilling to address the current realities of the newspaper business, and sadly a loss for Gannett and its shareholders."

In retrospect, the furor over Alden's bid for Gannett had the unfortunate effect of allowing GateHouse Media—the original private equity newspaper owner—to fly under the radar, despite relying on many of the same predatory tactics and at times cutting even more deeply than Alden. GateHouse Media was by then the largest newspaper owner in the country by number of publications, which made

Fortress Investment Group at least arguably the most powerful company in American media. (In 2017, Fortress was purchased by the Japanese tech investment firm SoftBank, though it continued to operate independently.) Just like Alden's Digital First Media, Fortress's GateHouse had laid off swaths of journalists and shuttered entire newspapers—in fact, GateHouse closed more newspapers between 2013 and 2018 than any other company, Alden included.

Yet when *GateHouse* came calling about a potential acquisition, neither the Gannett board nor the general public reacted with outrage. The talks were made public just days after Alden gave up on its second takeover attempt. Gannett's profits were slumping, its executives knew they needed a buyer, and GateHouse was offering more than a billion dollars. And GateHouse wasn't the industry bogeyman, even if it had killed off *more* newspapers than Alden. So GateHouse and Gannett agreed quickly on terms, and the deal "breezed through the regulatory process," coming together "with remarkable speed," in the words of the *New York Times*. On November 19, 2019, the largest newspaper owner in America was born. It would control one of every six papers in the country.

The combined company kept the Gannett name because it had the cultural cachet GateHouse lacked. That led many employees, Natalia included, to conclude that little had changed except that more newspapers were moving under their corporate umbrella. In spirit, though, the combined entity was GateHouse through and through: a private equity–funded company obsessively focused on profits and not much else. GateHouse had also considered a deal with the Tribune Company, which owned the *Chicago Tribune* and *Los Angeles Times*, but favored the Gannett deal because it owned more newspapers, which meant more opportunities to cut costs.

And to make the numbers work, they would have to cut many, many costs. When the ink dried, all those Gannett newspapers were now responsible for $1.79 billion in loans, provided by Apollo Global Management at an eye-popping interest rate of 11.5 percent. Fortress would be in charge of managing the company—Mike Reed, the CEO, would officially be employed by *Fortress*, instead of Gannett, the company he officially ran—in exchange for millions in management fees and incentives. (The previous year, Gannett had paid Fortress $10.7 million in fees.) The new Gannett became a public company, but Fortress would control all its major decisions. Earnings would pay not one private equity firm, but two: Fortress's management fees, plus Apollo's debt.

It was easy enough to understand the agreement's upside for Fortress, Apollo, and Reed—their salaries and fees were guaranteed. It was more difficult to see how this would ever work out for Gannett's newspapers, who were now on the hook for tens of millions in interest payments *and* tens of millions in management fees every year. Toys R Us had collapsed under the weight of its loan obligations barely a year earlier, but despite widespread news coverage of the saga, few people were talking about how private equity debt makes it more difficult for companies to survive.

In the beginning, Reed suggested that saving money wouldn't require cutting much staff: simply selling newspapers' physical newsrooms and renting out smaller spaces, often in less-desirable areas of town, would save as much as $125 million within two years, he said.

Much of the rest would come from eliminating "redundancies," which often meant competition. In the *New York Times* story on the deal, Reed gave one example, focusing on Upstate New York—where both he and the original Gannett company were born. In Rochester, the *Democrat and Chronicle* had been owned by Gannett. In suburban Canandaigua, thirty miles away, the *Daily Messenger* had been owned by GateHouse. Both covered the local minor-league baseball team. "Do we need two people covering the Rochester Red Wings?" Reed asked reporter Marc Tracy. "So that's where we potentially redeploy assets."

Within a few years, neither newspaper would have a Red Wings reporter.

—————

THE UNION CONTRACT AT THE *Indianapolis Star* was scheduled to expire in August 2020. So a few months after the Gannett/GateHouse merger, the Indianapolis NewsGuild began negotiating a new one. Now on the bargaining committee, Natalia was responsible for meeting with leadership from the *Star* and Gannett and trying to win the best possible deal for her colleagues.

The goal was to hammer out a new two-year contract by the start of September, avoiding a period with no agreement. Natalia and her colleagues had agreed on their priorities. At the top of the list was higher salary minimums—the lowest-paid reporters were still making just $32,000 a year—and a comprehensive pay study to determine whether there was a wage gap between male and female employees, and white and nonwhite ones. They also wanted to put a stop to the centralization that had become a hallmark of Gannett's cost-cutting strategy since the merger. The company had recently announced the creation of a "Midwest Digital Optimization Team" designed to eliminate city-specific producer roles. "Digital producers live, work and play in Central Indiana. They are Hoosiers like you," the union wrote in a blog post. "They keep track of the content you want to read. They write the personalized newsletters you love and find in your inbox every week. . . . And their jobs should remain local."

The union members knew they were facing a steep climb to improve their working conditions. The last time they had bargained, in 2018, they lost the ability to buy health insurance through the NewsGuild, which meant journalists had to rely on Gannett's more expensive options. The union also couldn't prevent the layoffs in 2019, nor get more than paltry severance for the affected employees.

The guild also knew that conditions at many other Gannett and GateHouse newspapers were getting worse. A round of layoffs in February 2020 had spared the *Star* but cost jobs at twenty-seven other newspapers. Many other Gannett newsrooms had already suffered huge cuts: 30 percent at the *Arizona Republic*, 70 percent at the *Sarasota Herald-Tribune*, 70 percent at the *Providence Journal*. At Gannett's papers that weren't unionized, the damage was undoubtedly worse; they had both fewer protections and less data tracking. One study found that roughly half of all newspaper jobs disappeared between 2004 and 2019, and one in four newspapers altogether. Thousands more had devolved into what the study called "ghost newspapers," which continued printing in order to make money on ads but carried essentially no local news. Thanks to consolidation and cost cutting combined with the most loyal subscribers continuing to pay regardless of quality, many of these papers remained profitable without producing any journalism.

By that standard, the *Star* was doing well. Despite losing more than half its staff, it was still producing newsworthy coverage of Indianapolis and its major suburbs. In early 2020, Natalia started a new job in the newsroom, covering immigrant communities throughout the region. When she proposed writing some stories in Spanish to attract more readers among Central Indiana's growing Latino population, the editors suggested launching an entire Spanish-language newsletter, written in Natalia's voice, that wouldn't require a subscription to read. "I wanted to write it in a way that would appeal to my aunts in Mexico, so they'd understand the references," she said. The newsletter was popular from the beginning, and Natalia was soon hearing from readers who either hadn't previously known the *Star* existed or didn't think it had anything for them.

Even so, morale and working conditions at the *Star* were deteriorating, and the union was determined to codify some basic protections. But in the early days of contract negotiations, Natalia said, the NewsGuild's arguments didn't seem to be making any headway with Gannett's fleet of lawyers. In fact, the Gannett negotiators often wouldn't even respond to emails about scheduling negotiation sessions. When they did show up for meetings, the company rarely made any proposals or responded substantively to the ones from Natalia and her colleagues. They didn't seem to care that the clock was ticking.

The contract deadline came and went. The *Star*'s union chair's term ended at the end of 2020, three months after they were supposed to have a new contract in place, and Natalia agreed to become the new chair. Now she was in charge of trying to get their employer to respond. On the rare occasions when Gannett's lawyers did suggest a new contract provision, it was often ridiculous to the point of offensiveness: in early 2021, a year into the Covid pandemic, Gannett proposed eliminating sick days.

Occasionally, the company seemed outright contemptuous of its staff. Since 2014, when Gannett sold the *Star*'s historic headquarters to help pay down its debt, the staff had worked out of a former Nordstrom store in the Circle Centre Mall, which required each employee to pay $80 a month for a parking spot. When Covid closed the office, Gannett just kept withdrawing money from people's paychecks, and never responded to the union's demands to stop. For more than a year, every employee paid $80 a month for parking they could not use.

While Gannett leadership dragged their feet with the Indianapolis NewsGuild, employees at other newspapers started to think about unionizing for the first time. Record numbers of newsrooms formed new unions in the first year of the pandemic, including at multiple Gannett newspapers, though just 16 percent of all journalists were unionized by 2022. Newspaper workers were worried about pandemic-related safety protocols, and they brought a renewed focus on racial justice after George Floyd's murder in May 2020. The most important reasons for the wave, though, were the same everywhere: too much work, not enough pay.

One of the biggest new Gannett unions was formed at the *Austin American-Statesman*, in Natalia's home state. When the pandemic began, a number of *Statesman* journalists were furloughed for one week every month, effectively cutting their pay by nearly 25 percent. A month later, seven more were laid off, including a sports reporter who had worked at the paper for nearly thirty-four years, a culture writer with eighteen years' experience, and an editor who was overseeing two different towns' newspapers. In February 2021, the remaining union-eligible employees voted 36–12 to form a unit of the NewsGuild. Natalia was part of a caucus of the chairs of every Gannett union; as a Texan, she was thrilled to see a *Statesman* representative join for the first time.

Austin's population was booming; thousands of people were moving to the city to work in the burgeoning tech sector. As a result, the city's cost of living was skyrocketing. In 2022, the average monthly rent for a one-bedroom apartment increased 108 percent in a single year, the biggest jump of any city in the country. But at the *Statesman*, some journalists were making as little as $40,000. Management didn't have to abide by a minimum salary, in part because the paper had never been unionized. Now the new Austin union demanded no one make less than $60,000, higher than almost any other unionized local paper ($28,000 more than at the *Star*).

The union's vice chair estimated that a third of employees couldn't afford to live in Austin. One full-time photographer said she was driving for DoorDash on nights and weekends; a former reporter said she was getting up at 4 a.m. to do shifts as a curbside shopper for a local grocery store before working all day in the newsroom.

In 2021, Gannett CEO Mike Reed earned $7.74 million in total compensation: $900,000 in salary, a $767,052 performance bonus, and a stock grant worth more than $6 million.

———

AT THE *STAR*, NATALIA WAS spending hours upon hours working with the union committee and other NewsGuild units across the country while also reporting stories. The work was exhilarating, but she was tired. Gannett wasn't listening to its employees; there was no union contract in sight; colleagues across the country were still being laid off en masse. She wanted to stay in Indianapolis, wanted to keep developing her beat, but she couldn't see a path.

So Natalia started applying to reporting jobs in other cities across the country. She nearly got a job in Philadelphia. She interviewed with a startup media organization covering education in Indiana. Then, in the summer of 2021, she got an offer. She would be reporting on immigrant communities in Texas, her dream job. There was just one problem: the position was at the *Austin American-Statesman*, another Gannett paper. Yet again, she would be part of a newsroom with a shrinking staff, private equity investors who didn't seem to care about their work, and a union but no contract.

When she first applied for the job, Natalia told the editor she would need $62,000 to consider moving. When he offered her the role, he said they'd pay her $52,000, "which was, like, so offensive," she said later. When she didn't call back right away, he upped the offer, unprompted, to $56,000. She knew that was still barely enough to make ends meet in Austin. But she wanted to be in Texas, to be closer to her mom and her boyfriend, Robert. Working at the *Statesman* would be a way to get there. She thought maybe she could do it for a year, just until she could find something else in her home state. She took the job, found an apartment, and moved to Austin.

Right away, her new colleagues asked her to join the bargaining committee. They knew her experience at a more established union made her invaluable; she could help work through the *Statesman*'s first contract. She turned them down. Working with Gannett management when she was in Indiana had been so demoralizing. And they hadn't even achieved their goals; the *Star* still didn't have a new contract. She didn't have it in her to fight again. "I came to the *Statesman* and I was so defeated," she said. "I didn't care about it. At the *Star*, I cared about making that place better. And when I came to Austin I didn't give a fuck."

She gave her all to the job, reporting dozens of stories about how government policies were impacting people of color across central Texas, but she stayed out of newsroom politics as best she could. That didn't mean she didn't care for her colleagues. She made it clear to them she would show up for every union action and scream as loud as she could. But from her very first day, she spent her extra energy looking for the next thing, not trying to improve conditions where she was. She couldn't see a future at the company. "This wasn't where I was going to stay."

By the time she arrived in Austin, Gannett was no longer technically operated by a private equity firm. The company paid $30.375 million to end its management agreement with Fortress Investment Group at the end of 2020, a year earlier than planned. After paying at least $145.6 million in management fees, incentives, and expense reimbursements to Fortress over eight years, Reed said Gannett needed to save the money it had been spending, and that it was ready to operate independently. But Fortress still owned 40 percent of the company's outstanding debt, and

Gannett still owed roughly a billion dollars of principal on its loan from Apollo Global Management. Decisions about the company's financial future were still fundamentally shaped by two different private equity firms.

Neither the *Statesman* nor the *Star* signed a union contract while Natalia worked there. (In early 2024, after more than three and a half years of bargaining, the Indianapolis NewsGuild finally won a new contract. The Austin NewsGuild agreed to a deal with Gannett in late 2024, after its own three-and-a-half-year wait.)

By the end of 2022, just 11,200 employees worked for Gannett in the U.S., down from 24,338 at Gannett and GateHouse combined in 2018. In an effort to pay down its loans to Apollo and Fortress, the company had wiped out more than half its workforce in four years.

EIGHT

LOREN

___

SOUTHERN TOWERS IS FILLED WITH STRIVERS. NEARLY 60 PERCENT of residents are immigrants, three-quarters of them from Africa. Many speak limited English; it's common to hear Amharic and Somali at the mailboxes or the bus stop in the parking lot. Just like Loren's parents, they moved to the United States chasing a better life. Just like Loren, they saw Southern Towers as the place where they could find it.

In early 2023, Loren and Rashad left public housing and signed a thirteen-month lease for Apartment 230 at the Sherwood, one of Southern Towers' five apartment buildings. The Sherwood looks like many other apartment developments from the 1960s: sand-colored brick, identical rows of windows marching up each side. It is home to three wings of apartments; from the air, Southern Towers looks like a row of Y's hulking over Seminary Road and Interstate 395. The rent was $2,850 a month for their three-bedroom apartment, twice as much as at their last place, and enough to make Loren nervous after so many ups and downs with their jobs. But things were different now: she was a year into working as an associate organizer at VOICE, earning more than she ever had. Rashad was working in IT for the city of Alexandria. Things were more stable than they had been at any point in her adult life.

Loren was aware that Southern Towers had some negative reviews online. But what gigantic apartment complex doesn't have negative reviews online? No one goes to the trouble of creating an ApartmentRatings.com account because they love their landlord. And

Apartment 230 was everything she'd been looking for, in a convenient location, at a price they could—*finally*—afford. Anonymous complaints were not going to stop her from giving Jaxon and Cameron a nice home, one outside of public housing, one with their own rooms and a swimming pool downstairs.

What she didn't know when she signed the lease was that the problems with Southern Towers weren't limited to routine complaints like slow responses to maintenance requests, broken elevators, or poor soundproofing. She didn't know about the cascade of attempted evictions during the pandemic, or the mold, or the mice, or the roaches, or the rent hikes. She didn't know that multiple elected officials had issued public statements demanding that the buildings' private equity owners treat its residents better. She didn't know that her new landlords were infamous among affordable-housing organizers for how ruthlessly they wrung profits out of working-class Americans. She didn't know that the stability she and Rashad had worked so hard to win would shatter in under a year.

———

SOUTHERN TOWERS HAD BEEN IN the news for months by the time CIM Group bought the complex from a smaller private equity firm, Bell Partners, in August 2020. When Covid lockdowns began that March, the buildings became a symbol of the national rent crisis caused by the pandemic.

Sami Bourma, a Sudanese immigrant and longtime Southern Towers tenant, had been furloughed from his job as a cook at the National Institutes of Health and had stopped driving for Uber because he feared getting his family sick. When he talked to his neighbors and realized that many of them were also unable to pay rent, he took the lead, organizing a petition that demanded rent cancellation for all 2,346 apartments at Southern Towers, as well as strengthened health and safety measures.

Bell Partners' only response was a statement about how they would work with tenants to establish payment plans and waive some late fees. But Bourma and his neighbors didn't have the money for partial payments either; they had been living paycheck to paycheck before Covid struck, and now they were running out of money entirely. So instead of accepting the offer, they persuaded three hundred tenants to sign on to a rent strike, staging protests in the complex's parking lot. They also enlisted the organizing power of a food service workers' union based in nearby Washington, D.C., and African Communities Together, a nonprofit that works with immigrants and refugees.

The strike ended quickly, without convincing Bell Partners to suspend rent, but it did draw local officials' attention to the predicaments of working-class Virginians living at Southern Towers. Those five buildings made up 6 percent of Alexandria's rental units and housed an even larger percentage of its low-income residents. A 2021 report found that the median income of families living at Southern Towers was just over $60,000, compared to the city median of $100,939. Thanks in part to Bourma's work, Alexandria dedicated $450,000 for emergency rent assistance to low-income residents, while the state of Virginia implemented eviction protections until 2022.

Those protections were still in place when Bell Partners sold Southern Towers to CIM Group in the summer of 2020, the largest apartment housing transaction in the history of the D.C. region. But the law was temporary, and the ongoing affordable housing crisis made residents and their advocates fear what would happen afterward. Amazon had announced plans to build a new headquarters, with more than 25,000 employees and an average salary of $150,000, just a few miles away, and CIM had said that it liked to invest in developments that could support "outsized rent growth." CIM management had told Southern Towers residents they should expect rent increases of 3 to 4 percent a year, but some residents would eventually report 9 percent annual jumps.

Even though actual evictions generally weren't yet allowed, eviction *proceedings* appeared to rise dramatically once CIM took over. The company wanted to start the clock, informing nonpaying tenants that they'd be thrown out the moment it was legal unless they caught up on rent. An African Communities Together report found that during

CIM's first eight months in charge, the company brought 541 eviction proceedings against Southern Towers residents. That was more than one in five of the total filings in the entire city of Alexandria during that time. Another building a few miles away, also owned by CIM, was responsible for another 6 percent, meaning that nearly 30 percent of all Alexandria eviction proceedings were filed by a single company based on the other side of the country.

Bourma and the African Communities Together organizers argued that CIM could easily afford to wipe away the rent obligations of some of the most vulnerable people in society during a public health emergency. On one level, that's true: average rent at Southern Towers was $1,467, and a researcher looking into the eviction proceedings estimated that more than 200 households had cases against them. If that number was 250, it would cost less than $4.5 million to cover all of their rent for an entire year—a pittance for a company with some $30 billion in assets.

But the definition of success is loftier in the private equity world: not just making profits, but maximizing them. Sixty-eight percent of the cost of acquiring Southern Towers was covered by its low-interest loan from Freddie Mac, but most of the remaining $160 million came from CIM Group's limited partners, and they expected to earn money from their investment. The Korean Teachers' Credit Union, which put $50 million in the Southern Towers deal, told members it expected to earn 13 percent returns from the acquisition. By that standard, giving away $4.5 million to low-income tenants wouldn't be benevolence, but an unforgivable breach of CIM's obligations. "Our empathy for residents must be balanced by our fiduciary responsibility," the company wrote to a local news outlet.

The choice between making people homeless during a global pandemic or angering investors was no choice at all.

———

WHEN LOREN AND HER FAMILY moved into Southern Towers in early 2023, the apartment had been freshly painted white. She liked the clean look so she didn't hang much on the living room walls. The place soon looked lived-in, the boys' sneakers sitting next to boxes they never found room for in the closet, the kitchen table stacked with textbooks and Amazon packages and half-empty water bottles. Neither Loren nor Rashad had ever been fastidious housekeepers. Their home was never *dirty*—her father taught her better than that, and she passed the lesson on to her kids—but it was cluttered. She didn't mind. Rashad and the kids were happy, so she was happy.

There were bad signs from the start, though. The leasing agent had boasted that the Southern Towers staff was uncommonly warm and responsive, and that residents were encouraged to bring any problems to building management. So it seemed strange that the CIM office door on the first floor was always closed. Most of the time, no one answered when someone knocked. They didn't pick up the phone very often either. One day, when talking to a professional acquaintance, Loren mentioned that she lived at Southern Towers. The woman was surprised. "I wish you had asked me about it first," she said. "There have been a lot of issues there." Loren brushed off the comment.

But as the weeks went on, some problems became hard to ignore. A few months after the De Pina–Jackson family moved in, the building turned on the air-conditioning, which made the bulky HVAC unit in their living room belch ink-black gunk onto the windowsill and floor. Loren would wipe it away, and more would come out. The maintenance staff swore it was dust, not mold. She had never seen dust that color, or smelled dust that swampy.

Then came the water. At first it was just a few drops here and there, so little that she was convinced Jaxon and Cameron were just being careless. It was weird, though: the water always seemed to appear at the seams between the gray laminate floorboards. By this point Loren had already filed several maintenance requests to get the air conditioner fixed. She was worried that building managers were becoming annoyed with her, so she just kept wiping up the water and going about her day.

Then, in late June, brown streaks appeared along the baseboards between the kitchen and the living room. It was clear now: there was water in the walls, and the problem was spreading. The streaks grew in two directions at once: up toward the kitchen counter, like so many beanstalks, and outward toward an adjoining wall. But maintenance wasn't even responding to the repair tickets Loren had filed in the residents' portal online. At the end of August, her dad came to visit. He took one look at the splotches, which now smelled swampy too. Ever the engineer, he told her in no uncertain terms that they had to be mold.

As it turned out, leaks and mold had been constant problems at Southern Towers. At a protest in the complex parking lot a few months before Loren and her family moved in, Sami Bourma told a couple dozen people that he had taken his child to the doctor because of breathing problems and was asked if there was mold in their apartment. When he got home that day, he said, he looked in the air-conditioning unit and found mold everywhere. So he started knocking on neighbors' doors and asking to check out their air conditioners. About 60 percent of them were moldy too, he said.

A CIM Group spokesperson told a local journalist that Bourma had most likely seen mildew, not mold. Most importantly, the company said, the previous owners were to blame for any issues. The spokesman added that management had found some leaks in the building and had been notified of "a limited number of mold issues" left over from the Bell Partners era, and was addressing them immediately.

Shortly after Loren moved in, African Communities Together led local politicians on tours of several tenants' apartments, showing them mold, leaks, damage caused by rodents, a flooded elevator, holes in the walls, bugs, broken appliances, and more. Alexandria city council member Alyia Gaskins followed up with a letter to CIM Group leadership, writing, "As a councilmember and mother, I do not want anyone living in conditions that compromise their health, safety, and stability. What we observed is unacceptable." (A CIM spokeswoman posted a comment beneath an article about the politicians' visit saying that residents had misrepresented the issues in their apartments; she also blamed several tenants—by name—for not reporting problems sooner.)

Local officials like Gaskins are among the only politicians in the U.S. with anything negative to say about private equity. On Capitol Hill, eight miles northeast of Southern Towers, the industry is the prom queen. That's because of its generosity to members of Congress on both sides of the aisle. Private equity and other investment firms spent $42 million on congressional races in the 2020 election cycle, two-thirds of which went to Democrats. Just four senators and sixty-two representatives *didn't* get any private equity donations, a mere 12 percent of all elected members. In 2022, New York Democrat Chuck Schumer, the Senate majority leader, pulled in more than $1.2 million in industry contributions, three times more than the runner-up. Kyrsten Sinema, the Arizona Democrat-turned-independent who killed the 2022 provision that would have closed the carried-interest loophole, received more than half a million dollars in private equity donations in the previous election cycle.

The industry's primary lobbying group, meanwhile, has long boasted about its ability to stave off efforts to regulate private equity's favored strategies. The American Investment Council spends as much as $3 million a year lobbying in Washington on top of what firms themselves shell out; its CEO, Drew Maloney, wrote an opinion piece in the *Arizona Republic* urging Sinema and fellow Senator Mark Kelly to help preserve the carried-interest loophole. When Sinema did, Maloney crowed that "our advocacy helped prevent punitive tax increases that would make it harder for investors to continue to support jobs, small businesses, and pensions in every state."

———

IT'S DIFFICULT TO KNOW HOW many issues at Southern Towers—the floods, the mold, the insects and rodents, the broken heating and cooling systems and elevators—happened because of inattention on the part of the complex's previous owner, as CIM repeatedly alleged. The complex was built in the 1960s; older buildings often have older systems that are more prone to problems if they aren't maintained and upgraded. But if the buildings were in such terrible shape, why had CIM spent half a billion dollars on them?

There's another strange thing about the story that all the problems at Southern Towers happened before CIM bought it, and that the firm did its absolute best to clean up after them. According to data provided by the city government in response to a Freedom of Information Act request, in the four years before CIM bought the complex, the building department found 2 violations there. In the three and a half years afterward, it found 185.

Negligent landlords are hardly a problem unique to private equity, especially when it comes to low- and moderate-income tenants. But private equity firms promise greater rates of return than other types of owners, which means increased pressure to cut costs and boost revenue. In real estate, that often means some combination of delaying expensive upgrades and catering to higher-income tenants.

Many Southern Towers residents believed they were becoming the victims of both tactics at once. Aside from all the maintenance issues, there were also rent hikes and the looming threat of eviction. In 2020, the first federal pandemic relief bill required landlords to give many tenants thirty days' notice before an eviction, up from the traditional five days. Yet the eviction notices posted on people's doors at Southern Towers said "5-Day Notice to Pay Rent or, Alternatively, to Terminate Lease and Vacate Premises." The only reference to the thirty-day period came midway through a lengthy paragraph. No information about whether the tenant qualified for the thirty-day window, or how to find out, was included. In some cases in which the tenant owed rent but hadn't reached the eviction-notice stage, CIM's letters didn't reference the extension at all. African Communities Together wrote a letter to CIM pointing out the obvious: many tenants "found themselves under the impression that they only have five days to pay the rent owed or leave the premises."

Residents were also being hit with new charges. Before CIM bought the complex, tenants said, they paid $20 per month per person for water and $15 for trash. Under CIM's system, management divided the total bill based on apartment size and number of occupants. For larger families, that meant a huge increase, regardless of how much water they actually used or how much trash they produced. Parking costs spiked too. Some charges seemed almost cruel: if a family had to be temporarily relocated to a different apartment because of repairs, and the only available unit was more expensive than the one they rented, they would have to pay the difference for as long as the work took. A growing number of the African immigrants and refugees who lived in the building told African Communities Together they were being priced out.

In statements to media outlets and politicians, CIM denied that it was violating the thirty-day eviction notice requirement. But with regards to the firm's responsibility to its low-income residents, its leaders were defiant. "Southern Towers is not now, nor has it ever been subsidized affordable housing," a spokesman wrote in an email to Vice News. "The residents at Southern Towers are our clients and they have chosen to live in this community and enter into a lease agreement with rents that are below the market average."

Loren and Rashad had factored the higher charges for parking and utilities into their budget when they moved in. But they were increasingly frustrated by their inability to get basic repair work done—especially once CIM started performing cosmetic upgrades while seeming to ignore more necessary fixes. In late 2023, workers started renovating their building lobby. A sign near the front door promised the space would "become a visual focal point, featuring sleek lines, modern materials, and an inviting atmosphere. It will set the tone for the entire building, welcoming residents and guests with style and sophistication." Next to the sign, renderings showed a lobby that looked like a hotel catering to business travelers, with modern chandeliers and artfully arranged club chairs. A third sign displayed renderings of other planned renovations, including a gussied-up mail room, a gym and yoga studio, and a "club room" with inset TVs and a bar area.

During construction, the lobby was mostly unheated, well into the winter; Loren brought blankets down to the front desk staff. Thinking about it months later still made her voice rise in anger. "You can't get anything to function the way it's supposed to and you're worried about a yoga room?"

———

AT THE SAME TIME PROBLEMS were mounting at Southern Towers, Loren's public profile was on the rise. She led VOICE's lobbying efforts to get the city of Arlington, which borders Alexandria to the north, to allocate $750,000 to expand after-school programs. She was part of a successful campaign to convince the Alexandria City Council to eliminate single-family-only zoning, which studies show limits housing supply and contributes to segregation. "I don't take losses," she liked to say, and her record was bearing that out. People she worked with, including elected officials, kept suggesting *she* run for office.

In October 2023, the VOICE staff was honored by the local branch of the NAACP at the group's Freedom Fund gala. Loren, not usually one for glamour, picked out a glittery blue jumpsuit with a deep V-cut, long silver earrings, and bright coral lipstick. In a photo from that night, she posed with Wanda Durant—an inspirational speaker and the mother of NBA star Kevin—beaming and clutching her glass plaque.

The event was a reminder that she had found a career she loved, and that she was making a real difference. She came home still buzzing with excitement, but she needed to get to bed: Rashad's birthday was the next day, and they had planned a family brunch. The kids were already asleep; she and Rashad went straight to their room. She drifted off, but around 1 a.m., she woke up thirsty. She got up and headed to the kitchen for a glass of water.

All the lights in the apartment were off, but the streetlights shining in through the living room window were bouncing off something, as if the floors were made of glass. She kept seeing weird reflections wherever she looked.

Then she realized her foot was wet.

She flipped on the overhead light, ran down the hall to wake Rashad, and dragged him out of bed and back to the living room. There was water *everywhere*. There was no obvious leak in the ceiling, but the water didn't look to be coming from a single source anyway. It seemed like it was coming from all over, all at once.

They scoured their leasing documents for a phone number for after-hours emergencies, but there wasn't one, so Loren threw on some clothes and ran down to the lobby to ask at the front desk. Two other people were already down there trying to figure out what to do about the shallow lakes in *their* homes. But if there was an emergency number, the person working the desk didn't know it either. He had no idea how to contact *anyone* from maintenance or management at 1 a.m. on a Sunday. It was becoming clear that this problem was not going to be solved until the morning, so she and Rashad piled every towel they could find on top of the water and tried to get some sleep.

In the morning, things were worse. The couple's bedroom was now flooded, as was one of the boys' rooms. Water was running down the walls, bubbling the paint in the entryway and bathroom. Everything on the floor was soaked: furniture, clothes, suitcases, and boxes that didn't fit in the closets. By midmorning, when they had to leave for Rashad's birthday brunch, there still wasn't anyone from CIM to be found—nor by the time they came back a few hours later.

By this point, more than a dozen people were milling around the lobby trying desperately to get help. A Southern Towers security guard called the on-site manager's cell number, but it went to voicemail. The group sat there for hours, people occasionally running up to their apartments and seeing even more water than the last time. Fourteen apartments had flooded. "I started to panic, almost feeling like I was being suffocated," Loren remembered. "After hours, they don't answer calls, even if we're on fire in here."

She also couldn't help but notice that most of the people sitting in the lobby with her were not native English speakers, and they looked even more panicked than she felt. Someone needed to take action. She was the one who had built a career out of refusing to accept the status quo, refusing to be afraid of pissing off people in power. And she didn't take losses.

So, late Sunday night, she picked up her iPhone and dialed 911.

She knew the flooding wasn't a life-threatening emergency. But she also knew that no one else was coming to help, that things were going to continue to get worse until someone turned off the water, and that no one on-site had any idea how to do that. She also wanted official documentation of the problem, who responded, and when. Nearly twenty-four hours after the flooding started, the fire department came, turned off the water, and wrote up an incident report. Now she had proof of CIM's negligence. Now she was ready for a fight.

After all the hours of leaking water, her family's apartment was unlivable: every room but one was flooded. The kids were already at their grandmother's house; they could spend the night there. She and Rashad booked a hotel room, planning to demand reimbursement later. The people who could afford to did the same, while others stayed with family or friends. One man, a student from Turkey who lived on the third floor, slept in his car.

Maintenance finally arrived on Monday morning. They set up industrial dryers and fans in the fourteen flooded apartments, and in the halls, where water had seeped out and soaked into the carpet. Gaskins, one of the city council members who had toured Southern Towers the month before, showed up, along with a leader from African Communities Together, and offered to help communicate with CIM to make sure residents had places to stay. That afternoon, close to forty-eight hours after the flood started, Gaskins texted Loren to say that CIM had told her everyone had now been relocated to temporary apartments, along with their furniture and clothes. "I'm calling you back on FaceTime," Loren responded, and then flipped the camera so the council member could see all fourteen families still sitting in the lobby. A couple of hours later, residents got an email that management was still working on getting them into other units at the complex.

In the lobby, a woman who worked in the Southern Towers

management office recommended that the tenants file renters' insurance claims as soon as possible. Several didn't have renters' insurance, but others pulled out their phones to contact their insurers right then and there. Loren stopped them. "Why should they file their own claims, which could increase their premiums, when the flood was the management company's fault?" she asked. CIM should be responsible for paying for everything they needed. She told her neighbors to put their phones away. Everyone did. The woman from the management office looked irritated, but she didn't say anything.

Finally, at 10:30 on Monday night, Loren said, she got a call that her temporary residence was ready and the movers were waiting for her. But it was late, she was already back at the hotel, and she and Rashad both had to work the next day. So she told the CIM employee she would be over in the morning. That annoyed the woman, Loren said, but they agreed that she would meet the movers then.

Loren and Rashad threw clothes and toiletries for the four of them into whatever suitcases and bags were handy. Everything they didn't need was left behind, strewn around the apartment in their rush and their attempts to avoid the most badly flooded parts of the floor. The maintenance staff was going to be tearing out walls anyway; housekeeping hardly seemed like a concern. On Tuesday, the family of four was moved into a one-bedroom one floor above their actual, three-bedroom, home. The company estimated they'd be there between three and six weeks.

Jerry Thomas, CIM's managing director for on-site management, suggested to local reporters that, like previous problems, the flood was the fault of Southern Towers' previous owner. They hadn't kept up with maintenance, he said, which had caused an aging pipe to burst. He added that there was no good way to prevent it from happening again: the only way to fix all sixty worn-out pipes would be to open all the walls at once—leaving the building uninhabitable, and CIM without months' worth of rent from more than four hundred tenants. "And that's not an option."

LOREN HADN'T LIVED IN THE building that long, and didn't even know that many of her neighbors, but now the other thirteen flooded families were looking to her as a leader. She organized a WhatsApp chat for everyone and told them to text or call her with any questions or requests for help dealing with CIM. She was already a professional organizer for other people; it felt natural to apply her skills to her home community. But by publicly calling out the management company, she also put herself on CIM's radar. She doesn't regret that, but from a distance, she can see exactly what it cost her and her family.

After everyone was resettled in temporary apartments, CIM announced a residents' meeting to discuss its plans to repair the broken pipes and damaged apartments, as well as other scheduled renovations. The meeting was in the middle of the workday, but Loren made sure to show up, both because she wanted answers and because she knew the other tenants were following her lead. CIM sent three employees from upper management to address the group, but Thomas did all the talking. Loren remembered him framing the situation as an "unfortunate event" but never once apologizing on the company's behalf. She also thought he was dancing around people's questions, especially the ones about what led the pipe to break and what they planned to do to avoid similar situations in the future.

The flood, the failure to respond, the months' worth of maintenance issues, the delay getting people into temporary accommodations, her kids sleeping next to the kitchen because they no longer had their own bedrooms, her upstairs neighbor spending the night in his car— Thomas was talking about the state of things as if it were a minor inconvenience, not a destabilizing crisis. Loren raised her hand, stood up, and faced her neighbors. "How did we get here? Why are we sitting here right now?" she said. "What they failed to tell you is that it's negligence, big-corporation negligence. They put profit over people."

Thomas tried to cut her off, saying that wasn't true. She kept going, turning to address him, fully shouting now. "At the end of the day, we're working-class Americans. I came here from the projects, and I give you three thousand dollars a month of my income, and this is the treatment we receive. When this is all said and done, and people mention Southern

Towers or CIM management, what are they going to correlate with it? That's what I want to leave you with."

As she spoke, she watched Thomas's face twist into annoyance, then anger. She knew she was now officially the problem tenant, the "agitator." Or, in her hyperbolic summary of his reaction, "this bitch needs to die."

Loren being Loren, though, she still didn't back down. Worried that contractors wouldn't do a thorough repair job, which could lead to more mold in her apartment, she demanded to be present whenever workers were in her apartment. Thomas responded that such a request was impractical. When she learned that CIM wasn't going to replace the floor in her unit because, they said, it hadn't been sufficiently damaged, she bombarded the company with calls and emails until they capitulated. When she had yet more water issues in the temporary accommodations—the toilet and bathtub both backed up and wouldn't function—staff initially sent maintenance to the wrong apartment because the one her family was in was listed as unoccupied. Loren yelled at the woman at the front desk.

At the same time, African Communities Together was drawing up a full catalog of demands, with contributions by Loren, to send to management. The final list included twenty-one items related to mold, pests, security, heating and cooling, plus lowered charges for water and trash. Some were reasonable, if unlikely to happen, including inspecting every apartment for mold and eliminating any issues within two months. Others veered into the realm of fantasy for a private equity landlord: agreeing to a maximum 2 percent annual rent increase and undoing previous increases that exceeded that amount, giving tenants two months to catch up on rent before an eviction, and eliminating all utility fees.

On November 9, slightly more than three weeks after the flood, a moving crew brought Loren's family's belongings back to Apartment 230. It still wasn't fully put back together, though. A large hole in her bedroom wall had been covered by plastic, but she could see through it into her neighbor's unit. The wall above the kitchen cabinets had holes. The hallway lights were flickering. Most urgently, the heat didn't work. The maintenance staff gave them space heaters, but running them tripped the circuit breaker, knocking out the power.

That week, a conversation with her son nearly broke Loren. Cameron, who was a month shy of his ninth birthday, suggested that maybe they should just move back to public housing, where their apartment was smaller but had never flooded or grown mold.

She sobbed. "I'm trying to give my kids a better life, and for my eight-year-old to be so stressed-out that he says, 'Mommy, can we just go back to the projects?' That is not what I wanted to hear from my child."

But at that moment, she knew her boy needed reassurance. So she looked him in the eye and said, "Don't ever think or allow people to make you feel that you should go backwards. This is a challenge we're going to overcome. They *want* us to say we're going to give up and just walk away, and we're not going to do that. You're not going back to the projects if I can help it."

In an email Loren sent to Thomas and cc'd to several city officials and African Communities Together staff members a few weeks later, she told them about the conversation with Cameron. Then she reiterated her complaints. "I do not have peace of mind and am living in fear that something significant will happen in this building and we will pay with our lives. What is CIM doing to address these issues?" she wrote. "Clearly, a human's life only matters if you get your rent money. CIM continues to put Band-Aids on bullet wounds, and the Band-Aids are leaking from EVERYWHERE. What you all are doing to us tenants is criminal and inhumane, and you all must be stopped."

BY MID-DECEMBER, LOREN AND RASHAD had been back in their apartment for a month, but they hadn't yet fully settled in. Contractors were still coming in and out regularly trying to repair the heat; there was still a hole in the wall. A lot of the stuff the family had taken to the temporary unit upstairs was still in suitcases on the floor; the apartment remained too much of a wreck to fully unpack.

That's when they got the first 21/30.

In Virginia, a 21/30 notice is the first step for a landlord who wants to evict a tenant for violating the terms of their lease, rather than for failure to pay rent. It requires the tenant to fix the specified problem within 21 days, or else the lease will be terminated in 30 days. (Tenants can also issue 21/30s to their landlords for failing to fix major problems.) The idea is to protect renters from being evicted for correctable issues.

The 21/30 affixed to Loren's door on December 13, 2023, cited two paragraphs from the lease she had signed eleven months earlier. One required her to keep her home in a clean and safe condition; the other specified that all trash and other waste must be removed and disposed of. The notice read: "Upon inspection of your unit, you have allowed incredible amounts of waste, trash, and/or other items of garbage to collect and build up throughout the unit to such a degree as to impede and severely limit the ability to ingress and egress through your unit. Such a condition is a potential fire hazard, creates potential pest control issues, and constitutes a violation of your obligations as noted above. Further, we have multiple contractors that have tried to do work but due to the housekeeping issues the contractors' work has been delayed."

Even months later, she could not read over that single sheet of paper without practically short-circuiting from rage. Yes, there were piles of stuff on the floor. There had always been piles of stuff on the floor, and the saga of the flood and the multiple moves and the ongoing repair work had made them worse. She had moved some things out of the way of where the workers needed to be, creating new piles. But the stuff was their personal belongings, not *garbage*. And nothing was impeding movement through the apartment. There were four people coming and going from school and work and basketball practice and friends' houses and community meetings, and managing to use every room. The notice made it sound like the house was unlivable, but Loren, Rashad, Jaxon, and Cameron were living there just fine.

Besides, no "inspection" had been done, at least with her knowledge, and Virginia law requires seventy-two hours' notice before a landlord enters a tenant's home. In an email sent several weeks later, a lawyer for CIM said the violation notice was based on a report by a member of the maintenance staff, not a formal inspection, which is not sufficient under state law.

Part of Loren wanted to tell CIM off, to leave and find a new place to live. But despite everything, her kids loved their home, and she did not want to uproot them again. Though it offended her sense of justice to appease CIM, her sons came first. She had until January 4 to remedy the alleged violation; she figured she'd handle it after Christmas. When Jaxon and Cameron got out of school for winter break at the end of that week, the family headed up to New England to visit relatives. They were gone for almost two weeks.

It wasn't a relaxing vacation. Her dad, Victor, had to have emergency triple bypass surgery on Christmas Eve, so the family spent Christmas with him in the hospital. But the doctors said he was recovering well, so the DePina–Jacksons headed home on December 28. Suitcases in tow, they walked through the construction zone that was the lobby, took the elevator up one floor, and walked down the hall to Apartment 230.

Tacked to the door, they saw three official-looking pieces of paper. One was a copy of the same 21/30 from two weeks earlier. One was a new 21/30, for a new violation. The last was a "notice of non-renewal and lease termination."

The second 21/30, dated December 22, said Loren and Rashad were violating the terms of their lease by smoking cannabis in their apartment. A neighbor had reported smoke coming from their door, it said, and a leasing agent had smelled it while leading a prospective resident on a tour. A third-floor tenant, meanwhile, said they had seen smoke wafting from their temporary unit during the three weeks they lived there.

This, Loren said emphatically, was "bullshit." Rashad had left a tin of THC gummies out when the maintenance workers were around—he uses it to manage pain from an old knee injury, and recreational weed is legal in Virginia—but they had never, ever smoked in their apartment. The neighbors who allegedly saw the smoke from their home had moved out weeks earlier; Loren called them in front of the assistant property manager, and they said they had never reported her for anything. And it's not uncommon to smell weed in the Southern Towers halls. Walking toward Apartment 230 one day two months later, the aroma was pungent throughout the second floor—until entering Loren's apartment and closing the door.

The details of the 21/30s didn't much matter, though. The third notice, which informed them that they would not have the option to renew their lease when it expired on March 24, 2024, was definitive. "You must vacate the premises by the Termination Date," it read. "If you fail to vacate by the Termination Date, your continued occupancy will be in violation of this notice. You will be liable for rent as it accrues and all other damages permitted by your lease and applicable law, including attorney's fees." Less than a year after moving in, they were being told they had under three months to find a new place to live.

Landlords aren't legally obligated to renew anyone's lease. But as far as Loren could tell, the only reason they weren't renewing hers was that they didn't like her. They hadn't even given her time to resolve the first 21/30 before kicking her out. She was seething, so angry she was shaking. But now Rashad—always the calm, steadying force in their relationship—was even more furious. Without needing to discuss their strategy, they dropped their suitcases by the front door, told the boys to stay inside, marched straight downstairs, and banged on the management office door.

When the assistant property manager—the same person who had signed the 21/30 letters—opened the door, Loren and Rashad unloaded. They yelled at her, insulted her. Rashad crumpled up each of the notices and threw them. (CIM said he flung them toward the door; he said toward the trash can next to the door.)

A lawyer representing CIM said later that the couple displayed "threatening and/or aggressive behavior" toward management that "made them fearful of their safety." (It's unclear who "them" is; only the assistant property manager was in the office.) "Additionally," the lawyer wrote, "your husband balled up the notices and threw them at the door while threatening to blow up the building." Both Loren and Rashad denied making any threats, and said he *certainly* did not say anything about blowing up the building. Several security guards patrol the Southern Towers complex around the clock; if the assistant property manager felt threatened, she didn't call any of them for help. "How much are we supposed to deal with? How much are people supposed to endure before they snap?" Loren wondered months later. "Then when they snap, you feel it's unwarranted. You feel threatened now? I've been threatened since October 14, 2023, when I came home to a flooded apartment."

Yet Loren knew even in the moment that they were committing a grave strategic error. Until that day, they had mostly declined to fight back beyond a few strongly worded emails, silently gathering evidence that they were being retaliated against. The moment they began yelling at the assistant property manager, they lost the moral high ground. The next day, they received a fifth notice: a cease-and-desist letter prohibiting them from contacting their own landlord. Except in cases of emergency, any communication would have to go through an outside lawyer representing CIM.

Loren and Rashad discussed their options. They could fight to stay—a tempting route for someone constitutionally incapable of admitting defeat—but they would be up against a $32 billion company with a fleet of highly paid attorneys. And the dispute in the management office wouldn't help their cause.

So they gave up.

Landing an apartment at Southern Towers had felt like a dream come true, but it was over. In March 2024, they moved to an apartment complex just down the road. Their new landlord was another huge corporation based thousands of miles away.

PART III
AFTER

NINE

LIZ

LIZ WASN'T NAÏVE. SHE KNEW THAT WEALTHY AMERICANS HAD AD-
vantages that were never offered to her. She knew that Toys R Us executives were making orders of magnitude more money than all the
workers in her store combined. She knew that competition sometimes
drives companies out of business, and that people sometimes lose
their jobs. After spending her entire adult life working in retail, she
understood the realities of a capitalist system.

But the more she read about what caused Toys R Us's failure, the
less it seemed like an inevitable result of capitalism. When the company was under threat from Amazon, its leaders responded not with
a new business strategy or major technological advancements or even
basic and much-needed store renovations. Instead, they sold off the
stores' real estate and took out such massive loans that the interest
payments alone quickly became crippling. The employees at her store
had kept things running while management seemed to flounder. Yet
the suits walked away with seven-figure bonuses, while she and her
colleagues couldn't even get the relatively paltry severance their contracts had promised.

The enduring myth of the lone business genius creating a Fortune
500 company, or saving one from destruction, has benefited private
equity immeasurably. Think of Gordon Gekko in *Wall Street*, the only
person clear-eyed enough to come up with a future strategy for failing
companies without allowing his emotions to get in the way. Think of
how finance titans like Blackstone cofounder Stephen Schwarzman,

former Apollo Global Management chairman Leon Black, KKR co-creator Henry Kravis, and former Bain Capital CEO Mitt Romney are rewarded with seats in the Senate and board positions at some of the country's most august institutions. For centuries, celebrating the "free market" has been one of the strongest uniting forces between Republicans and Democrats. With help from the donations it throws at politicians of both parties, the private equity industry has been allowed to operate with little scrutiny, charming people in power while taking advantage of the workers below.

Before she lost her job in late 2018, Liz didn't have much interest in activism. She already had plenty of people to take care of. Besides Henry and their three kids—eighteen, thirteen, and six when she was laid off—there was her extended family, a growing number of whom had also left Alaska for the northwest corner of the American mainland. Her younger sister, Mindy, had settled near Portland with her husband and two children. Their father often came down from Anchorage to stay with Liz and her family. Henry's parents had left Colombia and moved in. At work, she was perfectly content to be "just a retail employee," as she put it, doing what she was told.

But she had always had a hard time holding back when people needed help. She wondered, indignantly, why so few of the people in power seemed to have any interest in helping the little guys. So when she began reading more about what caused Toys R Us's death, learning for the first time about how private equity operates and how the country's political leaders help them do it, she saw no choice but to get involved. Because of the seemingly inexplicable decision to saddle her employer with a crushing amount of debt, her friend Annmarie Reinhart Smith couldn't afford the inhaler she needed to treat her asthma. Because of them, she was out of a job she loved.

———

LIZ HAD MET MICHELLE PEREZ a few years earlier, when they were assigned to help with the holiday rush at a Portland Toys R Us store. Michelle was a decade younger, with brightly dyed hair—the color depended on her mood—and a personality to match, always trying to make work fun for everyone else. Liz found herself inventing little tasks that would require her to run over to where Michelle was working. The two women soon became best friends. Every time Liz hosted a family gathering, Michelle was there too, blending in as seamlessly as a blood relation.

Michelle was the one who told Liz the story of what really drove Toys R Us out of business. After the company announced plans to liquidate but before most of the stores had closed, a group of laid-off employees had started a Facebook group they called the Dead Giraffe Society, and Michelle had become an early member. The group began as a place for Toys R Us workers to share memories of their time with the company and stay connected to colleagues. Pretty soon, though, it morphed into a space to express their outrage at the company's owners and swap ideas for what to do about it. Members posted articles about the executive bonuses and about Toys R Us's tremendous debt. Michelle felt energized and empowered when she saw all those people who wanted to fight back.

Annmarie, who had worked at Toys R Us since 1988—first on Long Island and then in Durham, North Carolina—was in the Facebook group too. She knew about Bain Capital from the days when its founder, Mitt Romney, was running for president; Barack Obama's campaign had released ads blaming Romney for 350 job losses at an office supply manufacturer in Indiana and 750 at a steel factory in Kansas City, Missouri, and making tens of millions of dollars in the process. She knew Bain was part of the group that bought Toys R Us in 2005. But Toys R Us wasn't a steel factory; the story she'd been told was that the acquisition was meant to help her company grow. Now—thirty years after she started her career with Toys R Us, thirteen years after Bain, KKR, and Vornado bought the retail icon, and six years after Romney lost his presidential bid—Toys R Us was becoming another victim of private equity. And Annmarie wanted people to know.

Annmarie, Michelle, and a handful of other Dead Giraffe Society members began telling people what the private equity firms had done to their employer, hoping to attract public outrage and media attention that would help them get their severance. They printed flyers, which they hung in their stores and handed out to customers. "I was taping them onto the registers, and the manager would tear them off at night," Michelle said. "But I was the first person to touch every single till in the morning, so I just put them back up." Michelle knew management couldn't do anything to her; she was losing her job anyway, and the stores needed people to get them through until closing.

That's when Michelle convinced Liz to join her in protesting Toys R Us's private equity owners. Before her employer decided to liquidate, Liz couldn't have named Toys R Us's parent company if she tried. Why would she have needed to? She worked for Toys R Us. Her bosses worked for Toys R Us. She had never spoken to anyone from Bain Capital, KKR, or Vornado, had never even heard of those companies. The idea that these faceless executives in New York and Boston could take away her job without even paying her the severance she was owed lit a fuse in her. In her first post in the Dead Giraffe Society group, she wrote about her revelation.

> My name is Liz, and I'm from Alaska. I was raised believing
> "when life hands you lemons, make lemonade." I just dealt
> with whatever was happening in the world around me.
> I stood up to bullies. I took sides with the underdog. But I
> never thought to stick up for myself, for my rights. Not until
> my favorite job at Toys R Us was taken away. Not until my
> second family was spread to the four corners of this country.
> Not until I started looking into the actual history of the Toys
> R Us/Babies R Us saga. I found out that this is an economic
> crisis that some politicians are trying to ignore and, yes, even
> hide due to their investment or involvement.

Inspired by Michelle and Annmarie, she began taping up flyers in her stores and tucking them in customers' bags. She also knew, felt in her bones, that this was just the start. She wanted to confront the firms' executives directly.

IN THE SPRING OF 2018, around the time Annmarie's Toys R Us store closed and a few months before Liz's did, a group of former and soon-to-be-former employees who were Dead Giraffe Society members got Facebook messages from organizers with a group called Rise Up Retail. The private equity firms were acting unethically, the organizers said. And Rise Up Retail wanted to help. Liz got one of the messages, which excited her. The Toys R Us workers weren't powerful enough to beat back multibillion-dollar corporations on their own, she knew. KKR and Bain executives didn't go to Toys R Us stores; they would never see those flyers. But Rise Up Retail was an established, well-connected nonprofit; they were playing in the big leagues. The organizers seemed excited about Liz too. Her story was irresistible; she had moved across an ocean and supported a family of five on a Toys R Us salary. And she was a captivating speaker, at turns warm, funny, and emotional.

Rise Up Retail grew out of a group formed in 2011 called Organization United for Respect at Walmart, or OUR Walmart. Its objective was as straightforward as it was ambitious: to improve working conditions for the million-plus Walmart employees across the country. At the time, the average Walmart associate made $8.81 an hour, and even many full-time employees required food stamps to survive. The company had become known as the archetype of American corporate greed hurting workers.

In many industries, lobbying for employee rights would be the job of a union, but the retail world has been wildly successful at beating back efforts to unionize. Just 4 percent of retail workers were union members in 2024, according to the Bureau of Labor Statistics. Among the ten largest retail chains in the United States, only one has a union open to a significant number of employees: at Costco, more than fifteen thousand workers are represented by the Teamsters. Store clerks and warehouse workers are seen as easy to replace, making union-busting campaigns particularly effective. And employees of large chains are geographically dispersed, with limited access to the tools that white-collar office workers use to communicate across borders, which helps companies prevent retail workers of big chains from strategizing with each other.

OUR Walmart was in fact the product of a union; it was created as an offshoot of the United Food and Commercial Workers International Union (UFCW). But their idea wasn't to unionize Walmart's workers. The group took a different approach: holding protests in front of stores and company headquarters in Arkansas and demanding meetings with executives. When Walmart agreed to raise starting salaries to $9 an hour in 2015 and $10 an hour in 2016, OUR Walmart claimed the announcement as a major victory, though there was no formal agreement between organizers and the company. (News articles at the time mostly attributed the increase to the company's need to boost its woeful customer service ratings.)

In 2016, new leadership at UFCW shifted the organization's strategy. They planned to focus almost exclusively on building union membership, which meant scaling back on nonunion organizing campaigns. Union enrollment was declining across the country, and UFCW needed more dues to survive. OUR Walmart wasn't bringing in any money, and organizers and demonstrations don't pay for themselves. As the *Washington Post* put it, the union's return on their investment in the Walmart employees, "besides the satisfaction of having helped workers more broadly, is essentially zero." OUR Walmart would continue to exist in diminished form, UFCW announced, but without the focus on on-the-ground organizing. Two of the group's leaders, Andrea Dehlendorf and Daniel Schlademan, were fired.

So in early 2018, with funding from the progressive nonprofit the Center for Popular Democracy, Dehlendorf and Schlademan launched their own organization. They called it Rise Up Retail. The name change signified an expansion of the mission, backed by a coalition of progressive foundations: to help *all* retail employees make their companies better places to work. Seeing the rising power of private equity in the retail world, Dehlendorf and Schlademan also wanted to focus directly on financial firms.

The new group happened to launch the same spring that Toys R

Us began liquidating all its stores and laying off employees without severance. Just as Liz and her friends were starting to coalesce around the loss of their jobs and their beloved toy store, Rise Up Retail organizers were on the hunt for workers interested in joining the front lines of a fledgling movement against private equity ownership.

———

IT WAS EASY FOR THE Toys R Us workers and the Rise Up Retail staff to home in on their first goal: to shame KKR, Bain, and Vornado into paying severance to the 33,000 employees they had laid off. Organizers asked workers and their supporters to bombard the firms with phone calls, demanding they pay the estimated $75 million it would cost to cover the total promised severance. Rise Up Retail provided executives' phone numbers, along with a sample script: "You created this crisis. I will continue to fight for the severance pay our families need. I hope you do the right thing by our families."

This was a ragtag group of workers and organizers taking on some of the most powerful financial firms in the country, but they had one huge advantage: people cared about Toys R Us. The story was egregious, but it was hardly unprecedented. Plenty of other businesses had gone under following private equity acquisitions—A&P, once the largest grocery chain in America, declared bankruptcy twice in five years before shuttering completely in 2015 and offering employees just $300 a year in severance. But no one loves their grocery store.

Toys R Us, on the other hand—*everybody* loved Toys R Us. The company had been around for sixty years; people who had fond memories of strolling the aisles as kids later visited to pick out toys for their grandchildren. Regular customers knew longtime employees, like the woman who named her baby after Liz. Geoffrey the Giraffe was one of the most recognizable corporate mascots in America, which gave the activists an opportunity: it put a cute, fuzzy, universally beloved face on how private equity destroys community institutions. Geoffrey attracted plenty of headlines—a feat activists and workers had struggled to achieve for decades. News stories didn't settle for the party line about how the rise of Walmart and Amazon doomed Toys R Us; many suggested that the debt piled on by its private equity owners played a major role. A CNN headline put it bluntly: "Amazon didn't kill Toys R Us. Here's what did."

Rise Up Retail was determined to take advantage of the opening. The group provided media outlets with poignant quotes from laid-off workers across the country and staged protests in front of the firms' offices. In one short speech outside a KKR office tower, Liz told a group of supporters, "I have given my whole self to Toys R Us. I wish Toys R Us treated us the way I treat my team." At the same event, Michelle spoke about her customers. "I believe that our relationships made Toys R Us and Babies R Us the company it was. My team members and I provided immense emotional support, and gave a new meaning to 'retail therapy' because we were there to listen and to offer vital support."

Henry's schedule didn't allow him to care for the couple's youngest child, Daniyel, by himself, so Liz would often take him along when she traveled. In one photo, Daniyel and a girl with braided pigtails are seen from behind, their arms slung over each other's shoulders in front of a San Francisco office tower—co-owned by Vornado Realty Trust and the Trump Organization—where KKR leased space. Daniyel has a buzz cut and cherubic cheeks; his free hand is raised in a fist, a tiny revolutionary.

Of course, if KKR and Bain Capital had cared about what laid-off workers and progressive critics of American capitalism thought of them, they would have changed their business practices decades earlier. Liz and her former colleagues staged protests at Toys R Us's corporate office in New Jersey and at KKR headquarters in New York, but they never got to speak to anyone beyond weary security guards at the front desk. Even with media support, the little guys had no good way to make the billionaires in charge take them seriously.

What those corporate executives *did* take seriously was the need to keep the money faucet flowing. Because a private equity firm puts in only a tiny fraction of the money necessary for a leveraged buyout, it relies on outside investors for much of its capital. Many of those investors are pension funds, and pension funds have boards. When those boards are unhappy, *that* is a real problem for the firms. So, taking a page out of the labor union playbook, Rise Up Retail organizers started appearing at pension fund board meetings.

———

EIGHTY-EIGHT PERCENT OF PUBLIC PENSION funds have some private equity investments, according to a study from the industry's lobbying group. The California Public Employees' Retirement System, or CalPERS, paid out nearly $30 billion in retirement funds and health benefits in the fiscal year ending in 2021, to 775,000 members, making it not only the largest public pension fund in the country but one of the most powerful investors overall. About $3 billion of CalPERS's money currently sits in various KKR funds.

The private equity industry argues that working people would be far worse off without it, because the returns it generates allow them to retire. Take it from Blackstone, the largest private equity firm in the world, in its annual SEC filing: "To the extent our funds perform well, we can support a better retirement for tens of millions of pensioners, including teachers, nurses and firefighters." In a 2023 interview at KKR's office in Manhattan's Hudson Yards development, Pete Stavros, the firm's cohead of global private equity, said his firm can't simply raise salaries at portfolio companies even when workers are underpaid because it would be irresponsible to pensioners. "If you're managing teachers' pension money and you want to just raise everyone's salary, that is on the backs of teachers, which is not ethical, and it's not our money."

Almost every state pension fund has a major shortfall—$1.5 trillion altogether as of 2023. That makes private equity's promise of higher-than-average returns on investment hard to turn down. (Pension plans for employees of private companies, meanwhile, are largely extinct—in part because private equity firms set out to eliminate them in 1980s-era leveraged buyouts. Killing off Revlon's employee pension plan in 1985 earned Ronald Perelman $100 million.)

BAD COMPANY

Yet the idea that private equity funds consistently outperform the stock market is controversial at best, with academic papers coming to a wide range of conclusions. Critics of the industry point out that rate of return is an easy metric to game, making them skeptical of those rosier studies. And public pension funds tend to generate worse returns from private equity funds than governments and private investors do. While it is true that millions of pensioners *do* rely on private equity returns, the evidence is far less clear that they *must*.

Those returns also aren't generated in a vacuum. Private equity often makes money by cutting costs and raising prices, both of which take the heaviest tolls on working-class people. In the retail world, cutting costs almost always means layoffs—not of executives, but of low-level employees like Liz. If private equity does in fact help pensioners lead better lives, it does so in part by hurting workers. Stavros and other private equity executives often talk about their responsibility to public employees who have served their communities—*don't all those teachers and firefighters who served their communities for decades deserve a nice retirement?*—but what they are in fact describing is a sort of zero-sum game in which cutting wages for working- and middle-class employees in one place helps working- and middle-class retirees in other places, a phenomenon labor journalist Hamilton Nolan has termed "capitalism's washing machine."

And while the pensioners make for a tidier narrative, the reality is that no one benefits nearly as much from private equity as private equity itself. The system is designed so that firms put in less money and shoulder less risk than anyone else, yet reap the lion's share of the profits. Benefiting retired teachers and firefighters might be a desirable side effect, but the point is to earn returns for private equity executives. Stephen Schwarzman didn't earn $37 billion by putting teachers' and firefighters' interests first.

———

UNLIKE MOST GROUPS THAT CONTROL billions of dollars, the boards of pension funds include "participant representatives"—actual beneficiaries of the fund, who are generally rank-and-file workers and retirees. Rise Up Retail knew those people were more likely to be sympathetic to a campaign organized by laid-off employees than private equity executives had been. So organizers like Liz, Michelle, and Annmarie began showing up at their board meetings and signing up to speak during the public comment portion.*

During the spring and summer of 2018, Liz spoke at pension fund meetings in Oregon, Washington, California, Minnesota, and Ohio. Toys R Us's owners weren't harmed by the company's demise, she told the boards, but she didn't know whether she'd be able to pay her rent the next month. Her former coworkers were struggling just to put food on the table. Rise Up Retail estimated it would cost $75 million to pay the severance the workers' contracts promised. Surely KKR and Bain could find $75 million—pocket change to firms that big—to fulfill their obligations.

Liz had never been much for public speaking, but her outrage outweighed her nerves. She told the Washington pension board about how she insisted on answering every phone call at her store in the last few weeks of the company's life to protect her coworkers from angry customers, about how she was scrubbing toilets because they were so short-staffed. "You will go down in history as a hero for standing with thirty-three thousand employees trying to change laws for the next generation, or you will go down as the enablers who refused to stand up to Wall Street greed," she told the board of the Oregon Public Employees Retirement System.

Looking back years later, Liz still seemed awed by how she wound up traveling the country—a country she had seen very little of until then—speaking to so many powerful people. Once she was asked to appear on a keynote panel in front of two thousand people at a conference to tell the Toys R Us story from a worker's perspective. Rise Up Retail suggested another former employee go instead, she said, a

---

* Annmarie Reinhart Smith died in 2021, at age sixty-one, of Covid-19. In an obituary, the New York Times cited her as a key voice in the fight against KKR, Bain Capital, and Vornado.

white woman who could show "a softer side." But the panel organizers insisted: they wanted Liz. She started to panic, intimidated by the idea of posing as some sort of expert in front of all these scholars and activists and people who knew *way* more about private equity than she did. Then Jim Baker, the executive director of the watchdog group Private Equity Stakeholder Project, explained why he asked for her by name. "You know how to talk to all of us," he told her. "You know the ins and outs. We are here because of you." She began to protest, but he cut her off. "It's the truth. You are always about the truth. *We are here because of you.*"

All the speeches seemed to be having an impact. Pension boards were paying attention. On several occasions, Liz remembered, individual board members asked her to stick around after a meeting to answer more detailed questions about the experiences of Toys R Us workers. After all the protests outside KKR and Bain offices failed to even get them into the buildings, the interest felt thrilling.

Just weeks into Rise Up Retail's nationwide tour, organizers achieved a breakthrough. Minnesota's $93 billion public employees' pension board voted to pause all new investments in KKR funds because they were concerned about how the firm had treated Toys R Us workers. The decision didn't get much mainstream attention, but to Liz and her colleagues, it was huge—a crucial first step on the road to winning their severance. "That happened because we went and fought and told them 'we can all fight back, we don't have to take this,'" Liz said, her voice still radiating pride years later.

A few days later, another accomplishment: the Washington State Investment Board interrogated KKR executive Nate Taylor after they heard Liz's speech about the Toys R Us workers. "Did anyone at KKR lose their job over the failure of Toys R Us? Did anyone have their bonuses cut, did anyone have their compensation cut significantly? Because that's one of the consequences of free market capitalism," board member Stephen Miller asked Taylor. (Taylor did not directly answer the question.) Liz even got the chance to briefly address Taylor herself. "How can you sit there and tell me you're sorry when your shoes can pay my rent?" (He didn't answer that question either.)

Then, in November, after months of campaigning, the workers landed their biggest victory. Citing "an extraordinary set of circumstances," KKR and Bain had struck a deal with Rise Up Retail to pay the laid-off Toys R Us employees after all. (Vornado, the third partner in the deal, would not contribute.) Technically it wouldn't be severance, but a "hardship fund"—the firms wanted to make clear that they didn't legally owe anyone anything: they were *choosing* to help. Perhaps they were doing it out of the goodness of their hearts. Or perhaps they wanted to avoid more bad press and problems with pension boards.

Under the terms of the deal, each firm would contribute $10 million, which meant a total pot $55 million smaller than what Rise Up Retail had calculated the workers were owed. It was less than twice what Toys R Us CEO Dave Brandon had earned during the last year of the company's life, and it would be split among 33,000 employees. But the idea of a private equity company voluntarily paying workers after driving a company out of business was all but unprecedented. It may have been a partial victory, but it was $20 million better than nothing.

———

A FLURRY OF HEADLINES CREDITED Rise Up Retail and its pension fund strategy with winning private equity concessions once considered unthinkable. But to Liz's mind, that wasn't quite right. She and her former colleagues were the ones who did the work, not Rise Up Retail's full-time staff. They were the ones who had recruited new protesters, spoken in front of pension boards, spent nights and weekends writing speeches and creating gift bags of Toys R Us merch to hand out to politicians along with flyers outlining their grievances.

And they had done all of that work for free. Rise Up Retail raised $2.5 million from foundations and individuals in 2018—they would nearly triple that the following year—but the vast majority of Toys R Us organizers weren't paid beyond travel expenses. Liz was paid $6,000 from the hardship fund, minus taxes, far less than what her contract said she would receive if she was laid off after six years of service.

Multiple people involved in the organizing effort say most workers wanted to hold out for more money from KKR and Bain, but Rise Up Retail's core team overruled them in favor of striking a deal. "I think for them it was transactional: Let me use your face. Let me use your image. Let me use your story," Liz said. "Where for me it was more like, okay, your life was affected by this. How do we fix it?"

Several months into the Toys R Us campaign, Liz took a job doing janitorial work at an Intel campus in the Portland area. She mostly liked the job, in part because her boss encouraged her activism and always found someone to cover for her when she had to jet off for a protest or speaking engagement. But she had also gotten a taste for organizing, and realized she was good at it. She wanted to make a career out of it. She, Michelle, and other former organizers both said Rise Up Retail would dangle the possibility of full-time jobs whenever someone started to grow tired of doing so much work for free. "The minute you'd pull back, they'd be like, 'Hey, we have this position that we're creating in two months and we want you to be a part of it. But you've got to be active so your name's the one they think of, you know,'" Michelle remembered. "So then you'd continue to do things and then nothing would ever come of it."

Liz did eventually get hired as a part-time organizer in 2019. (By then the group had renamed itself United for Respect.) But she didn't last long. She felt left out from strategic decisions, which she said were always made by senior leaders who had never even worked in retail. She felt like a cog in a machine controlled by people who knew far less about what actual working conditions were like than she did. She had never expected a global corporation to prioritize her interests, but she had genuinely bought into United for Respect's mission. Now she was walking away feeling more burned than she ever had been by Toys R Us.

She wasn't alone in her frustration. In 2019, United for Respect's staff unionized, citing complaints including high rates of burnout among organizers, a lack of input in overall strategy even on campaigns at companies they'd worked for, a failure of the organization to retain people of color, and a fear of questioning senior leadership. After three years of bargaining, the union won its first contract in 2022. The following year, the organization laid off thirteen employees, including every field organizer. The excitement over one scrappy nonprofit going head-to-head with corporate retail giants felt like a distant memory.

———

YET SOMETHING SURPRISING HAPPENED IN the years during and after the Toys R Us debacle: private equity largely got out of the retail game. As of early 2025, KKR's private equity portfolio included exactly one U.S.-based brick-and mortar retailer, a small chain selling outdoor and home improvement in the upper Midwest. Bain Capital, Toys R Us's other former owner, also owned just one, a small discount furniture chain in the Northeast (plus Canada Goose, a winter clothing manu-facturer that operates a few dozen retail stores in the U.S.).

It wasn't worker activism that had driven firms out. Private equity wants growth industries that are recession-proof, like housing and health care. Retail fit the bill, until it didn't.

Stavros did not work on the Toys R Us deal, but he nonetheless gets visibly frustrated by the idea that private equity killed the company. "Of course [Toys R Us] was a bad investment. It was a stupid invest-ment. Of course, KKR screwed up. They should never have bought it," he said in 2023. "But with some balance, I would have thought people would say, 'Okay, but there's like ten big retailers that disappeared. No major toy retailer survived.'"

But accepting the narrative that Amazon doomed retail chains requires ignoring the companies that continued to perform well into the 2020s, a group that includes not only Walmart but specialty re-tailers like Home Depot, Lowe's, and CVS. All of them compete with "the everything store," yet all have thrived. Their success is, in large part, a result of evolving along with their customers: developing user-friendly websites, desirable in-store experiences, and perks like curb-side pickup—exactly the kinds of advancements Toys R Us could never afford to make because of the crushing debt that private equity took out in its name. Of the twenty largest retailers in 2024, none were owned by a private equity firm. (In early 2025, Walgreens, the eighth-largest, was in talks to be acquired by Sycamore Partners, one of few firms that still specializes in retail.) Brick-and-mortar retail will never again be as lucrative as in Charles Lazarus's day, but a smaller industry is not the same as a nonexistent one—until private equity gets involved.

Toys R Us's demise pushed some progressive politicians to take aim at private equity more broadly, looking to prevent similar stories from playing out in the industries that still appealed to firms like KKR and Bain Capital. In 2019, Senator Elizabeth Warren became private equity's most prominent foe when she introduced the Stop Wall Street Looting Act. As she announced the bill in D.C., workers knelt in front of the lectern holding a banner announcing "Wall Street Killed My Job."

"There is a part of Wall Street that has figured out it can make millions of dollars, billions of dollars by going into businesses that are already established, that are up and running, and suck all the value out of them, sell the pieces off for parts, leave the employees behind, leave the pensioners behind, leave the communities behind, line their own pockets, roll on out of town, and go to the next business and the next business and the next business," Warren said in her opening remarks. "And Washington keeps helping them. They give them special tax breaks, loopholes, multiple ways that they can take more value out of these corporations, put it in their own pockets, and leave everyone else behind."

At the event, series of speakers, including a few from Toys R Us, recounted how their lives were upended when their private equity–owned employers shut for good. One talked about her experience working for a small California newspaper owned by Alden Global Capital, which had become infamous for pillaging American newsrooms. In videos of the event, Liz is visible on the left side of the frame, beaming and occasionally nodding her head emphatically.

Warren's bill would have upended the way the private equity industry operates. It would tax the monitoring fees that firms charge companies they own at a rate of 100 percent, effectively ending the practice. It would ban dividends to investors and real estate sales in the first two years after an acquisition, requiring firms to stick with a company in order to make a profit instead of selling off its assets and shutting it down. It would prioritize employee severance in bankruptcy packages and close loopholes that allow private equity firms to lower their tax rates.

Most terrifyingly to private equity executives, it would force firms to share responsibility for the debt they take out in a company's name: if an acquired company declared bankruptcy or liquidated, the firm that owned it would no longer be off the hook for repaying debtors. In the case of Toys R Us, that would have meant Bain and KKR would have lost their respective $31 million in profits from the deal, and instead be forced to pay back at least some of the $5.2 billion in debt they took on in the retailer's name. The Stop Wall Street Looting Act would end leveraged buyouts as we know them.

That's exactly the reason Warren's bill stood no chance of passing. Private equity employees and analysts scoffed at the idea, saying it would create too much risk and not enough potential upside to be worth taking a chance on struggling companies. Later in 2019, when Warren briefly surged in presidential polls, even Democrats in the finance industry started to grow worried. "Everyone is nervous," former Obama economic advisor Steven Rattner told the *New York Times*. "What scares the hell out of me is the way she would fundamentally change our free-enterprise system." The bill never made any headway in the House or Senate. Warren reintroduced it in 2021 and again in 2024, but didn't get any further. Barring a dramatic change in the composition of Congress, the proposal to fundamentally change the private equity industry had no future.

The Stop Wall Street Looting Act did help breathe new life into a less radical proposal many people *did* think would eventually pass: closing the carried-interest loophole, which allows private equity firms and their executives to benefit from a dramatically lower tax rate. The exact amount of additional tax revenue such a plan would generate is the subject of a contentious debate, but even the most conservative estimates put the figure at nearly $15 billion over a decade, while the most optimistic put it closer to $200 billion. It wouldn't be a lethal hit on private equity, but it would be the most significant regulation in decades.

The idea of closing the loophole has bounced around Capitol Hill since 2007, when Democrat Max Baucus and Republican Chuck Grassley introduced a Senate bill to tax all of a firm's profits as income, not capital gains. Though the measure didn't pass, the private equity industry was spooked enough to immediately, and dramatically, increase the amount of money it spent on lobbying. The House passed a version of the bill four times, but it could never get through the Senate.

In 2022, closing the loophole came closer than ever to becoming a reality. Democrats wrote it into the American Families Plan bill, which was designed to fund social services ranging from paid family leave to free prekindergarten programs. The American Families Plan passed in the House with the carried-interest provision intact, but Arizona senator Kyrsten Sinema, then a Democrat, managed to kill the Senate version at the eleventh hour, making her an industry hero. (The bill eventually failed altogether, though some elements ended up passing later.)

Since then, no one has tried to mess with private equity's favorable taxation structure. For the foreseeable future, even a relatively minor cut to private equity's profit margins is too politically unpalatable to consider.

———

LIZ DIDN'T STAY AWAY FROM retail for long. After a spell cleaning the Intel campus near Portland, her family moved to the Tacoma, Washington, area, where her husband, Henry, began work as a pharmacist. Liz took a job at WinCo Foods, a regional grocery chain locally famous for its low prices—and for being the second-largest employee-owned company in the country, behind Publix supermarkets.

She also discovered that she did in fact have the skills to make a career as a professional organizer. When she was hired at WinCo, she took part-time hours because she needed to make room for another offer: to join the staff of a tiny advocacy group called Seeding

Sovereignty, which works on issues affecting Indigenous Americans like her. After a few years there, she struck out on her own, taking on individual organizing projects and running trainings for groups looking to translate online activism to the real world. Every day, she sits at the computer in her tiny home office, surrounded by Toys R Us memorabilia, and works on campaigns designed to pressure powerful people and companies to improve conditions for less powerful ones.

She doesn't have a multimillion-dollar budget or powerful politicians on speed dial, but she chooses her projects based on her own values. In addition to workers' rights issues, she spends much of her time trying to raise awareness of missing or murdered Indigenous women: putting ads online, sending letters to police departments and local politicians, and writing media releases.

She also fiercely protects her time with her family. She dotes on Daniyel, whom she calls Son-Son, and hosts her sister, Mindy, and her family as often as possible. She flies to Alaska as frequently as she can for family events and Tlingit tribal celebrations. Toys R Us didn't give her the stability she hoped for, but she found it anyway.

TEN

ROGER

AFTER YEARS OF TRYING TO IMPROVE RIVERTON'S HOSPITAL—FIRST
as a doctor, then as a board member and volunteer activist—Roger
was ready to give up.

As one of the few Democrats in deep-red Fremont County, he
had gotten used to his neighbors lovingly teasing him about being a
bleeding-heart liberal. But he wasn't marching in the streets to support
Medicare for All; he had never argued that SageWest should be unconcerned with making money. All he was saying was that they should
make money by providing actual health care. Even the neighbors *he*
lovingly teased for being heartless conservatives agreed with that.

The PowerPoint slides Roger found in 2018 showed that LifePoint
had no interest in operating a real hospital in Riverton even before
private equity got involved. Under Apollo Global Management's
ownership, things were getting even worse. "It seemed like they
were killing it softly, and then all of a sudden we realized it was an
orchestrated effort," he said. "This hospital and this community are
a very personal thing to me, and I felt absolutely betrayed."

Vivian Watkins's faith in LifePoint had run out long before
Roger's. Where he is warm and gentle, always assuming the best
about people, she is more discriminating, and more blunt. While other
members of Save Our Riverton Hospital were trying to negotiate with
then–SageWest CEO Alan Daugherty, Vivian—who calmly described
Daugherty as "arrogant, smart-mouthed, disrespectful"—wasn't going

to bother. "The group said we've got to try. And I said, 'God bless you. Go with my love. I'm not wasting my time on the man,'" she said.

They met with him twice a week, trying to get him to promise to restore the services the hospital had lost or at least not cut any more. "And every time they would come back to our meetings and say, 'What an idiot,'" Vivian remembered. "So finally I said, 'Okay, so you guys either have the patience of Job or you're stupid as a box of rocks.' How much longer are we going to do this?" After six months of these exchanges, they finally told her they were done.

To Vivian, it seemed like the SageWest hospitals in Riverton and Lander weren't very important to their parent company's bottom line, and LifePoint evidently wasn't interested in growing them. So, she thought, perhaps they'd be willing to sell SageWest Riverton? She had spent her entire career in banking; she knew she could find the money. On multiple occasions over a period of months, she asked Daugherty and his bosses to name a number at which they would consider selling or leasing the hospital. But every time, they said they weren't interested at any price. If LifePoint and their private equity owners at Apollo wouldn't listen to money, she knew they weren't going to listen at all. She was ready to escalate.

By the end of 2018, Roger was all in. He had learned the hard way that LifePoint executives would say whatever they needed to get what they wanted. They had appealed to his fundamental belief that rural places deserved comprehensive health care. Then they used him to win the trust of his colleagues, neighbors, and friends, all while gradually cutting off Riverton's access to basic medicine. The only way to ensure that future Rivertonians had a functional hospital, he decided, was for locals to build one themselves.

WHEN PEOPLE HEAR THAT YOU want to create a hospital from scratch in a small town with no corporate support, they tend to react with cheery enthusiasm that belies pity for your naïveté. "Wow, that's amazing; I didn't know that was possible," they'll say, but all the while their eyes are saying, *That's not possible. How are you crazy enough to believe that's possible?*

Fremont County is the third-poorest in the state, and building a hospital is a remarkably expensive undertaking in the best of circumstances. Even small rural hospitals with no frills typically cost upwards of $75 million, not including land or operational expenses. Even in places with fast-growing populations, which Riverton isn't, hospitals most often expand to accommodate increased patient load; few create new ones from scratch. And, as the executives at LifePoint and Apollo were quick to point out, the only way for a hospital to be sustainable without being part of a larger company or government entity is to control costs or increase prices. The deck is stacked in favor of the status quo—and against the Rogers and Vivians of the world.

Even Roger and Vivian weren't sure whether they could ever raise the money to build a community-owned hospital. But true to form, Vivian was the first to suggest they would never find out unless they tried. "My perspective was, stupidly, that I bet I could build you a pretty darn good bank and run it. How different can a hospital be?" she said later. Roger couldn't argue with that. He started quoting the anthropologist Margaret Mead—possibly apocryphally, but no less inspirationally—at meetings: "Never doubt that a small group of thoughtful, committed citizens can change the world. Indeed, it is the only thing that ever has."

The first step was to solidify the loosely organized Save Our Riverton Hospital into something resembling a real nonprofit. In October 2018, they incorporated, renaming the group Riverton Medical District. Roger and Vivian became board members; so did several other Rivertonians who had helpful connections and professional experience. There was Eric Ridgway, who had practiced family medicine in Riverton since 1994. There was Susan Goetzinger, who had spent fifteen years as the chief financial officer of Riverton Memorial, before and after the LifePoint acquisition and merger with Lander's hospital. And there was Corte McGuffey, the youngest of the group and the biggest celebrity in town.

Corte looks like the platonic ideal of a retired athlete: six-foot-one and stocky, gelled hair just starting to gray. He spent his early childhood in Reno, Nevada, then lived in Pinedale, on the other side of the Wind River Range. But many people forget that he isn't an actual Riverton native because of his heroics after moving to town in tenth grade.

Corte grew up playing football, often coached by his dad, and by the time he enrolled at Riverton High in the fall of 1992, he was a promising quarterback. As a senior, he led the Riverton Wolverines to the first state title in school history. Better yet, they won the championship game against the school's—and the town's—archrival: Lander. Corte went on to win a national championship and national player of the year honors as a senior at the University of Northern Colorado. In the process, he set nearly every school record, throwing 93 touchdowns and 8,766 yards and rushing for 956 yards and 14 more touchdowns. He briefly played professionally, first with the St. Louis Rams and then in the short-lived XFL, then hung up his cleats for good and became a dentist in Colorado. He worked there for a dozen years, but he missed Wyoming. So when his wife's father asked him to take over the family trucking company back in Riverton, the McGuffeys moved home.

Corte was still getting settled when a family friend told him he needed to come to a meeting about improving the hospital. His in-laws had told him something about SageWest Riverton getting worse, but he hadn't paid much attention, so when he showed up at the community college auditorium, he was shocked to see three hundred people there. Speaker after speaker testified to the scope of the problem, from the loss of the labor and delivery unit to the skyrocketing number of air ambulance trips. Corte was in his early forties, with two young kids, and he wanted his family to plant long-term roots in Riverton. They needed a functional hospital.

While Roger talked about a hospital's value from the perspective of a caregiver, Corte took a more business-minded approach. He was in charge of a company, and he knew recruiting talent to small-town Wyoming would be much more difficult if he couldn't promise decent health care. Fewer services at SageWest Riverton also meant fewer local jobs in a place that already loses a huge number of its young people to bigger cities.

Aside from his notoriety, Corte brought two major advantages to the Riverton Medical District campaign. One was that he was young, which meant he could get other young people invested in the effort, which he did. The other was that, unlike Roger and Vivian, he was a good Republican. In a town where more than three times as many people voted for Trump as for Harris in 2024, that mattered: Roger was beloved, but he was still a liberal. Corte, though, had the credentials. When *Corte* said this Wall Street firm whose executives didn't know anything about small-town Wyoming was trying to take their hospital away, his neighbors listened.

So with Corte newly ensconced on the board alongside Roger, Vivian, and eleven others, the group set out to raise money. Not enough to build a hospital—even Vivian wasn't sure they could do *that*—but enough to commission a study of the area's health care needs and whether a new hospital could *theoretically* be financially viable.

Vivian began cold-calling hospital CEOs across Wyoming, looking for advice on where to start. One told her that she should go straight to Stroudwater Associates, a Maine-based consultancy with a specialty in rural health care finances. Hiring Stroudwater to conduct a study was expensive, the CEO warned her, but they were the country's leading experts in small-town hospitals. Whatever Stroudwater said about the prospects for a new hospital in Riverton would be treated as incontrovertible fact. That, Vivian knew, would be powerful if—*when*—the group set out to raise orders of magnitude more money for the real thing.

"Expensive," the group learned, meant $150,000 for the study alone. The fourteen board members didn't have $150,000 between them. They saw two choices: quit right then, or ask their neighbors. "If you want this done, break out your checkbook, and don't even try to tell me you forgot your checkbook," Vivian announced to a few hundred neighbors at a meeting in late 2018. "If you truly walked out without your checkbook, ask your neighbor to borrow one of his checks. He'll give it to you."

The line became a town-wide joke, but it spoke to a deeper truth about Riverton, something that made Roger think the group might just pull off something amazing. The community meetings felt like a family reunion, everyone hugging and asking about each other's kids, the kind of place someone really would loan you a check. Roger couldn't remember the last time he had seen so many Rivertonians so invested in a cause. People were stopping him in the grocery store to ask how fundraising was going, pressing checks into his hand. They'd tell him stories about how SageWest Riverton had let them down, and they'd beg him to do whatever it took to get a new hospital, a *real* hospital, in town. The exact factors that had made LifePoint and Apollo Global Management neglect their community—its small size, its remote location, its lack of serious wealth—made Riverton Medical District feel like the rare kind of group project where everyone actually pitches in.

Within two months, the board had raised their $150,000.

———

THE CONVENTIONAL WISDOM ABOUT RURAL hospitals in the twenty-first century is that they are, in a word, screwed. Young people move away; older residents left behind need more expensive care and are less likely than urban and suburban residents to have private insurance, which is more lucrative for providers than Medicare and Medicaid. A study from the U.S. Government Accountability Office in 2020 found that the rate of rural hospital closures doubled between 2013 and 2017, and the ones that remained were in much worse financial shape than their nonrural counterparts. As a result of all these closed hospitals, the report found, Medicare recipients in affected areas had higher rates of every one of the ten most common chronic conditions—including hypertension, diabetes, depression, and rheumatoid arthritis—compared to Medicare patients whose rural communities still had hospitals. Emergency funding during the Covid-19 pandemic improved the financial health of rural hospitals, but only temporarily: after the extra income from emergency funding programs dried up, many were left facing labor shortages and supply-chain problems that increased prices.

The ability to stave off closure at a time of mass rural hospital die-off has been the chief value proposition of private equity firms in the health care industry. The story that LifePoint and Apollo told Riverton residents is common: *Without us, you will be left with no hospital at all. Yours is running out of money, and our ability to consolidate and find efficiencies across our ever-growing system is the only thing that can keep it alive. Your community is too small and poor to support an obstetrics department, or general surgery, or mental health services, so you won't have those anymore, but isn't* something *better than nothing?*

After nearly thirty years working with rural hospitals, though, Stroudwater Associates chairman Eric Shell has a different, surprising take. Sure, there are plenty of challenges, he believes, but the idea that there is no way to make it work is just wrong. The real problem, as he sees it, is that too few hospital executives think creatively about solutions. Over and over, he's seen cuts damage a hospital's business further: "You win the battle, but you lose the war," he said.

Chopping more and more services, Shell said, comes from a "scarcity mentality"—a term coined by *The 7 Habits of Highly Effective People* author Stephen Covey—while making rural hospitals work in twenty-first-century America requires an "abundance mentality." Applied to rural hospitals, a scarcity mentality means cutting costs by "doing more with less," to use the corporate jargon for layoffs and overworking employees. An abundance mentality, in Shell's parlance, means increasing profits by expanding a hospital's business.

Asked to sum up Stroudwater's approach to health care, Shell cited a different self-help book beloved by business leaders: Simon Sinek's *The Infinite Game*, which uses the phrase "just cause" to mean a specific, idealistic, service-oriented vision of the future. Shell's just cause is building a health system that works for everyone; he is fervent in his belief that his approach leads to higher profits *and* better care. While the language he uses feels more like that of private equity executives than progressive-minded doctors and Medicare for All activists, the underlying philosophy feels radical in a world where a single firm in

New York can control dozens of hospitals in communities its leaders have never been to.

One of Shell's go-to examples of an abundance mentality in action is Mahaska Health in Oskaloosa, Iowa, a nonprofit hospital in a city slightly bigger than Riverton. When the pandemic hit in 2020, hospitals across the country were overwhelmed with critically ill Covid patients, but also saw a decline in other types of cases. The result was a huge unexpected loss of revenue for many hospitals, and a correspondingly huge number of layoffs: 1.4 million health care workers lost their jobs in April 2020 alone. In southeast Iowa, many hospitals joined the layoff trend when revenues crashed. At Mahaska, though, CEO Kevin DeRonde—a former NFL linebacker—ran the opposite direction: he hired many of the providers who had been laid off from other area hospitals. His hospital took a short-term financial hit, but that was part of the plan. He wagered that patient volume would recover once the worst of the pandemic eased up.

The bet paid off. After the drop in 2020, the number of non-Covid patients skyrocketed. Now many hospitals were understaffed, but not Mahaska. The hospital hadn't been doing well even before the pandemic, losing more than $5 million in 2017. By 2023, it was making $7.5 million in net income. The following year, DeRonde continued to expand the hospital's offerings, adding twenty new providers. One of the new hires, an emergency physician who had previously worked at a hospital twenty miles away, told the local newspaper that Mahaska had become the dream destination for a lot of local providers. "There's a culture here of value and appreciation, and they show that in a lot of different ways," he said.

When rural hospitals approach Stroudwater for help, Shell and his team encourage them to think about how to attract more patients, through new services or convincing more locals to turn to them first. That doesn't mean that he won't ever recommend cuts, or that joining a larger system is always the wrong call, but his primary focus is on how to make any given hospital sustainable on its own, which usually means growth.

Growth, though, is more difficult at hospitals owned by private equity firms because of the need to keep shareholders happy through quick returns. Stroudwater has worked with hospitals owned by LifePoint, but Shell says their options are more limited. "When I look at what they're doing in Lander and Riverton, I shake my head and say, 'That's not the way I'd be running the company,'" he said. "But I'm not running the company, and they're driven by an external force. If they're not beating the market rate of compensation for their investors, their investors are going to walk. They're doing what they have to do to maintain their investment pool." In other words, they have no choice but to maximize profits in the short term.

———

RIVERTON MEDICAL DISTRICT WAS NOT Stroudwater's typical client. Shell and his team usually work directly with rural hospitals, occasionally with a larger chain looking for system-wide strategic planning. The Wyoming group didn't have a hospital, didn't have concrete plans for a hospital, didn't even have any money for a hospital.

Thanks to donations from their friends and neighbors, though, they did have enough cash for a study. And Shell was intrigued by the ambition of what they were dreaming up; he couldn't even think of more than a couple examples of "greenfield" hospitals—ones that start from scratch—especially in towns that weren't booming. Riverton's population grew by sixty-seven people, or 0.6 percent, between 2010 and 2020. And the town *already had a hospital*, one backed by a private equity firm worth hundreds of billions of dollars. The Stroudwater team had no idea whether a competitor could be viable, but they agreed to fly out to Wyoming and figure out the answer.

Still, the risks, and the brazenness of the Riverton Medical District plan, made Shell nervous. "Guys, instead of building a new hospital, can't we approach LifePoint to partner around ownership or do *something* that isn't two brick-and-mortars in the same community?" he remembered asking over breakfast on his first day in Riverton. The response from Roger and Vivian, birthed from years of frustration with LifePoint's cutbacks and layoffs and secret plans and failure to listen, was resounding. "We have tried working with them," the pair told Stroudwater. "We have tried to buy the existing hospital. We are done trying to negotiate with people who don't care about our community."

Like so many people faced with Vivian's bravado and Roger's quiet insistence, Shell acquiesced. "Okay, we'll run the numbers," he told them.

At breakfast and over the next few days, Roger told the Stroudwater team how Riverton Memorial Hospital used to work, back before it became SageWest Riverton. He described how the lack of obstetrics, general surgery, and other basic services hurt the community he had treated for decades. He explained providers' obligation to treat residents of the Wind River Reservation, and how LifePoint was neglecting them. Shell and his team took all that they had heard, gathered up data from the federal and state governments, and began to develop an expert opinion as to whether a new hospital could succeed.

One of their most important findings was that, although SageWest Riverton was the only hospital in town, it was serving a surprisingly small number of local residents. Data from the Centers for Medicare and Medicaid Services showed that in 2017, just 44 percent of Medicare recipients in the area who needed treatment at a hospital got it in either Riverton or Lander. Four years earlier, that number had been 60 percent. More than one in three Medicare patients in the region were driving to Casper, 120 miles away. Information on patients with employer-sponsored insurance is harder to capture, but the percentage of Rivertonians relying on Medicare is likely to rise significantly. The town's population is aging fast.

That shift is often tough on local economies, but it's difficult to overstate the value of a growing number of older residents when making the case to build a new hospital. Increased demand is not sufficient to make a hospital financially sustainable; patients must also have a way to pay. Medicare reimburses at lower rates than private medical insurance, but the checks always clear.

Of course, having a strong base of privately insured residents is even better, fiscally speaking, but that can be elusive in poor rural areas. Here too, Riverton has a unique advantage: the Northern Arapaho and Eastern Shoshone, the two tribes that share the Wind River Reservation, provide private insurance to tribal members. Because Native Americans have higher rates of most chronic diseases than white Wyomingites, the people most likely to need hospital care in Riverton are also the most likely to have private insurance. From the start, Eastern Shoshone chairman John St. Clair vocally supported the Save Our Riverton Hospital campaign and the Stroudwater feasibility study, providing valuable credibility to the effort.

Riverton Medical District organizers wanted their hospital to be a nonprofit, which would mean no obligation to shareholders. But it would still need to break even to survive. And the presence of SageWest—even at reduced capacity—was going to limit the earning power of a potential new hospital. They would have to pick off a significant share of SageWest patients, plus those driving to Casper or elsewhere.

Even if the new hospital offered more services, it would have to give the 44 percent of locals still relying on SageWest a compelling reason to switch. What's more, Riverton's proximity to SageWest Lander meant the new facility wouldn't be eligible for extra funding paid by the federal government to hospitals that are the only provider of acute health care within thirty-five miles. *And* there was the looming threat of Apollo Global Management. If LifePoint decided one day to bring back the labor and delivery unit or round-the-clock surgical services, they could put Riverton Medical District out of business practically overnight.

In June 2019, after months spent digging into every aspect of Riverton's economy, population, and existing health care options, Stroudwater handed over its report. Its takeaway: the area had the ability to "support a financially viable rural health system with a range of medical, surgical, and specialty services." The Riverton Medical District team had the answer they wanted, from a company with unimpeachable bona fides in the rural health care world. Roger and Vivian were jubilant. They were going to build a hospital.

THEY WERE GOING TO BUILD a hospital *if* they could find the money, that is—lots and lots of money. Friends and neighbors had banded together to cover the $150,000 Stroudwater study, but a whole new hospital was going to cost tens of millions. There were only two options for that kind of funding: a bank or a government.

Despite his finding that a new hospital could hypothetically be sustainable, Shell didn't think they could pull it off. He told them so outright. He's an accountant, which means always assuming the worst. He couldn't fathom why either a bank or a government would give Riverton Medical District a loan considering the competition risk.

The board, though, was unanimous: Shell's fears about what might, possibly, *theoretically* happen at some unspecified time in the future sure weren't going to stop them from acting now. They were the ones who lived there; they were the ones who, in Roger's words, felt an obligation to leave Riverton better than they found it.

At the community meeting where they presented the results of the feasibility study, Corte showed photos of his son. The boy, he explained, had been doing flips on the living room couch and landed face-first on the edge of the coffee table, splitting his forehead open. The photos showed a tiny grinning blond boy, a close-up of the injury, and the emergency room at SageWest Lander. Riverton didn't even have the capacity to stitch up a cut. If Riverton's existing hospital wasn't able to treat perhaps the most classic childhood injury, Corte, Vivian, and Roger were going to give their neighbors one that could. The group set out on a quest for $35 million.

As the former banker, Vivian did her due diligence on bank loans. But even with the Stroudwater seal of approval, commercial lenders weren't likely to take a pricey flier on an independent rural hospital. For months the team pursued hospital revenue bonds, but decided their high interest rates would be too risky. When the pandemic began, nine months after the feasibility study had been completed, they thought they might be able to get funds from the economic stimulus bill, but the legislation only specified funding for *existing* health care providers. That meant LifePoint *was* eligible; despite being owned by a private equity firm worth half a billion dollars, the company got $535 million in government grants and an additional $941 million in subsidized loans.

That left what Vivian called the "lender of last resort": the United States Department of Agriculture (USDA). Along with overseeing farming and food issues, USDA is the primary government funder of projects affecting rural Americans, from broadband access to waste-water disposal to new housing. A community hospital in an under-served rural area fit the portfolio, which could qualify Riverton Medical District for low-interest loans. Applying for government money, however, required navigating government bureaucracy, which, Vivian knew well, meant months if not years of back-and-forth, and the potential to crush the souls of everyone involved.

Sure enough, the process was a nightmare. The USDA rural de-velopment regional director for Wyoming, Lorraine Werner, was encouraging but exacting. Their Stroudwater feasibility study, the gold standard for project evaluations, was initially rejected: it turned out they *also* needed a third-party audit, which ate up three months and $50,000 the board hadn't planned for. Every time Werner needed more documents, the group would scramble to get them to her. Then she would demand even more. It took Riverton Medical District more than a year to have their application accepted—not for funding, just for consideration.

All the while, the projected costs of the hospital were rising, and rising, and rising. Inflation was causing the cost of seemingly every-thing to spike, and supply-chain issues in the construction and medi-cal technology industries weren't helping either. Plus, the pandemic had changed the standards for new hospital construction. The facility would need a more advanced HVAC and air filtration system than the team had planned on, and more room in the intensive care unit. A proj-ect they had forecast to cost $35 million a year earlier was looking like it would require more like $60 million.

Yet somehow, even with the delays and skyrocketing costs, Riverton residents never seemed to grow tired of what looked to many outsiders like a quixotic scheme. To house the hospital, the Eastern

Shoshone tribe agreed to sell eight acres in a planned business park on the north end of town for a song. They donated four more acres outright. And people kept handing over money, frequently five or ten bucks at a time. "Often you'll see a lot of people get excited and involved in something for two or three months or six or whatever, but then they get disillusioned and quit," Roger said, the pitch of his voice rising with emotion. "And I think that's what LifePoint thought we were doing. And they underestimated that failure was not an option."

━━━━

FINALLY, IN APRIL 2022, AFTER an application process that took nearly two years, USDA announced its ruling. The federal government agreed that a new hospital in Riverton could be financially viable, agreed strongly enough that the agency was committing to fund the lion's share of the costs. Riverton Medical District would receive a low-interest federal loan for $37,195,000, plus a $1 million grant. It was the largest USDA rural development loan ever awarded in the state of Wyoming.

The money would fund a hospital offering every routine service Rivertonians had lost. It would have thirteen patient beds, a full surgical department, two labor and delivery rooms, two rooms equipped for intensive care, and space for physical and speech therapy. At 73,000 square feet, it would be 9,000 square feet smaller than SageWest Riverton, but it would be staffed to perform surgery and deliver babies twenty-four hours a day. And the building would be designed to accommodate future growth, with the potential to add eleven new patient rooms, additional surgery space, and more parking. Within two years, the hospital would employ 135 people, including 17 doctors and 44 nurses. The Billings Clinic, a Montana-based nonprofit health care system, would provide many of the administrative services, but the hospital would be owned by a local trust.

In its report, USDA was more bullish than Shell and Stroudwater had been; the agency's official assessment of the project barely referenced the threat of competition from LifePoint, which had in 2021 spun off the SageWest hospitals and nearly eighty other rural facilities into yet another new portfolio company it called ScionHealth. Citing numbers provided by the Riverton Medical District board, USDA found that the hospital could break even with just 30 percent market share, far less than SageWest's 44 percent.

In a list of strengths and weaknesses at the end of the assessment, USDA briefly acknowledged the "existing competitor in the same community" and "duplication of some services" as separate bullet points under "weaknesses." The strengths list, though, was twice as long, ranging from "involved board" to "strong community need" to "support from the Eastern Shoshone tribe." The Riverton Medical District project, evaluators wrote, had generated a remarkable level of local support; the agency noted donations from individuals and businesses that added up to more than $1 million, and more than two hundred letters of support. "Without this life saving addition to our community, I fear my value as a citizen would be diminished in favor of someone with more money or potential," one resident wrote. Several said that without a new hospital, they would move out of Riverton. Multiple business owners wrote that the lack of a fully functioning hospital left them unable to recruit and retain workers.

The overall impression the report created was one not just of approval, but of genuine enthusiasm. Most of the document was written in bureaucracy-speak, but at one point the author slipped into first person: "The applicant started a true grassroots movement to bring back essential services to the community and has exhibited a level of community support, both monetarily and otherwise, that is unseen in my experience."

Of course, even the biggest loan in Wyoming history wasn't enough to fund the entire new hospital, but the thing about locking down $38 million is that it makes an extra $22 million a lot easier to come by. In November 2022, seven months after the USDA loan was awarded, the Wyoming State Loan and Investment Board approved a $10 million grant for Riverton Medical District. A half-cent county sales tax earmarked for economic development funded another $880,000. Combined with contributions from businesses, foundations, and individuals, plus in-kind donations like the Eastern Shoshone land, Riverton Medical District raised $54 million by the beginning of 2023—the entire amount it needed to break ground.

By the time RMD completed its fundraising, Stroudwater chairman Eric Shell had pretty much forgotten about the project. He was busy flying around the country trying to save other rural hospitals, and he assumed the well-intentioned but out-of-their-depth locals in Riverton wouldn't find anyone to give them the money they needed. When he heard in early 2024 that they had in fact raised $54 million, he fell silent for a moment. Then he exhaled, seemingly stunned, and let out a long "Wowwwwwwww."

Across the country, some 460 hospitals are owned by private equity firms. Many of them, especially ones in rural areas, are suffering the same fate as SageWest Riverton: their owners are cutting costs, eliminating services, making more money by providing less health care. Building a new locally owned hospital isn't a scalable way to help all those communities. During the Biden administration, USDA had an annual budget of just under $400 million for rural development projects, nowhere near enough to award low-interest loans to every community at risk of losing its hospital even if that was the division's only priority. Most towns, even tight-knit ones, don't have people like Roger and Vivian. The particular combination of ingredients in Riverton Medical District's recipe baked into something resembling a miracle.

But to Roger's mind, following Riverton's example doesn't require building a new community hospital in every rural county in the country. What it does require is people banding together to dream up solutions, and being unafraid of pursuing more radical options.

One of the developments he's most excited about is renewed interest in strengthening restrictions on the corporate practice of medicine. Thirty-three states place limits on companies' ability to own or control hospitals and doctors' practices, though enforcement of the laws ranges from porous to essentially imaginary. Progressive physicians and health care advocates want to tighten those strictures by introducing them to new states, filing lawsuits over their interpretation, and pushing for a national ban. An activist doctors' group is pushing the American

Medical Association—the largest and most influential physicians' association in the country—to call for a complete prohibition on the corporate practice of medicine nationwide. In late 2023, delegates at an American Medical Association meeting voted to refer a resolution on the topic to the organization's board for further study.

Meaningful federal action on corporate practice of medicine—or, to name an even more ambitious moonshot, Medicare for All—is not on the immediate horizon. But a growing number of doctors, Roger included, see private equity as an existential threat, and they're committed to the fight—even if the payoff doesn't come until after they're gone.

Even Riverton's little miracle still has a ways to go before it's fully realized. RMD hoped to break ground in the spring of 2023, kicking off two years of construction, but personnel changes at USDA and the need to move a drainage ditch running through the property pushed plans back. For a year and a half afterward, the lot remained empty, a sign advertising the new hospital growing increasingly weathered by the harsh Wyoming winter. Finally, in December 2024, just before the soil froze for the season, construction workers broke ground on Riverton's new community hospital.

No one in town will voice anything but optimism about the future, least of all Roger. When he moved to Riverton fifty years ago, as a Texas boy who didn't know the first thing about life on the High Plains, he committed to leave the place better than he found it. During his three-decade career as a doctor, he felt like he was doing exactly that. Then LifePoint and Apollo tore down everything he helped build, and he began to question how much of an impact he had truly made.

As he nears ninety years old, Roger's perspective has shifted again. He knows Riverton Medical District will, within the next few years, become a hospital that can deliver babies and perform surgeries and care for patients the way Uncle Austin taught him. He also knows it will inspire other towns. He'll leave Riverton—and communities far beyond—better than he found it.

ELEVEN

NATALIA

AS A REPORTER AT THE *AUSTIN AMERICAN-STATESMAN*, NATALIA spent most of her free time looking for a way out. Taking the job made sense; it had gotten her back to Texas. But she was determined to escape Gannett, to report for a publication focused more on journalism and less on shareholder value. She was sick of spending so much time fighting the bosses that were supposed to be supporting her work, and all for $56,000 a year. In Indiana and Texas, she loved reporting on government policies and immigrant communities. She wanted another job doing exactly that.

When she was at the *Indianapolis Star*, a recruiter had asked her to apply for a job at Chalkbeat, a newsroom covering education policy and local school systems in eight American regions, with a focus on students who had limited access to high-quality schools. Chalkbeat was created when two existing education news sites, in New York and Denver, merged, then added outlets in Memphis, Indianapolis, Detroit, Chicago, Newark, and Philadelphia. The goal was specifically to fill the gap left by newspapers owned by Gannett and Alden Global Capital, many of which had scaled back their coverage of schools as they made deep cuts to their reporting staffs. Intriguingly, the site was also a nonprofit; it relied on funding from foundations rather than a big financial firm.

Natalia could see herself working there; Chalkbeat was the rare publication that genuinely prioritized covering marginalized communities. And she was disillusioned with the private equity business model in media, which so often seemed to mean serving investors at the expense of readers. But she had never covered education, didn't know the first thing about how to work the beat. She said exactly that to the recruiter, assuming the conversation would end there, but the woman didn't seem dissuaded. "We'll teach you; we'll get you caught up," Natalia remembered hearing. So she threw her hat in, but she didn't end up with the job; Chalkbeat hired someone with more experience. Which is why, when that very same recruiter called a few years later to ask her to apply for a reporting job at a publication that didn't even exist yet, Natalia was skeptical. In fact, she remembered later, she was actively annoyed.

The new site would cover voting—not polls and election results, but how elections are administered, who gets to vote, who is disenfranchised, efforts to make sure ballots are stored securely and counted properly, efforts to delegitimize the outcomes. Just as they had with education reporting almost a decade earlier, the journalists who ran Chalkbeat saw a hole in mainstream media coverage. They ran a pop-up site covering voting access during the 2020 election. Then, after Donald Trump's attempts to invalidate Joe Biden's victory—and the attack on the U.S. Capitol on January 6, 2021—became the defining story of the cycle, they decided to make the voting news organization permanent. They called it Votebeat. To start, they would hire reporters in Arizona, Pennsylvania, Michigan, and Texas.

When the recruiter reached out in early 2022, Natalia thought the job sounded fascinating, but she assumed she'd never get it. Why call her, again, about applying for a role covering a beat for which she had little relevant experience? She had never covered election security, had never been a politics reporter. In fact, she had less direct engagement with American elections than almost any reporter in the country. She was a green card holder, not a citizen; she had never voted in her life. Still, she couldn't resist applying.

THE SEEDS OF THE 2020S nonprofit online news boom had been planted nearly two decades earlier. When Voice of San Diego launched in 2005, it was described as a bold new solution to America's burgeoning local journalism crisis. For most media watchers, though, the innovation wasn't the Voice's tax status, but its platform: it didn't publish a print edition.

At the time, local newspaper reporters wrote for print first, the length and deadline of their stories determined by layout needs. Most of the money came from print too; ads in the physical paper commanded a much higher price than those online. But by the early 2000s Craigslist was gobbling up what used to be a thriving classified ad market, while Google had figured out how to precisely target the right ads to the right people. Newspaper leaders were doing shockingly little to adapt to the new world, providing their stories online for free rather than attempting to develop web revenue strategies of their own. But although newspaper profits were declining, many *were* still profitable—just not profitable enough for the private equity firms who were swallowing a growing swath of the industry.

The radical theory behind Voice of San Diego was that local news shouldn't have to be profitable at all. If journalism is a public good, argued founders Neil Morgan and Buzz Woolley—a journalist and entrepreneur fed up with the declining quality of the *San Diego Union-Tribune*—publishers' priority should be providing the most news to the most people, not making more money for investors. Running a digital-only outlet would save money that could be spent on salaries and reporting expenses; passing up the opportunity for print ads would limit revenue, but that was a trade-off they were happy to make, because they weren't looking to maximize profits. As long as the staff could afford to keep the lights on and keep pumping out stories, they'd be fulfilling their mission.

At first, Woolley funded Voice of San Diego himself, but he knew that sustainability would require philanthropy money. The site's co-founders pitched their project as an experiment that could help solve America's dwindling supply of local news. It worked. The site's first major grant came from the John S. and James L. Knight Foundation, which had been funded by local newspapers in their glory days and was looking to repay the favor by supporting innovation in the news industry. Within a few years, Voice of San Diego had inspired a flood of new web-only nonprofit news sites to launch in its image, in New Haven, Minneapolis, St. Louis, and more.

In 2009, the Texas Tribune became the new standard-bearer for digital local news startups, launching with a nearly $4 million budget and nineteen staff members. Cofounder John Thornton framed the move toward nonprofit journalism as a moral imperative: "The apostles Peter and Luke both admonish against that most common of human frailties—the allure of attempting to serve God and Mammon simultaneously. From roughly 1960 to about the middle of this decade, newspaper publishers seemed to think they had managed somehow to roll this dictate back," he wrote a few months before the Tribune's official debut. "With newspaper margins now plunging into the single digits on a very large base of (largely leveraged) capital, nobody is talking about public service nearly as much as paying the bills. When it comes to the news business, God and Mammon are no longer BFFs." Thornton was hardly a foe to the finance world—he had made his fortune in venture capital and would go on to start a private equity firm investing in tech companies. He just didn't believe local news outlets should be corporations in the Milton Friedman sense, prioritizing shareholder value over the public good.

IN THE TINY WORLD OF journalism funders, this noble view of local news was beginning to spread. In the larger world, the more ruthless private equity philosophy about journalism's value was becoming ever more dominant. After GateHouse bought Gannett in 2019, the combined company owned 260 daily newspapers; Alden Global Capital owned another 200. The top twenty-five chains, led by the two companies that had become most infamous for destroying local newsrooms, now controlled one out of every three newspapers in the nation. In

2020, a small New Jersey–based firm, Chatham Asset Management, bought McClatchy, the fifth-largest newspaper chain in the country. It was clear who was winning the battle for American newsrooms, and it wasn't the philanthropists.

Private equity executives argued that slashing costs was the only option to make up for all those decades of screwups by all those high-minded newspaper leaders too smug about their own importance to bother building a good business. "I would love our team to be remembered as the team that saved the newspaper business," Alden managing director Heath Freeman said in a 2020 interview, one of the only ones he's ever given. Freeman and his counterparts at Gannett blamed forces beyond their control for the cuts they inflicted: declining ad rates, declining subscriptions numbers, Google, Facebook, mismanagement by their predecessors.

Yet despite the conventional wisdom that journalism is just an outdated industry driven into the grave by market forces, plenty of American newspapers remained profitable well into the 2020s. Some ads were still coming in; some people, especially older ones, would never stop subscribing to their local newspaper no matter how little actual reporting it carried. While Gannett does not break down its revenue numbers by individual newsroom, the company's earnings grew by nearly $60 million from 2022 to 2023.

It's true that profit margins declined dramatically from the 20 or 25 percent that was common in the 1990s. It's true that the trend line hasn't stopped pointing down, and the long-term prospects for for-profit local media look bleak no matter who's in charge. But Alden and Apollo and Fortress don't get into industries to be saviors; they do it because they see an opportunity to make a quick buck.

Which makes it unsurprising that neither Gannett nor Alden ever seemed to have any plan for actually improving the product they sold. They didn't invest in new technologies or new types of content; they didn't attempt to reinvent what a twenty-first-century newspaper looks like. They gave no indication that journalism meant anything to them. The only strategy was cutting their way to profits. The more newsrooms the firms shuttered, the more journalists they laid off, the more local stories they replaced with syndicated ones, the better the business.

Alden and Gannett also adapted other strategies that had helped private equity firms profit from other industries—often at the expense of the companies they owned. Gannett sold more than $150 million worth of real estate between 2015 and 2019, including buildings that had housed major American newspapers for more than a century. Alden moved even more aggressively into the real estate business, creating a company called Twenty Lake Holdings, which takes control of its portfolio companies' newsrooms and printing plants, then develops the properties and sells or leases them. The newspapers are forced from the historic headquarters they once owned, then charged rent for downsized offices. In one bleakly amusing case, Gannett sold the office of one of its newspapers, the *Asheville Citizen-Times* in western North Carolina, to Twenty Lake for $3.2 million; Twenty Lake flipped the same property to a local developer for $5.3 million the very same day. It was a financial win for both firms. The only loser was the newspaper, which signed a lease to pay rent for part of the building it had previously owned.

Gannett also took advantage of dividend recapitalizations, a common private equity strategy in which a firm takes out new loans specifically to pay dividends to shareholders. Like all loans at private equity–owned companies, the portfolio company itself is solely responsible for this additional debt, even though it never sees any of the money. When a company goes public or sells for a profit, dividend "recaps" can result in a bigger payout than the exit itself. And when a company is at risk of failing, recaps can be even more appealing: the payments can help firms recoup their initial investment if the company itself isn't bringing in enough cash. After the Gannett-GateHouse merger, CEO Mike Reed boasted of the company's track record of continuously raising dividend payments.

Gannett and Alden didn't have to fix the broken media business model to make money: there were already plenty of assets and plenty of cash flow to work with. All they had to do, in the words of one industry analyst, was "get in inexpensively and strip the assets and liquidate buildings and liquidate the lightbulbs, and squeeze as much cash out as possible."

——

NATALIA FIGURED VOTEBEAT WOULD NEVER hire a voting reporter who couldn't vote; better to get it out of the way up front. But as she explained her situation to the recruiter, she realized she was pitching herself for the job. "And that's actually a good perspective to have," she said, as smoothly as if she had planned it. Now her mind was flooded with memories of stories she had written about immigrants who were fighting for their rights, for recognition of their hard work, for full inclusion in the American project. She thought about articles she had written in Corpus Christi and Indianapolis about new citizens voting for the first time, about how she longed for the chance to vote herself someday. She thought about her first days in an American middle school, about how desperate she was for someone to explain how things worked. Maybe she did have a valuable perspective on voting after all. Votebeat's editors seemed to like the stories she pitched too.

A few weeks after her interviews for the job, in the summer of 2022, Natalia was in South Dakota meeting her boyfriend Robert's family and friends for the first time. The next day, the couple was heading to Wyoming to visit Devils Tower—Natalia had wanted to see it ever since *Close Encounters of the Third Kind* became one of her favorite movies as a kid. They were still dating long-distance, but she and Robert were getting serious, even talking about marriage.

Votebeat was due to get back to her any day, and she was trying and failing not to get her hopes up. The more she talked to the editors there about their plans and aspirations, the more excited she grew. While Votebeat was new, with $3.1 million in startup capital from several nonprofits that cared about elections and local journalism, Natalia and her colleagues wouldn't have to build an audience from scratch: in each state, Votebeat had developed a partnership with an existing nonprofit news outlet. If she got the Texas job, her stories would be published by the Texas Tribune, the most prestigious local news nonprofit in the country. There was just one catch. Votebeat wanted their Texas reporter to work from one of the state's big cities. Natalia wanted to move home to Corpus Christi and live with Robert.

Natalia and Robert had just gotten to Wyoming and settled into their hotel when her phone rang. It was Votebeat's editor in chief, Chad Lorenz. He was calling with a job offer. He even had a solution for the geographic conundrum: what if she stayed in Austin for the first year, to establish sources at the capital, and then moved south to Corpus Christi? That sounded good to her; she and Robert could wait one more year to make a home together.

Votebeat had listed the maximum salary for the position at $80,000, so, emboldened by her understanding of the disparities at Gannett, that's what she asked for. Lorenz offered $72,000, a 25 percent raise over what she was making at the *Statesman*. She pushed back. Covering Texas by herself would be a huge responsibility, and her fluency in Spanish would elevate the site's coverage. "You're not going to find another reporter like me," she said. She told him she couldn't take the job for less than $75,000 (though she told Robert privately she'd accept regardless). Within an hour, Lorenz called back with a new offer: $76,000. She said yes on the spot.

After seven years at Gannett, she walked away from the company for good.

The next day, Robert proposed at Devils Tower. She said yes to that too.

———

BY THEN, THE SLOW DEATH of American newspapers had escalated into a full-blown crisis—thanks in large part to the two biggest chains in America, Gannett and Alden. It didn't matter if a given newspaper was the only source of reliable information in its community. It didn't matter if the paper had been sustainable until its private equity owners sold off its real estate and captured its remaining profits as dividends.

If a paper was underperforming compared to shareholder expectations, it would be downsized or shut down. Nearly a quarter of local newspaper jobs, about 27,000 total, disappeared between 2008 and 2017. Two and a half newspapers were disappearing from American communities *every week*.

Gannett and Alden knew their slash-and-burn strategy wouldn't last forever, but they weren't innovating either. They were happy to cut until there was nothing left, then close the doors for good. "You have to look at Gannett and the other big newspaper chains not as media companies but as financial firms," media scholar Jay Rosen said. "They see newspapers as declining assets, and they ask themselves how they can squeeze a few more years of profit out of those assets."

As private equity firms wiped out newspaper staffs at an ever-faster clip, dozens of new local outlets cropped up. In 2018, a report from the Institute for Nonprofit News identified more than two hundred non-profit newsrooms covering local and national stories, three-quarters of which had been around for less than a decade. The report called the blossoming of nonprofit news a "silver lining story." But its authors also acknowledged the limitations of the publications it studied: half of the eighty-eight newsrooms surveyed employed eight or fewer staffers, nowhere near what serious newspapers had, even by that point. With a few exceptions, nonprofit outlets were not remotely compensating for the demise of local newspapers.

The American Journalism Project set out to change that. In February 2019, two of the most prominent figures in local news announced that they had raised $42 million from the Knight Foundation, Craig Newmark Philanthropies, Facebook, and other major funders, which they would use to support dozens of nonprofit newsrooms around the country. Chalkbeat founder Elizabeth Green and Texas Tribune founder John Thornton had built two successful nonprofit newsrooms, but they weren't satisfied. They wanted to fund publications that would quickly expand from 8 to 80 to 800 journalists, ones prepared to actually replace local newspapers. Startups wouldn't be selected for funding out of a sense of benevolence or even an evaluation of which communities had the greatest need, but rather based on a cold-blooded assessment of where startups were most likely to grow quickly, a philosophy known as venture philanthropy. Thornton and Green were out to prove that local news wasn't beyond repair after all—as long as private equity wasn't in the picture.

Venture philanthropy is a touchy topic in the nonprofit world. It takes not only its name but much of its ethos from venture capital, the private equity cousin that invests in early-stage companies and expects exponential growth in return. Groups like the American Journalism Project argue that too many nonprofits are ineffective because their soft-hearted funders aren't willing to apply cold, hard business strategies. Opponents counter that the opportunities for financial growth, and the techniques used to maximize it, should not decide which causes are funded, like which communities get a news outlet. "Many of the practices associated with the attitude and style of this new form of giving endanger some of the most essential benefits and values the nonprofit sector brings to society," legal scholar Garry W. Jenkins wrote in an influential 2011 paper.

In local news, the rise of venture philanthropy transformed who got funded and how, in ways that left out many newsrooms in towns in desperate need of more coverage. Among other requirements, American Journalism Project grantees must have strong financial support from local foundations. Requiring local buy-in makes sense strategically, but it means that places without deep philanthropic networks don't fit the model. Only funding newsrooms that demonstrate a clear path to financial growth means declining to fund the ones in many of the communities most neglected by local media.

Being picky has paid off for the American Journalism Project and the newsrooms it does support. In the organization's first four years, its leaders raised $134 million to back forty-one local newsrooms, many of them in cities where the unholy trinity of Gannett, GateHouse, and Alden Global Capital had decimated local news coverage.* One of the group's splashiest launches of 2023 was Mirror Indy, which now

* Disclaimer: I have worked as a consultant for the American Journalism Project on a handful of projects related to editorial strategy, newsroom management issues, and hiring.

competes head-to-head with the *Indianapolis Star*, Natalia's former employer. Votebeat received a three-year grant from the group, as did its older sibling Chalkbeat.

The American Journalism Project boasts that its grantees grow by an average of 67 percent in their first year and double revenue by year three. The rise of venture philanthropy has clearly demonstrated that local newsrooms *can* thrive financially, no matter what private equity firms say to justify the latest round of cost cutting.

———

WHEN NATALIA MOVED BACK TO Texas in 2021, it had more places without local news than any other state: of the 225 counties across the country classified as "news deserts," nearly 10 percent are in Texas. And among the 440 newspapers that remain there, many no longer publish any local news. As many as 20 percent of all American newspapers—a disproportionate number of them at Gannett and Alden—have no staff and no local stories, just syndicated articles from larger newspapers in the chain.

A 2022 study found that low-income communities were the most likely to lose their newspapers; the median household income in news deserts was $15,000 less than in other counties. But even in Austin, by then one of the wealthiest and fastest-growing cities in the nation, Gannett had shrunk its news coverage so much that it was impossible for a resident to get an in-depth sense of what was going on in the region. According to a NewsGuild filing with the SEC, the number of *Austin American-Statesman* employees dropped from two hundred in 2013 to forty-one just ten years later. The number of *Statesman* stories about Austin plummeted even further, from thirty-seven a day in 2013 to just *nine* in 2023. Everything else in the paper came from Gannett's wire services.

Until Natalia was hired at Votebeat, there was no full-time reporter covering elections and voting in Texas—not at any newspaper, not at the Tribune, not at the handful of other nonprofit outlets that had popped up across the state. The *Statesman* had a single reporter dedicated to covering the entire state capitol, with its 181 elected representatives and senators, plus a governor who loved to make news.

The chance to report on a topic no one else was covering was a huge part of what drew Natalia to the Votebeat job. During one interview, she told an editor about one election night when she worked at the *Caller-Times*. The rural areas around Corpus Christi didn't put election results online, so her job was to drive out to a neighboring county and collect the vote totals for the next day's paper. She expected local officials to give her a printout, but instead she found a harried election worker hand-counting ballots and yelling out the totals, which were written on a whiteboard. Natalia copied the numbers from the board, then called them into a colleague in the newsroom. If she hadn't done that, no one would have known how that tiny county voted. She liked that feeling.

She also relished the chance to explain the basics to readers. In a field dominated by white, American-born, college-graduate native English speakers from middle- or upper-middle-class backgrounds, Natalia is none of those things. Just 8 percent of American journalists are Hispanic, compared to 19 percent of Americans and 40 percent of people in Texas, where she has now lived for more than twenty years combined. In a state where nearly 30 percent of people speak Spanish at home, Natalia is one of far too few journalists who grew up that way. "In the U.S., there's a system of things that sometimes people just know and I don't," she said, becoming more animated by the word. "I feel like that's going to be the same thing for people walking into a polling location for the first time. Imagine someone in their sixties or seventies becoming a citizen, and they've never done it before. It's all super obscure and complicated."

Many of the first wave of nonprofit digital startups focused on deep investigations: the kind of expensive, time-consuming work that cash-strapped newspapers often cut first and that appeal to funders interested in exposing corruption (and winning prestigious prizes). In the American Journalism Project era, though, the most common types of coverage have changed. The local foundations the group partners with often have never funded traditional journalism, focusing instead on direct services. Votebeat's parent organization, now called Civic News Company, describes its mission as part of a movement that "prioritizes community benefit instead of commercial gain" and "thinks of readers as community members, not consumers."

As a result, many startup newsrooms publish more service journalism than Pulitzer-caliber investigative work: a chart about what to do if you can't pay your electric bill, a call for reader questions for political candidates, a map of where to find Narcan. As AJP executive Loretta Chao put it, "People are like, 'If my trash hasn't been picked up in two months, who am I even supposed to call?' It's not that people want investigative reporting to go away, they just need so much other stuff."

Natalia spends much of her time talking to average voters about what they want to know, and choosing story topics accordingly. Every Election Day, she runs a basic guide about how to vote. When conspiracy-minded Trump supporters pushed for Texas counties to count ballots by hand, she wrote two thousand words explaining why hand-counting would make elections less accurate and less secure. Her articles are written not for awards committees or state officials, but for that sixty- or seventy-year-old first-time voter who doesn't understand how the system works. Because maximizing profit margins isn't Votebeat's goal, she and her editors have the freedom to focus on the people left out of mainstream journalism. "*This* is what I always wanted journalism to be—getting information to people who need it," she said. "That's supposed to be the whole point."

BY THE TIME NATALIA ACCEPTED the job at Votebeat, a growing number of people, including very powerful ones, believed that the nonprofit model—and specifically the American Journalism Project's growth-focused venture philanthropy—was the way forward for media. Few local newspapers had figured out how to make money on ads and subscriptions alone. At the two biggest chains in America, journalists couldn't even try to innovate because their private equity investors were systematically starving them of resources while selling off their assets. The only hope many people saw started with divorcing journalism from shareholder value entirely.

Just a few weeks after Votebeat published its first stories in the summer of 2022, a group of forty-two journalists launched the Baltimore Banner, the best-funded local news nonprofit in American history. Stewart Bainum, the chairman of one of the world's largest hotel chains and the former CEO of one of the nation's largest nursing home chains (which was bought by the private equity firm Carlyle Group seven years after Bainum stepped down), pledged to raise a total of $50 million, much of it from his own donations, over three and a half years to fund the Banner.

Starting something new wasn't Bainum's original ambition. In 2021, he tried to buy the *Baltimore Sun*, the city's 184-year-old newspaper, from the floundering Tribune Publishing Company. He lost out to Alden Global Capital, which paid $633 million for the entire chain, including the New York *Daily News*, the *Orlando Sentinel*, and the flagship *Chicago Tribune*. So instead, Bainum decided to compete. "There's no industry that I can think of more integral to a working democracy than the local news business," he said in 2021. By 2024, the Banner newsroom had grown to roughly eighty journalists, comparable to the *Sun*.

Though major foundations lent legitimacy to the cause of nonprofit news, it was clear early on that even the wealthiest philanthropists weren't going to keep newsrooms alive single-handedly. So in addition to appealing to the people who control multibillion-dollar budgets—and in some cases competing for ad dollars with legacy newspapers and TV news networks—nonprofit outlets also beseech their readers for support. Most of these newer publications, especially those that report on communities with high levels of poverty, feel strongly that they shouldn't lock their stories behind paywalls, as most local newspapers do. Instead, they strike at wealthier readers' sense of civic obligation, like NPR or the local art museum or food bank do.

While some nonprofit media outlets have always asked for donations, the language of their appeals—and their target audience—has evolved over time. First-generation startups put the onus on foundations and very wealthy individuals: "a bunch of financial titans," as Texas Tribune founder John Thornton put it. Votebeat, meanwhile, suggests donations of ten, fifteen, or twenty-five dollars a month, writing that "we hope you will consider a tax-exempt donation so that we can focus on providing the accurate news and information that voters need to participate in a healthy democracy."

But because wealth is unequally distributed across the country, and because groups like the American Journalism Project focus on scale, true news deserts are not the communities benefiting most from the nonprofit news boom. There appear to be zero American Journalism Project grantees specifically dedicated to cities or counties that don't already have some form of a local newspaper. (Several publications in the portfolio do cover entire states.) "Of course, we entertained visions of getting big grants from Big Philanthropy. But it didn't take us long to realize that wasn't going to happen," Corinne Colbert, the cofounder and editor of the Athens County Independent, which covers a poor, mostly rural area of southeast Ohio on a budget of roughly $139,000 a year, wrote in 2024. "It seems that when folks talk about the 'local news crisis,' they're not talking about Athens County, Ohio; they're talking about cities the size of Salt Lake or even bigger. But small, rural and/or poor areas are at the center of this phenomenon of journalistic decline."

Media scholars can rattle off scores of data points about the dangers of shuttering newsrooms: People who have access to reliable sources of news are more likely to vote. Towns without a newspaper see fewer candidates run for office. Political polarization increases as news coverage is scaled back. Private companies violate more laws after their local newspapers close; government becomes more corrupt. Having a strong local news outlet increases residents' feelings of social cohesion.

And while journalists can sound overly sentimental when they talk about the "value" of local news, there is literal value, in the capitalistic sense, to it too. When Gannett or Alden closes a newspaper and creates a news desert, the void doesn't just result in more division and corruption. Research shows that towns without local news pay more to borrow money, which in turn means higher taxes.

But taxpayers aren't shareholders. While less law-breaking and lower taxes might be important factors to residents of Appleton or Augusta, they don't mean anything to the private equity firm in charge. The firm's executives don't live there. In most cases, they've never even been there. Restoring local news coverage requires a level of community investment that goes far beyond money.

━━━

THIS REQUIREMENT MAKES JOURNALISM MORE similar to other public services than other types of businesses. As with town parks and fire departments, residents don't need to subscribe to their local publication to benefit from it. But unlike town parks and fire departments, media isn't funded by the government.

Public funding has long been seen as the ultimate taboo by many journalists, afraid that government money would come with government interference in stories. (NPR and PBS and their respective member stations are notable exceptions, though federal appropriations make up a small percentage of their respective budgets.) But if most people don't pay for news and most newspapers can't survive on digital ad rates and most news deserts can't get foundation funding, that leaves a looming question of how media is expected to survive even in the theoretical absence of private equity owners. As media scholar Nikki Usher puts it, "newspapers as an industry and news as a public good are an economic contradiction."

So a growing number of journalists have concluded, often reluctantly, that there will be no local news industry without some sort of government intervention. "It is time we accepted this basic fact: the collapse is so severe, the causes so complex and the consequences so catastrophic, that we also need First-Amendment-friendly taxpayer support," Steven Waldman, the head of a coalition called Rebuild Local News, wrote in early 2024. Waldman's group advocates for several ways of sending public money to local news outlets without direct governmental involvement: tax credits for newsrooms to hire reporters and for small businesses to advertise in community publications, vouchers for residents to spend on local news outlets of their choice, and requirements for government agencies to advertise in locally owned media.

Recognizing that such changes are unlikely on the federal level in the near future, some states are beginning to workshop solutions of their own. In 2024, New York's legislature approved a plan to provide tax credits to help cover reporters' salaries at local news outlets. The $30 million program was designed to cover 50 percent of the first $50,000 of a reporter's salary, up to $300,000 per newsroom. Yet nonprofit newsrooms are ineligible for the money, while Gannett and Alden can collect, undermining advocates' larger goal of helping small, independent local outlets survive. "We missed something all along here, and it was never quite set up the way any of us thought it was," Waldman said after the bill passed.

Another option is requiring tech companies like Google and Facebook to pay publishers in exchange for advertising next to news stories posted on their platforms, as Canada and Australia do. In 2023, California's lower house passed a bill that would require social media companies to pay for linking to stories, but it was put on hold because of concerns that the platforms would respond by blocking news stories (as Facebook and Google have done in Canada). The following year, the legislature agreed to a partnership with Google that would pay $180 million to California-based news outlets over five years in exchange for killing the bill that would have charged tech companies directly. The agreement also funded an artificial intelligence research program at the University of California, Berkeley, infuriating many journalists concerned about the prospect of Google developing AI tools that will eliminate even more reporting jobs.

None of these approaches—not benevolent billionaires, not foundation funding, not small donations, not tax credits, not partnerships with tech companies—will drive private equity firms out of local news, nor solve its underlying challenges. If there is any chance of staving off the industry's extinction, it will require a multipronged approach: a dramatic expansion in the number of nonprofit outlets and the amount of philanthropic dollars directed toward them; more experimentation with business models ranging from membership-funded worker cooperatives to new ways of attracting advertisers; continued explorations of legislative options to provide funding for journalism while protecting freedom of the press. It will also require trying to rescue individual legacy newspapers from private equity owners. Will all of that be enough, and will it happen soon enough that there is any local media industry left to save? Nobody knows.

NOW THAT SHE'S FOUND HER way to nonprofit journalism, Natalia has no plans to leave. In a tweet about a year after she was hired, she marveled at how far she'd come: "I am for the first time, finally, working in a healthy, supportive and uplifting workplace and I just want the same for everyone. It can be done. Starts with management."

When Trump-supporting local government officials in Texas suggest, as they do frequently, that the state's elections infrastructure is irredeemably compromised, Natalia is often the only journalist publishing articles that measure their arguments against demonstrable facts. She frequently interviews voters in Spanish, and has written Votebeat stories in her native language to make sure her journalism reaches as many Texans as possible. (In South Texas, where she grew up, as many as 90 percent of residents are primarily Spanish-speaking.)

In the fall of 2022, Natalia wrote a Votebeat story that ran in the Texas Tribune about the election administrator in Tarrant County, in and around Fort Worth. Heider Garcia was not well-known outside the area, but Natalia followed Texas election administration more closely than anyone, and she was fascinated by how Garcia dealt with conservative skeptics. What she found was that he engaged with them rather than tuning them out, spent untold hours patiently answering their questions, bought huge video screens for the election office so his detractors could watch the counting process, handed out his personal cell number to every "stop the steal" type in town so they could come to him before spreading misinformation online.

After weeks of reporting on Garcia, Natalia wrote a story no other reporter could have written, because no other reporter knew where to look for it. *This American Life*, one of the biggest podcasts in the world, asked her to report a version for their show, which played for millions of listeners. Garcia was asked to advise on federal election planning; after four months of that, he was hired to oversee elections in Dallas County, the second-most-populous county in Texas.

As her editor promised she could, Natalia moved home to Corpus Christi after her first year at Votebeat. In December 2023, she married Robert on a beach in Tampico, Mexico, where she spent the first thirteen years of her life. After a year and a half of reporting on voting, she also became a first-time voter. She was sworn in as a United States citizen in August 2023, then voted in Texas's presidential primary in March 2024 and the general election that fall. She wrote for Votebeat about her experience: "It took a lot of work, time, money, and patience to get here. . . . This time, no one can take this away." In the photo above the story, she grins widely, holding up her I VOTED sticker and flashing her wedding ring, glowing with pride.

TWELVE

LOREN

BACKING DOWN IS NOT IN LOREN'S DNA. A NEW ADDRESS WASN'T going to change that. Though she had accepted CIM Group's decision not to renew her lease, she was adamant that her former neighbors wouldn't go through what she did. She had lived in Alexandria for more than two decades. She had relationships with nearly every political leader in the area. She had the network to expand the fight. And she wanted payback. "I tell everybody, I can be your best friend or your enemy. But when you make me your enemy, please keep up."

CIM gave her a lot to work with. The problems at Southern Towers just kept coming. The week she moved out in March 2024, another second-floor unit in her former building flooded so badly that water poured into the communal hallway. A video from the same day shows water raining down the wall by the residents' mailboxes too. That summer, during a record-breaking heat wave that sent temperatures soaring to 102 degrees, the air-conditioning in one of the complex's five buildings broke, drawing more negative headlines in local news outlets.

Loren wanted to make agitating at Southern Towers part of her official responsibilities as an organizer at VOICE, but she represented Arlington, not Alexandria. So instead she committed to helping her former neighbors in her free time. When she heard about the flood on the second floor, she canceled a work meeting, drove over to help the residents get their stuff out of the water, then called local reporters.

"They're going to be sick and tired of me today," she wrote about CIM in a text message.

Her goal now is to drive the private equity firm out of Southern Towers, whatever it takes—legislation, court order, or just annoying its executives so much that they decide owning the complex isn't worth the hassle. She doesn't care *why* they leave; she just plans to make sure they do. "I'm not stopping until I have the satisfaction of the result, and the best result is for them to get out of Alexandria," she said, but she knows she's up against a formidable opponent. "They have some properties in Arlington too, and that's the thing: if we don't hurry up, they're going to keep buying more. We need them to stop and get out."

Few remaining tenants have Loren's fervor to keep fighting. Sami Bourma, who organized the rent strike and other protests against CIM when pandemic lockdowns began, bought a house and moved out of Southern Towers. Most of those who are still there are just trying to keep their heads down and preserve some semblance of stability. Several residents initially agreed to interviews but later backed out or stopped responding: "I have suffered a lot of financial and mental damage in this process," one wrote, explaining why she changed her mind about speaking to a journalist. They already feel demoralized enough by the problems at Southern Towers; losing their homes altogether wouldn't help.

But Loren did have one ally as motivated as she was to get CIM out of town. African Communities Together, the nonprofit group that helped stage protests at the complex and invited local politicians to witness the problems, wasn't ready to give up either. In fact, the organizers there saw Southern Towers as crucial to their larger mission of empowering African immigrants as leaders and citizens. The group initially focused on supporting newly arrived refugees and providing assistance with immigration cases. But when its leaders realized what was happening at Southern Towers, where a third of tenants are African, they leaned into housing issues. "Without a stable place to live, it's hard to focus on anything else," said Sosseh Prom, who was born in

D.C. and raised in Gambia, and worked as a family law attorney before becoming the group's first national housing justice director.

When Loren received the cease-and-desist notice barring her from communicating with Southern Towers management—even while they were still her landlord—Prom became her liaison; on email chains, Prom's smooth lawyerspeak replaced Loren's indignation. But Prom was also focused on the bigger picture: trying to improve conditions for the remaining residents, ideally by convincing—or forcing—CIM to sell the complex.

African Communities Together started with politicians. Some local elected officials had been keeping an eye on problems at Southern Towers since the pandemic began. But CIM's executives aren't Councilwoman Alyia Gaskins's constituents; they live three thousand miles from Alexandria. Getting *their* attention meant aiming higher. In June 2023, the group earned a meaningful win: their advocacy had convinced Virginia's U.S. senators, Mark Warner and Tim Kaine, to send a letter to CIM principal Bethany Chang. They wrote that they were troubled by reports of "declining conditions, unresolved mainte-nance requests, and significant pricing changes" at Southern Towers. They urged CIM to "take immediate action to address these issues by engaging directly and frequently with the tenants and working quickly to resolve outstanding concerns." In a response shared with local media outlets, CIM blamed the previous owners, as well as activists' "disinformation," adding that the company "will not be deterred from their commitment to the community they serve, their legal obligation and the fiduciary duty the company has to investors."

The letter didn't attract much notice outside of Northern Virginia, but it was a bold move for Warner especially. He is one of the richest members of the Senate and a prominent friend to private equity; he held $30.8 million in industry investments in 2022. For the last five years, Apollo Global Management has been among his largest donors. Warner wasn't exactly becoming a crusader for reforming the industry— a strongly worded letter is a far cry from legislation—but his willing-ness to go even that far was part of a noticeable shift among some Democrats to voice skepticism of private equity for the first time. And private equity circles paid attention: employees of the industry gave more money to Democratic candidates in 2020; during the 2024 election cycle, they favored Republicans.

Organizers at African Communities Together and similar groups were also encouraged by successful anti–private equity campaigns in other cities. They were keeping an especially close eye on Minneapolis. Minnesota attorney general Keith Ellison became a folk hero among housing activists when he filed a consumer protection lawsuit against a company called HavenBrook Homes in 2022. HavenBrook is an offshoot of real estate company Progress Residential—itself an offshoot of private equity firm Pretium Partners—and it had purchased hundreds of single-family houses in majority-Black neighborhoods in north Minneapolis. The company, Ellison alleged, had grossly overstated its home-repair practices as part of "a deliberate and calculated strategy to extract ever greater profits from their tenants by severely under-maintaining their homes." In 2024, HavenBrook agreed to settle the case by creating a $2.2 million restitution fund for current and former tenants, forgiving nearly $2 million in back rent, and committing to strict maintenance standards.

Most surprisingly, Pretium also said it would sell its Minneapolis homes to affordable-housing organizations. The largest landlord in town was packing up and leaving; hundreds of homes' worth of rental income didn't justify the cost of the political fight.

WHILE LOREN WELCOMED THE LETTERS from city council members and U.S. senators about conditions at Southern Towers, she wasn't holding out hope for more significant political action. She didn't have much trust in most politicians. As much as she dislikes the way conservatives have neglected or outright opposed services for poor communities, some of her strongest antipathy is reserved for people in power on the left. They're so blinded by their ideals, she said, that they forget the people on the ground. One of her go-to rants is about how Bernie Sanders needs to drop his advocacy of Medicare for All, a cause she supports in theory but thinks is a waste of time. "Everything that happens in this country, there's always going to be the big person and the little person," she said. "And when it's those types of fights, especially when it's tied to billions of dollars, you're not going to win it." It's ridiculous for Sanders to spend time on a pie-in-the-sky plan, she believes, when he could be focusing on "something that's doable in my lifetime."

It can be difficult to square her rejection of David-versus-Goliath fights with her drive to evict private equity from Southern Towers. Giant corporate landlords like Pretium and CIM own homes in dozens of cities, and the industry's control over housing is only growing. What is a company like CIM if not "the big person," and a low-income immigrant tenant if not "the little person"? Why would going after multibillion-dollar real estate firms end any differently than going after multibillion-dollar health insurance companies?

To Loren, though, getting private equity out of affordable housing looks increasingly achievable. Considering all the headaches owning Southern Towers has brought CIM, she thinks, why wouldn't they sell it for a nice profit and go do literally anything else? Ellison got Pretium Partners out of Minneapolis; the annoy-them-until-they-go-away strategy has actually succeeded in a handful of cases that pitted working-class little people against private equity's big people. In fact, around the same time CIM Group bought Southern Towers, a group of little people on the other side of the country pulled it off against CIM itself.

In April 2020, four months before CIM bought the Alexandria complex, it announced a new acquisition: the firm would pay more than $100 million for a struggling mall in Crenshaw, a neighborhood that has been called "the heart of African American commerce in Los Angeles." Baldwin Hills Crenshaw Plaza, once one of the largest shopping centers in the city, was a classic CIM project: after decades of neglect, the city was doing its best to encourage development in the neighborhood, including building a new light-rail line. CIM was already in the process of transforming West Adams, the historically Black neighborhood just north, so Crenshaw was the logical next step, a chance to draw higher-paying commercial tenants and wealthier shoppers and diners to the area. CIM cofounder Shaul Kuba was particularly excited to build office space. "There are very few large sites in the city that have a subway stop right in front," he said. "I think we have a tremendous opportunity."

Crenshaw, though, didn't want office space and wealthier shoppers and diners. Activists wanted housing and restaurants and retail that catered to the people who lived there, not people traveling in on the light-rail. "What CIM proposes is a hostile takeover of the most iconic African-American retail space west of the Mississippi River and the construction of a project that would ignore the community's needs and wishes and possibly wipe out dozens of minority-owned businesses that are now tenants in the Baldwin Hills Crenshaw Plaza mall," the president of the Southern Christian Leadership Conference of Southern California told reporters. More than ten thousand people signed a petition titled "Save the Baldwin Hills Crenshaw Plaza." A dozen local organizations and community leaders sent a letter to CIM asking its executives to allow a coalition of neighborhood non-profits to buy the mall instead.

Incredibly, the activists won. Just two months after agreeing to buy the shopping center, CIM announced in an Instagram post that it was dropping out. Much of the campaign against them, the firm wrote, was "based on falsehoods," but they weren't going to keep fighting overwhelming community opposition. "CIM has concluded that the community, the Mall, and CIM are best served by us stepping aside," read the four-paragraph caption under CIM's orange logo. "We wish the community great success in achieving all of its goals for the Mall." The following year, the nonprofits' bid to buy Baldwin Hills Crenshaw Plaza was rejected in favor of a local developer with financial backing from a Russian American oil baron, but community opposition died down significantly after the developer outlined plans for housing in addition to office space and retail.

It seemed like irritating CIM into submission *could* work, at least in some cases. But it hadn't worked at Southern Towers back in 2020, when Bourma organized his rent strike. And kicking out Loren and her family when *she* irritated them more than three years later didn't inspire hope that the firm was softening its stance on Southern Towers. Pushing CIM out, African Communities Together decided, was going to require a different kind of solution, one that more directly targeted the firm's sources of capital.

———

WHEN LAID-OFF TOYS R US employees appealed to the pension funds that invested in the company's private equity owners, helping win the severance fund they had been denied, other organizing groups took note. The genius of the Toys R Us strategy was understanding that the people who benefit from pension funds—teachers, nurses, firefighters, and other public employees—also hold seats on the boards of those funds, and that they might be inclined to side with other lower- and middle-income workers over billionaires. Housing advocates figured it couldn't hurt to see if that approach might work for them.

In the fall of 2022, Bourma spoke at a conference for the Council of Institutional Investors, an association of more than 135 pension funds and other benefit programs. The organization was born out of the rise in corporate takeovers in the 1980s; its members wanted to make sure pensioners had a voice in how their money was being spent. It is hardly a radical group; its mission is to "enhance long-term value for U.S. institutional asset owners and their beneficiaries," and representatives on its various committees come from Goldman Sachs, BlackRock, and Coca-Cola as well as the New York State Teachers' Retirement System and the Service Employees International Union. As a result of building a big tent, the group's recommendations tend to become industry standards.

At the conference, Bourma was part of a session called "Responsible Investing in Institutional Real Estate," speaking alongside a New York City government official, the CEO of a Canadian nonprofit, and a University of California, Berkeley, professor. Bourma talked about what living at Southern Towers was like under CIM Group ownership, from the mold to the rent hikes. He said he didn't object to investors making money, but that much of private equity's profits from housing was coming at the expense of low-income Black tenants like him. He didn't have the power to change the system, he said, but the people in that room did. As decision-makers for big pension funds, he argued, they had a unique opportunity to stop private equity from taking advantage of vulnerable residents.

That same year, Southern Towers tenants brought a special guest to a meeting with building management: a representative from the Pennsylvania Public School Employees' Retirement System, a $76 billion fund that had invested $250 million in CIM. The invitation seemed to pay off. Soon afterward, CIM leaders agreed to two more meetings with residents and even committed to fulfilling a few of their demands, including repairing the elevators and temporarily capping rent increases. Perhaps the fixes would have come with or without the watchful eye of a pension fund, but it certainly didn't hurt. After the flood that drove Loren's family and thirteen others out of their apartments, Prom spoke at a meeting of the Pennsylvania pension board. She told them about the water damage as well as other ongoing maintenance issues, and promised to return with updates.

In 2022, the Pennsylvania fund ranked in the bottom 1 percent of all large pension plans by return on investment. In response, the state hired a new chief investment officer, Benjamin Cotton, who pledged to trim the amount of the group's money that was being invested in private equity. He wasn't the only one. Across the country, a handful of public pension funds were downsizing their private equity investments. Their reasoning was about calibrating risk and responding to market fluctuations, not ethical concerns, but the result was the same: a bit less money from public employees in some states going to firms like CIM.

———

WORKING WITH PENSION FUNDS WAS a useful step in the right direction for tenants and activists. Yet the more important funnel of money for CIM's real estate investments comes from low-interest government-backed loans, like the $346 million used to purchase Southern Towers.

In 1992, Congress assigned Fannie Mae and Freddie Mac an obligation to develop affordable-housing programs. But although Fannie and Freddie do require buyers of multifamily buildings to reserve units for working-class people and set aside mortgages for lower-income residents, the law governing the programs is relatively toothless. The exact number of units designated for low- and moderate-income Americans is a "goal" set each year, not a legal standard. Fannie and Freddie do not limit how much landlords can increase rent, nor require them to report those increases. If a private equity firm lists a certain number of affordable apartments on its loan application, it makes no difference to the federal government how many of those units *remain* affordable. And while Fannie and Freddie require landlords to keep their buildings clean, safe, and functional, actual enforcement is rare.

To African Communities Together and other housing advocates, targeting Freddie Mac and its government overseers at the Federal Housing Finance Agency seemed like the most promising path toward protecting tenants at Southern Towers and the ever-larger number of apartment buildings owned by private equity firms. In November 2022, Prom wrote to Sandra Thompson, the agency's director, and Michael DeVito, Freddie Mac's chief operating officer. She made three requests: that they investigate CIM's predatory practices, refuse to fund future CIM projects, and consider demanding immediate payment on the loan used to purchase Southern Towers. "Freddie Mac is using taxpayer money to fund the displacement of working-class Black residents. This is unequivocally antithetical to Freddie Mac's goal of preserving affordable and stable housing," she wrote.

Prom didn't get much of what she asked for. But she got the agency's attention: Thompson visited Southern Towers in June 2023 on a tour hosted by Prom and progressive grassroots organizing group People's Action.

Around the same time, the Federal Housing Finance Agency asked for public suggestions about what steps it should take to better protect tenants in multifamily buildings financed by Fannie and Freddie. In its request, the agency wrote that it "recognizes that tenants can be exploited by housing providers who either do not abide by the law or their lease agreements, or who take advantage of opportunities created by a lack of legal constraints," and that low-income residents often have little recourse, which can mean losing their homes.

Among the respondents to the survey was a group of seventeen Democratic U.S. senators, including both Kaine and Warner as well as Elizabeth Warren and Sherrod Brown, then the chairman of the committee that oversees housing issues. In a letter addressed to Thompson, the senators asked for enforceable limits on rent hikes, remedies for residents when landlords fail to meet health and safety standards, additional disclosures about who owns which buildings, and a right for tenants to form unions.

The second bullet point on the senators' list happened to describe Loren's situation specifically: "Require good cause for evictions and lease non-renewals . . . such as serious and repeated lease violations provable in a court of law—to ensure that tenants are safeguarded against unfair, discriminatory, and retaliatory evictions." Considering the lack of evidence provided against Loren and Rashad in December 2023, seventeen United States senators were effectively arguing that CIM should not have been allowed to refuse to renew their lease.

In July 2024, after reviewing thousands of submissions, the Federal Housing Finance Agency announced three new tenant protections. Its leaders declined to implement the more progressive ideas, including good-cause evictions and nonrenewals. But it did require additional notice of rent increases or lease expirations, as well as a five-day grace period for rent payments. It wasn't much, but it was a sign that Fannie and Freddie were finally looking closely at the issues housing activists had been raising for years.

It's not clear how serious the agency is about stricter regulation of corporate landlords, especially under a second Trump administration, or how much it can do without involving Congress or the federal judiciary. Lawmakers may well be more likely to let the free market continue to govern federally backed housing for low-income tenants. Historically, the FHFA has mostly brushed off concerns about supporting private equity with low-interest loans. When a ProPublica journalist found that, over the previous ten years, 85 percent of Freddie Mac's biggest apartment complex loans went to private equity firms, a spokesman responded that the agency generally only makes a small handful of loans of that size every year.

That is true, but the biggest loans generally fund the buildings that are home to the most people. Private equity firms often also take out an array of smaller loans, which attract less scrutiny, to fund many separate acquisitions. As long as the Federal Housing Finance Agency continues to provide them an always-flowing spigot of cheap money, low-income renters will continue to suffer under private equity's thumb.

Loren knows that getting the government to act isn't impossible. She successfully pressured Alexandria's city council to ban single-family-only zoning and build more affordable housing. She won't stop fighting until more tenants get more protections, in Alexandria and nationwide. "I've organized tenants by my goddamn self in affordable housing without any know-how," she said, occasionally pumping her fist or pounding of the table in front of her to underscore her point. "From then to now, I've been educated, and I've actually applied it and had victories. So I know that if you organize the right way around these types of issues, the change can come."

=====

WHILE POLITICIANS HAVE PROPOSED VERY few ideas to meaningfully regulate private equity ownership of apartment buildings, there has been more movement in single-family homes and mobile home parks.

In December 2023, Representative Adam Smith and Senator Jeff Merkley, both Democrats, introduced a bill that would prohibit private equity firms and hedge funds from buying any single-family homes, and require them to sell the ones they currently own within ten years. Smith, who represents parts of Seattle and the surrounding area, and Merkley, of Oregon, framed the End Hedge Fund Control of American Homes Act as a necessary response to the lack of affordable homes in huge swaths of the country. They didn't accuse private equity of *creating* the crisis, which was primarily the result of building too few homes, and exacerbated by spiking interest rates. But they did paint institutional investors as vultures happy to take advantage of those conditions for their own gain at the expense of ordinary Americans. "Wall Street . . . is now going after sort of the last bastion of wealth creation that is available to your average working-class family, which is being able to buy a house and see it go up in value. Now Wall Street's coming in and buying it and forcing you to rent so that they get the increased value and you don't," Smith said.

There were two problems with Merkley and Smith's idea. One was that it stood no chance of passing. The influence of private equity lobbying and donations to members on both sides of the aisle meant that real regulation wasn't in either party's interest. The bill was referred to the relevant House and Senate committees, but there it sat, undiscussed and largely unnoticed. It expired at the end of the term.

A more fundamental issue, though, is that it's not clear that the bill would achieve its goals even if it did become law. Several studies have shown that private equity acquisitions shut out potential first-time home buyers in some areas of the country. But that research leaves out the experiences of people who aren't even close to affording a home of their own. That group includes most low-income residents of buildings like Southern Towers, which are among the hottest properties for private equity firms. In a 2023 Federal Reserve report, 65 percent of renters said they couldn't afford a down payment, and 44 percent said they couldn't afford monthly mortgage payments. Fewer than one in three said they were working toward buying a home. The End Hedge Fund Control of American Homes Act might help the relatively small number of families already on the cusp of buying homes, but it wouldn't do anything for the millions of perma-renters. The American Dream of homeownership already felt out of reach to millions of people; the growth of private equity in the industry has pushed it even further away.

Legislation and organizing around mobile home parks, meanwhile, offer other possible solutions to the problem of private equity taking advantage of low-income residents. Several states have passed laws giving mobile home owners new rights, including mandating more notice of lot rent increases, requiring management to maintain central services or else reimburse rent, and increasing transparency around who owns the land under parks.

Some states even now require mobile home park owners looking to sell to give residents the chance to buy their park collectively. Mobile home parks can cost as little as a single-family home in some communities, making ownership an achievable goal even for a group of low-income residents. In Maine, residents have two months to make a competitive offer, and three months to secure financing. In New York, residents have sixty days to declare their intention to make an offer, and 140 days to follow through. ROC USA, a nonprofit that helps mobile home tenants buy their parks, works with more than 330 resident-owned communities across the country, the largest of which is home to more than 400 families. Not a single park has defaulted on its mortgage or shut down.

Buying a mobile home park is far cheaper than buying an entire apartment building; even if apartment dwellers benefited from the same guarantees that mobile home residents have in a handful of states, few would be able to afford the opportunity. But the push for increased rights for mobile home tenants may indicate a growing desire to strengthen tenant protections more generally. Housing advocates are betting that policy solutions in one sector of the industry could inspire adaptations in another. They're also focusing on the local and state levels, where the private equity lobby has less power than on Capitol Hill, and where groups like African Communities Together can have more impact.

———

OVER AND OVER, ACROSS EVERY segment of the housing landscape, residents' victories came when they banded together—and not in a symbolic way. The laws that now allow residents to buy their parks require them to form a legal collective; it's impossible to take ownership without working as a unit. Activists are hyperaware that standing up to the "big person," in Loren's words, can't be done by one little person, or even a handful of them. "I can show a concern by myself, and you're going to tell me to shut up and go away," Loren said. "I'm going to bring five people, and you might stop to listen, but you're not really listening. When I show up with fifty to a hundred people, you're forced to sit down and listen and acknowledge. And then if I do it publicly, where there's other eyes, whatever you say, you're going to have to do."

The creation of America's first rent control program, in New York City in 1920, was the result of tenants modeling their tactics on those used by labor unions: rent strikes, pickets, public awareness campaigns. In the last few years, a small handful of tenant unions have won major victories against private equity landlords, offering a stencil for others to attempt to trace.

In 1971, shortly after New York passed a law largely eliminating rent-controlled housing, residents of Stuyvesant Town–Peter Cooper Village, known as StuyTown—the largest apartment complex in Manhattan, with more than 11,000 apartments spread over two zip codes—organized a tenants' association, which eventually helped repeal the law. When Blackstone, the largest private equity firm and largest landlord in the country, bought StuyTown in 2015 for $5.3 billion, its leaders promised that 4,500 apartments would remain affordable to middle-class families, and 500 to low-income ones. That got the firm a $77 million tax break and a $144 million loan from the city, with zero interest. The rest of StuyTown's units were designated as rent-stabilized—which means strict limits on how much rent can increase each year. That designation was set to expire in 2020, and Blackstone had no intention of renewing it.

The tenants' association sued, and won. A state supreme court judge ruled that under the terms of a 2019 state law strengthening tenant protections, Blackstone could not roll back rent stabilization, as it had planned. StuyTown would remain rent stabilized forever.

Though tenants' associations are still rare, the victory in New York helped drive a wave of organizing in private equity–owned apartment buildings across the country. In San Diego, residents formed the Blackstone Tenants Union in 2021 and began to fight rent hikes, evictions, and maintenance delays in several Blackstone buildings. Two years later, the city passed an ordinance increasing protections against evictions and rent hikes. In Kansas City, Missouri, a tenant association won a "Right to Counsel" program that guarantees a free lawyer to anyone facing eviction. In Minneapolis, the nonprofit that advocated for renters of HavenBrook homes is now working to create a city-wide tenants union. In a handful of other big cities, including Washington, D.C., Seattle, and San Francisco, tenants already have the legal right to organize unions, and landlords can be penalized for not bargaining with them.

Virginia law has long been hostile toward unions. In 2018, Oxfam, which works to address inequality and poverty worldwide, ranked it the worst place in America for workers, awarding it low marks on wage policies, employee protections, and the right to unionize. But the tide has begun to turn: Oxfam's 2023 ranking put the state in the middle of the pack, thanks in part to a 2021 law that dramatically expanded collective bargaining rights. After Princeton University's Eviction Lab drew national attention to Virginia's high rate of evictions, meanwhile, the state spent more than $335 million on rental relief funds and passed a law extending the grace period for late rent from five to fourteen days.

The push for better protections for renters in Virginia has been halting. Republican governor Glenn Youngkin vetoed a 2022 bill that would have allowed cities and towns to sue negligent landlords, and a revised version failed to make it past a state House committee. Even so, African Communities Together organizers are optimistic about the overall trend. The biggest hurdle may be keeping residents' energy up for a long, slow fight.

———

OVER HER LONG CAREER AS an unpaid rabble-rouser and her newer one as a professional organizer, Loren has seen over and over how people's motivation can flag when a crisis dies down, when the "big people" stall and dissemble. Low-income people must constantly triage issues in their own lives, she knows; if their housing situation is stable for the moment, yelling at the landlord isn't going to be a priority even if they are fully aware more problems are coming.

Loren is not built to triage, though she realizes life would be easier if she was. She moves through each day like a fire juggler who's constantly getting another blazing torch tossed her way. While eating lunch at her favorite local Mexican restaurant, strategizing her next move at Southern Towers, her phone pinged with a request to show up at a political candidate's kickoff event the following Sunday. She already had five other commitments on Sunday, a day when she tries to prioritize time with her kids, and she had less than a month to find a new place to live. She was annoyed that the candidate didn't give her more notice, but she quickly tapped out a gracious reply promising to swing by. Then she noticed the time: she should have left five minutes ago to pick up her younger son, Cameron, from the school bus. Throwing on her coat, she walked briskly to her car. Throughout the entire sequence, she never once lost her train of thought about how to get CIM out of Alexandria for good.

After CIM threw her out of Southern Towers *and* banned her from talking to its staff, Loren had to get used to not being able to barge ahead on her own. That's still difficult for her. She admires Prom but is often frustrated at how slow and deliberate African Communities Together can be. Her boss at VOICE has had to remind her, several times, to stay on her side of the border between Alexandria and Arlington; she left the organization in late 2024. But she's long known the "big people" of private equity are far too imposing to confront without an army of little people. So she decided to serve as their general.

Her first step, before she even moved out of Southern Towers, was to make sure her soon-to-be-former neighbors all knew to call her. Many of them were too scared to agitate with management directly, so every time she saw someone watching more water run down the walls, or heard someone inquiring at the front desk about when maintenance workers would arrive, she pulled them aside and told them to put her number in their phone, call her whenever there's an issue, and share her contact info with as many other people as will take it.

When someone new reaches out, she goes to see them as soon as she can. She takes photos and tells them step by step how to negotiate with management. Her phone is filled with pictures and videos: a chunk of the ceiling that nearly fell on someone's head in the hallway; a moldy heating unit; a shower curtain rod that came crashing down after maintenance supposedly fixed the wall it hung on; water dripping down by the mailboxes, by the management office, along an outside wall, in someone's kitchen. Walking through the lobby one afternoon, she ran into a girl around her son Jaxon's age, who was just getting into the elevator with some friends. "Tell your mom she needs to send me those photos!" she instructed. The girl promised she would.

Maybe once she collects enough evidence, she thinks, the residents could file a class-action lawsuit, though it isn't clear where they'd get enough money to take on CIM's fleet of lawyers. Or perhaps the city council could push for the type of legal regulation that would never fly at the state level—though this is tricky too; Virginia is a "Dillon Rule" state, which means cities can't pass any laws that the state constitution doesn't explicitly empower them to pass. She's happy to go to Richmond to lobby the legislature, if that's what it takes, or to step up the pressure on Freddie Mac and Virginia's two senators to push them to do something beyond writing a letter.

She's also considering running for office herself. Maybe she'll start with the school board, then make a play for a city council seat later. Her father—the man who built a multimillion-dollar business from scratch in a new country and became his eldest daughter's hero—always tells her not to complain about things that are broken. Step up and fix them instead, he likes to say. She thinks about that a lot. Long before private equity came into her life, she refused to back down from any fight, refused to be cowed by people in power, refused to take losses. She's not planning to start now.

CONCLUSION

IN THE SUMMER AND FALL OF 2024, AFTER I HAD FINISHED REPORTING on Liz, Roger, Natalia, and Loren and was editing this book, a new private equity story burst into public view.

Steward Health Care, the Dallas-based owner of thirty-three hospitals, had gone bankrupt that May. Federal lawmakers wanted to know what went wrong, and were exasperated by Steward executives' unwillingness to provide details. The company's CEO failed to comply with a congressional subpoena, and was held in criminal contempt.

Steward was created in 2010, when Cerberus Capital Management—the private equity firm named after the three-headed dog that guards Hades in Greek mythology—acquired a nonprofit Catholic health care system in New England, then began buying hospitals across the country. In 2020, Cerberus transferred the controlling interest in the company to a group of physicians led by Steward's longtime CEO, a heart surgeon named Ralph de la Torre. Steward boasted that it was now the largest doctor-owned health care system in the country; de la Torre called the move a "transformational moment."

Until 2024, few people realized that Steward Health Care was facing an existential financial threat. But then the owner of the real estate under Steward's hospitals—Medical Properties Trust, the same Alabama-based firm that owns the building Roger's former hospital occupies in Riverton, Wyoming—revealed in a press release that Steward owed $50 million in unpaid rent. After that, Massachusetts governor Maura Healey, whose state was home to nine Steward hospitals, said the company hadn't filed required financial disclosures in a decade.

Within a few months, Steward declared bankruptcy, putting hospitals in eight states at risk of closure.

It turned out that the company had been in financial trouble for years. Court filings and an investigation by a team of *Boston Globe* reporters revealed that Steward and Cerberus had gone to great lengths to disguise its struggles from employees, vendors, patients, the government, and even its own investors. In 2020, the year Cerberus transferred ownership of the hospitals to its doctors, Steward had lost $408 million, and had $1.5 billion more liabilities than assets. The "transformational moment" de la Torre bragged about had actually been part of a secret Cerberus scheme—complete with a code name, "Project Easter," and a byzantine set of transactions to disguise the real plan—to save Steward from financial ruin without drawing attention to its problems.

The *Globe* found fifteen cases in which patients had died as a result of issues with equipment or staffing. At the time of the bankruptcy, the company owed roughly $9 billion in loans, rent payments, bills from suppliers, and salaries. The company even hired corporate spies to target its opponents in Malta, where it had struck a deal to operate three hospitals and was now at the center of the largest corruption case in the country's history. The bill for the spies was passed on to Maltese taxpayers.

Meanwhile, over the decade it owned Steward, Cerberus Capital Management made $800 million for its investors. De la Torre, the CEO, earned a $3.7 million annual salary; a consulting firm he ran was paid an additional $30 million a year out of Steward's accounts. De la Torre and his family lived in luxury: he owned two yachts, together worth $55 million, while two private jets owned by Steward carried him to family vacations as well as on business trips. Steward bought de la Torre an €8 million apartment in Madrid. A $3 million donation to his children's private school in Dallas was credited to his family foundation but funded by his employer.

The scale of the alleged malfeasance by Cerberus and de la Torre made Steward the rare private equity story to break through into the public consciousness. Even more than the egregious nature of the alleged crimes, though, what struck me about the saga was how little we still actually knew about what happened. Even after all those bankruptcy filings and all that investigative reporting, it remains entirely unclear where a lot of the money went. Donald Berwick, a former Centers for Medicare and Medicaid Services administrator and an expert in hospital management, told a Senate subcommittee that he couldn't tell how the company's business model worked: Steward, he said, maintains a "lack of transparency that [makes] it very, very difficult to know what is going on."

═══════

MAKING IT DIFFICULT TO KNOW what's going on is exactly the point of so much about how private equity operates. For decades, the industry has invented its own rules: pioneering workarounds to tax and disclosure laws, slipping through loopholes, so thoroughly disguising its tactics that they're often incomprehensible to observers and even employees of portfolio companies. Few people understand what private equity is; even fewer understand the often-devastating consequences—to workers, customers, and communities—until they are forced to live through them.

In his famous 1970 essay about shareholder value, Milton Friedman justified his thesis using the language of freedom. Business owners, he wrote, are free to prioritize their company's interests above all. Workers, meanwhile, can choose whom to work for based on wages, job security, or whatever factors are most important to them. This, Friedman argued, is "the great virtue of private competitive enterprise—it forces people to be responsible for their own actions and makes it difficult for them to 'exploit' other people for either selfish or unselfish purposes."

In Friedman's free enterprise system, bosses and workers each have power over one another, each fully in control of their own destinies. "No individual can coerce any other," he wrote, "all cooperation is voluntary, all parties to such cooperation benefit or they need not participate."

But Friedman's stipulation that bosses and workers have equal power requires bosses and workers to have equal information. In the fifty-five years since his essay, the growing dominance of private equity has destroyed that precondition. Workers often don't know who their bosses are, much less what their business strategy is or whether they plan to drive the company into bankruptcy and profit off the scraps. If knowledge is power, private equity has managed to hoard full control for itself, with the blessing of the federal government.

Liz, Roger, Natalia, and Loren each occasionally grow agitated about how difficult it can be to convince other people of the severity of the private equity crisis. "It's like, I'm desperate to convince everyone else how bad this is, but they don't believe me because it's not their problem," Loren said a few weeks before she moved out of Southern Towers. The effect can be maddening, as if they're pointing to the monster looming just outside the window but everyone else thinks they're hallucinating.

———

REGULATING AN INDUSTRY WITH SO much power and wealth would require massive willpower, and willpower can be very hard to come by when it comes to private equity. A committed lobbying operation and generous donations to politicians of all political stripes have helped protect the industry's ability to operate largely unchecked; even support from both Donald Trump and Joe Biden wasn't enough to close the carried-interest loophole.

Ordinary people, though, don't benefit from those industry donations. And while support for private equity unites Republican and Democratic *politicians*, anger about wealth inequality and the disproportionate power of the ultrarich increasingly unites *all* Americans. A 2024 poll found that 59 percent of Americans believe billionaires are creating a more unfair society. Seventy-one percent said wealth inequality is a serious national issue, including 56 percent of Republicans. More than half of Republicans and nearly three-quarters of Democrats support higher tax rates for the richest members of society; the most popular answers for how the government should spend the hypothetical extra revenue were affordable housing and health care.

A separate survey the same year reported that just 32 percent of Republicans and 26 percent of Democrats believe that large corporations "have a positive effect on the way things are going in the country these days." Just five years earlier, more than half of Republicans had answered yes to the same question. Even the people who haven't directly suffered under private equity rule appear newly primed to accept that it negatively affects everyone.

The scope of the private equity machine, and the imbalance of power, can make people cynical about the prospect of ever fixing the problem. Every year, more bills designed to regulate the industry die in congressional committees. Meanwhile, more people lose their jobs, their local institutions, and their homes. But that also means that every year, a few more people like Liz, Roger, Natalia, and Loren start fighting back: reckoning with private equity's outsize role in the American economy, starting legal battles, pushing for new legislation, organizing grassroots campaigns, working to reinvent their industries from the ground up.

Even if private equity doesn't own your employer or your home, it may well control your dentist's office, your children's preschool, your grandmother's nursing home, or your public utilities. The industry's rapid expansion has given firms and their executives scores of new ways to line their own pockets at the expense of American workers. But it has also created scores of new people who can finally see the monster through the window. If it doesn't play a role in your life yet, just wait. Private equity is everybody's problem now.

ACKNOWLEDGMENTS

This book would not exist without Liz Marin, Roger Gose, Natalia Contreras, and Loren DePina, who welcomed me into their homes, answered my questions for days on end, and never shied away from the hard parts. I will always be grateful.

More than three hundred other people took the time to talk to me about their work, their scholarship, their advocacy, and their lives. All of those conversations—on the record, off the record, on background—shaped my thinking and my writing in profound ways.

Freedom of Information Act specialists, librarians, government clerks, and researchers are actual American heroes, the people who make sure the rest of us can take advantage of our right to know. I am also indebted to all of the journalists whose work informed my own, especially those in local newsrooms.

Anna Sproul-Latimer signed me as her client in 2012, stuck with me for a *decade* with no book to show for it, then kicked off the reporting for this one with an email saying, in its entirety, "This is a boookkkkk." I owe her the world—for teaching me how to write a book, for always being up for some gossip, for having the biggest brain and heart in publishing.

The team at Dey Street Books were unimaginably supportive during my reporting, writing, and editing process. From the moment we met on Zoom, Kate Napolitano's enthusiasm boosted my confidence that I could tackle a subject as sprawling and unwieldy as private equity. Stuart Roberts kept me out of the weeds and sharpened my argument and my sentences immeasurably. Anna Montague steered me through many of the most stressful days and always made me laugh. Libby Burton saved the day during the final push. Chelsea Herrera made sure things happened when they needed to. Thanks also to Rachel Meyers, Tom Pitoniak, Alison Bloomer, Melanie Bedor, Cari Elliott, Paul Miele-Herndon, Bill Adams, and the many other HarperCollins team members who helped put this book into the world. Thank you to the HarperCollins Union for making the industry better.

Maria Streshinsky is one of the greatest narrative editors in the business as well as a true friend; I'm so fortunate that she spent her nights and weekends editing my book. Having your work scrutinized by a world-class fact-checker is a priceless gift, and Linnea Feldman Emison is the best of the best.

Working with young people is one of the most joyful parts of my life, and several of them contributed immeasurably to this book. I am thankful to Victoria Feng for serving as my research assistant, and to the University of Chicago's Practitioner Program for funding the first phase of her work with me. Andrew DeMar, Elizabeth Harris, and Pablo Perez-Castro also helped with research projects and organization. The students, alumni, and staff of the Princeton Summer Journalism Program make me smarter and inspire me to do big things.

The Omidyar Network's Reporter in Residence Program provided additional financial support that bought me valuable writing time. Rachel Monroe and the Very Reverend Christian Schreiner offered me "residencies" in Marfa and Les Îles-de-la-Madeleine, the best places I've ever written.

Without the steady hands of my orthopedic surgeon, Dr. Amanda Walsh, this book never would have gotten done on time.

Slogging through any gigantic project is so much more fun when you're doing it at the same time as the most important people in your life. Maggie Gram, Amanda Hess, Kelsey McKinney, and Julianne Escobedo Shepherd, thank you for working in coffee shops with me and commiserating with me. I love you and your books.

Many friends talked me off many a ledge while I reported and wrote. Thank you to Charley Locke, Corey Sobel, Dayna Evans, Doug McGray, Harold Hayes, Kate Bergren, Katie Wilson, Lyz Lenz, Marin Cogan, Millie Tran, Richard Just, Seyward Darby, Tieisha Tift, and Tim Marchman. And, especially, to two people: David Chernicoff, who has read my writing and rooted for my success for more than two decades, and Scott Rosenfield, for having my back in every situation.

My parents, Jim and Gail Greenwell, taught me to love books and never seemed to regret it, even when I neglected everything else in my life because I couldn't put down a good one. My sister Emily Greenwell is my most faithful confidant. My brother-in-law Chris Quartly is always ready with a perfect cocktail and an encouraging word. The entire Heller family has offered unending support. I am so lucky.

Above all, thank you to David, for always being there and for always being you (and for downloading so many academic papers for me). I love you forever; I like you for always.

NOTES

INTRODUCTION

ix *Our company's previous owner:* Benjamin Mullin and Dana Mattioli, "Private-Equity Firm Great Hill Partners in Talks to Buy Gizmodo Media Group," *Wall Street Journal*, February 15, 2019, https://www.wsj.com/articles/private-equity-firm-great-hill-partners-in-talks-to-buy-gizmodo-media-group-11550246035.

xi *By that standard:* "Great Hill Partners #10 on HEC-DowJones Private Equity Performance Rankings," Great Hill Partners, December 17, 2019, https://www.greathillpartners.com/media/great-hill-partners-10-on-hec-dowjones-private-equity-performance-rankings.

xi *In less than five years:* "deadspin.com Ranking by Traffic," Similarweb, accessed October 24, 2024, https://www.similarweb.com/website/deadspin.com/#ranking.

xi *Great Hill Partners itself:* "Mid-Market Players with Sector-Focused Strategies Challenge the Dominance of US Based Funds in Latest HEC Paris–Dow Jones Ranking," HEC Paris, March 6, 2024, https://www.hec.edu/en/news-room/mid-market-players-sector-focused-strategies-challenge-dominance-us-based-funds-latest-hec-paris-dow-jones-ranking.

xii *Twelve million people:* "Economic Contribution of the US Private Equity Sector in 2022," EY, April 20, 2023, https://www.investmentcouncil.org/wp-content/uploads/2023/04/EY-AIC-PE-economic-contribution-report-FINAL-04-20-2023.pdf.

xii *These firms' influence:* "PESP Private Equity Hospital Tracker," Private Equity Stakeholder Project, accessed April 15, 2024, https://pestakeholder.org/private-equity-hospital-tracker/.

xii *America's production:* Alyssa Giachino and Riddhi Mehta-Neugebauer, "Private Equity Propels the Climate Crisis," Private Equity Stakeholder Project, October 2021, https://pestakeholder.org/wp-content/uploads/2021/10/PESP_SpecialReport_ClimateCrisis_Oct2021_Final.pdf.

xiii *Four of the five:* Elliot Haspel, "Toddlers and Investors Aren't Playmates: The Threat of Private Equity in Child Care," Capita, 2023, https://static1.squarespace.com/static/5936b0c92994cab8bfe601d4/t/640719a1497f12367db923c2/1678186913434/Toddlers+and+Investors+Arent+Playmates+Capita+Final+0307.pdf.

xiii *The central branch:* Sergei Klebnikov, "The Richest Private Equity Billionaires on the Forbes 400 List 2021," *Forbes*, October 5, 2021, https://www.forbes.com/sites/sergeiklebnikov/2021/10/05/richest-private-equity-billionaires-forbes-400-2021/.

xiii *Apollo Global Management cofounder:* Matthew Goldstein, "Senate Committee Presses Leon Black on Epstein Tax Advice," *New York Times,* July 25, 2023, https://www.nytimes.com/2023/07/25/business/leon-black-jeffrey-epstein-senate.html.

xiii *Dozens of people:* Maryann Feldman and Martin Kenney, *Private Equity and the Demise of the Local* (Cambridge: Cambridge University Press, 2024), 26.

xv *The sole interest:* Milton Friedman, "A Friedman Doctrine—The Social Responsibility of Business Is to Increase Its Profits," *New York Times*, September 13, 1970, https://www.nytimes.com/1970/09/13/archives/a-friedman-doctrine-the-social-responsibility-of-business-is-to.html.

xvi *Between 2013 and 2023:* Yang Liu and Lue Xiong, "Leverage in Private Equity: What Do We Know?" MSCI, September 9, 2024, https://www.msci.com/www/blog-posts/leverage-in-private-equity-what/04942552461#f1.

xvii *According to a report:* EY, "Economic Contribution of the US Private Equity Sector in 2022."

xvii *They left in 1976:* Carol J. Loomis, "Buyout Kings," *Fortune*, July 4, 1988, https://money.cnn.com/magazines/fortune/fortune_archive/1988/07/04/70748/.

xviii *What it did have:* Max Holland, *When the Machine Stopped* (Brighton, MA: Harvard Business School Press, 1989).

xviii *"The public documents":* James Sterngold, "A Pioneer in Leveraged Buyouts Quits the Fray," *New York Times*, June 19, 1987, https://www.nytimes.com/1987/06/19/business/buyout-pioneer-quitting-fray.html.

xviii *Later that same year:* "How Capital Gains Tax Rates Affect Revenues: The Historical Evidence," Congressional Budget Office, March 1988, https://www.cbo.gov/sites/default/files/cbofiles/ftpdocs/84xx/doc8449/88-cbo-007.pdf.

xviii *From KKR's vantage:* George P. Baker and George David Smith, *The New Financial Capitalists* (Cambridge: Cambridge University Press, 1998), 207.

xviii *"All of the Houdaille 'constituents'":* Max Holland, "How to Kill a Company," *Washington Post*, April 22, 1989, https://www.washingtonpost.com/archive/opinions/1989/04/23/how-to-kill-a-company/6c4ecddb-a0a6-47c7-a810-4c552f6e2205/.

xviii *All of them:* "Houdaille Industries to Move Headquarters," *South Florida Sun Sentinel*, March 27, 1987, https://www.sun-sentinel.com/1987/03/27/houdaille-industries-to-move-headquarters/.

xviii *About one in three:* Eileen Appelbaum and Rosemary Batt, *Private Equity at Work* (New York: Russell Sage Foundation, 2014), 27.

xix *Today, less than:* "McKinsey Global Private Markets Review 2024: Private Markets in a Slower Era," McKinsey, accessed April 17, 2024, https://www.mckinsey.com/industries/private-equity-and-principal-investors/our-insights/mckinseys-private-markets-annual-review.

xix *Blackstone, for example:* "Building Sustainable Businesses," Blackstone, accessed April 23, 2024, https://www.blackstone.com/our-impact/building-sustainable-businesses/.

xix *Private equity firms:* Karl Angelo Vidal and Annie Sabater, "Private Equity Buyout Funds Show Longest Holding Periods in 2 Decades," S&P Global, November 22,

2023, https://www.spglobal.com/marketintelligence/en/news-insights/latest-news-headlines/private-equity-buyout-funds-show-longest-holding-periods-in-2-decades-79033309.

xx *A 2019 paper found:* Steven J. Davis, John C. Haltiwanger, Kyle Handley, Ben Lipsius, Josh Lerner, and Javier Miranda, "The Economic Effects of Private Equity Buyouts," National Bureau of Economic Research, October 2019, https://www.nber.org/system/files/working_papers/w26371/revisions/w26371.rev0.pdf.

xx *Two finance professors argued:* Brian Ayash and Mahdi Rastad, "The Economic Effects of Private Equity Buyouts: A Comment," S&P Global Market Intelligence, November 1, 2019, http://dx.doi.org/10.2139/ssrn.3479467.

xx *Researchers found:* Brian Ayash and Mahdi Rastad, "Leveraged Buyouts and Financial Distress," *Financial Research Letters,* July 20, 2019, http://dx.doi.org/10.2139/ssrn.3423290.

xxi *Even Berle and Means:* Appelbaum and Batt, *Private Equity at Work,* 46.

xxi *"The manager of such a corporation":* Friedman, "A Friedman Doctrine."

xxii *"When [private equity]":* Feldman and Kenney, *Private Equity and the Demise of the Local,* 30.

ONE: LIZ

6 *Charles Lazarus:* The sections of this chapter about Charles Lazarus are drawn from an unpublished 2010 video interview with filmmaker Mark Aaron.

7 *Until the war:* Marc Fisher, "Chevy Chase, 1916: For Everyman, a New Lot in Life," *Washington Post,* February 14, 1999, https://www.washingtonpost.com/archive/politics/1999/02/15/chevy-chase-1916-for-everyman-a-new-lot-in-life/b59d9130-b374-4337-b784-f22f0960c653/.

8 *These big department stores:* Robert Spector, *Category Killers: The Retail Revolution and Its Impact on Consumer Culture* (Brighton, MA: Harvard Business Review Press, 2005), 12.

12 *a 1937 federal law:* "Resale Price Maintenance: The Miller-Tydings Enabling Act," *Harvard Law Review* 51, no. 2 (1937): 336–45, doi.org/10.2307/1334229.

12 *A 1962* Time *magazine cover:* "Retailing: Everybody Loves a Bargain," *Time,* July 6, 1962, https://time.com/archive/6873143/retailing-everybody-loves-a-bargain/.

13 *The infusion of cash:* Isadore Barmash, "Interstate Stores Tries Surgery for Survival," *New York Times,* August 3, 1974, https://www.nytimes.com/1974/08/03/archives/interstate-stores-tries-surgery-for-survival-surgery-is-tried-for.html.

13 *The company went bankrupt:* Barmash.

14 *Four years later:* Robert Metz, "Market Place," *New York Times,* March 12, 1976, https://www.nytimes.com/1976/03/12/archives/market-place-money-funds-weather-stock-surge.html.

14 *The company had been around:* Tracie Rozhon and Andrew Ross Sorkin, "Three Firms Are Said to Buy Toys 'R' Us for $6 Billion," *New York Times,* March 17, 2005, https://www.nytimes.com/2005/03/17/business/three-firms-are-said-to-buy-toys-r-us-for-6-billion.html.

14 *"All of retail"*: Nanette Byrnes, "Toy Story," Bloomberg, December 4, 2000, https://www.bloomberg.com/news/articles/2000-12-03/toy-story.

15 *The rent, meanwhile*: Charles V Bagli, "Toys 'R' Us to Build the Biggest Store in Times Sq.," *New York Times*, August 2, 2000, https://www.nytimes.com /2000/08/02/nyregion/toys-r-us-to-build-the-biggest-store-in-times-sq.html.

15 *Founded in 1994*: George Anders, "Amazon.com Unveils Plans to Open Two More 'Stores' on Its Web Site," *Wall Street Journal*, July 13, 1999, https://www.wsj .com/articles/SB931823473942188601.

16 *The retailer limped*: Parija Bhatnagar, "A Christmas Letdown," CNN, December 31, 2003, https://money.cnn.com/2003/12/31/news/companies/holiday_losers /index.htm.

16 *Toys R Us still controlled*: Rozhon and Sorkin, "Three Firms Are Said to Buy Toys 'R' Us for $6 Billion."

17 *"The inclusion"*: Joseph Pereira, Henny Sender, and Ray A. Smith, "Toys 'R' Us Narrows Suitors to Four," *Wall Street Journal*, March 1, 2005, https://www.wsj .com/articles/SB110964806953366810.

17 *KKR teamed up*: Rozhon and Sorkin, "Three Firms Are Said to Buy Toys 'R' Us for $6 Billion."

TWO: ROGER

23 *When Uncle Austin*: Paul Starr, *The Social Transformation of American Medicine* (New York: Basic Books, 1982), 261.

23 *"The doctors escaped"*: Starr, 24–25.

24 *"It is a dangerous device"*: Starr, 253.

24 *"No third party"*: Starr, 299.

25 *"Just think for a moment"*: Starr, 195.

28 *In 1878, the U.S. forcibly assigned*: "The Arapaho Arrive: Two Nations on One Reservation," WyoHistory.org, Wyoming Historical Society, June 23, 2018, https:// www.wyohistory.org/encyclopedia/arapaho-arrive-two-nations-one-reservation.

28 *A nurse and homesteader*: "Notice of Foreclosure," *Riverton Review*, September 17, 1919, https://wyomingnewspapers.org/?a=d&d=WYRTV19190917-01.1.5.

29 *On November 26, 1950*: Mick Pryor with Edward Jones, "#Lookback: Riverton Hospitals," County 10, November 12, 2021, https://county10.com/lookback -riverton-hospitals/.

29 *Riverton's poverty rates*: "Riverton City, Wyoming," U.S. Census Bureau Quick-Facts, accessed October 21, 2024, https://www.census.gov/quickfacts/fact /table/rivertoncitywyoming/HSG010223.

29 *Per capita income*: "Wind River Reservation," Census Reporter, accessed October 21, 2024, https://censusreporter.org/profiles/25200US4610R-wind-river-reservation/.

29 *compared to $77,000*: "Per Capita Personal Income in Wyoming," Federal Reserve Bank of St. Louis, accessed October 21, 2024, https://fred.stlouisfed.org/series/ WYPCPI.

30 *By 1966, the ratio*: Starr, *The Social Transformation of American Medicine*, 358.

31 *They soon did*: "Groups Sign Hospital Lease," *Casper Star-Tribune*, November 11, 1981, https://www.newspapers.com/image/446375407.

31 *"Obviously, HCA has no interest"*: Lutheran Hospitals and Homes Society of America v. Hospital Corporation of America et al. (United States District Court for the District of Wyoming, August 13, 1980).

32 *That was a radically:* "Our History," HCA Healthcare, accessed March 2, 2025, https://hcahealthcare.com/about/our-history.dot.

32 *the ratio of investment:* Greta R. Krippner, "The Financialization of the American Economy," *Socio-Economic Review* 3, no. 2 (2005): 173–208, https://doi.org/10.1093/SER/mwi008.

33 *A decade later:* Starr, *The Social Transformation of American Medicine*, 430.

33 *A key component:* Brett Kelman, "HCA: From Single Hospital to Health Care Behemoth," *Tennessean*, August 16, 2018, https://www.tennessean.com/story/money/industries/health-care/2018/08/16/hca-hospitals-nashville-health-care-company-timeline/986397002/.

33 *In 1986, 46 percent:* R. M. Mullner, R. J. Rydman, D. G. Whiteis, and R. F. Rich, "Rural Community Hospitals and Factors Correlated with Their Risk of Closing," *Public Health Reports* 104, no. 4 (1989): 315–25, https://www.pubmed.ncbi.nlm.nih.gov/2502801.

33 *And although poverty rates:* Mullner et al., 315–25.

34 *Without involvement from a corporation:* "Rural Hospitals: Federal Efforts Should Target Areas Where Closures Would Threaten Access to Care," U.S. Government Accountability Office, February 15, 1991, https://www.gao.gov/products/hrd-91-41.

35 *In 1994, HCA merged:* Bloomberg News, "Company News; Columbia Healthcare-HCA Merger is Completed," *New York Times*, February 11, 1994, https://www.nytimes.com/1994/02/11/business/company-news-columbia-healthcare-hca-merger-is-completed.html.

35 *In March 1997:* Associated Press, "Columbia/HCA Healthcare Says Agents Searched Offices," *New York Times*, March 20, 1997, https://www.nytimes.com/1997/03/20/business/columbia-hca-healthcare-says-agents-searched-offices.html.

36 *More than a dozen:* Kurt Eichenwald, "Whistle-Blower Lawsuits Aim at Big Provider of Health Care," *New York Times*, August 19, 1997, https://www.nytimes.com/1997/08/19/business/whistle-blower-lawsuits-aim-at-big-provider-of-health-care.html.

36 *The allegations included:* Kurt Eichenwald, "U.S. Contends Billing Fraud at Columbia Was 'Systemic,'" *New York Times*, October 7, 1997, https://www.nytimes.com/1997/10/07/business/us-contends-billing-fraud-at-columbia-was-systemic.html.

36 *In 2003, a decade after:* U.S. Department of Justice, "Largest Health Care Fraud Case in U.S. History Settled; HCA Investigation Nets Record Total of $1.7 Billion," press release, June 26, 2003, https://www.justice.gov/archive/opa/pr/2003/June/03_civ_386.htm.

36 *In 1997, HCA's rural hospitals:* "Columbia/HCA Finishes Spinoff of Hospitals," *Journal Record*, May 12, 1999, https://journalrecord.com/1999/05/12/columbiahca-finishes-spinoff-of-hospitals/.

36 *A company SEC filing:* "LifePoint Hospitals, Inc.—Form 10-K," United States Securities and Exchange Commission, accessed September 11, 2023, https://www.sec.gov/Archives/edgar/data/1301611/000095014407000885/g05360e10vk.htm.

38 *To incentivize safe transport:* Mary Childs and Kenny Malone, *Planet Money*, podcast, "Carried Interest Wormhole," NPR, August 12, 2022, https://www.npr.org/2022/08/12/1117305695/carried-interest-wormhole.

38 *Presidents Obama, Trump, and Biden:* Tim Murphy, "Biden and Trump Both Trashed Private Equity's Favorite Tax Dodge. Surprise! It's Still Here," *Mother Jones*, May 2022, https://www.motherjones.com/politics/2022/05/carried-interest-loophole-biden-trump-private-equity-tax-break/.

38 *Victor Fleischer:* Victor Fleischer, "Two and Twenty Revisited: Taxing Carried Interest as Ordinary Income Through Executive Action Instead of Legislation," September 16, 2015, http://dx.doi.org/10.2139/ssrn.2661623.

38 *As the* New Yorker: James Surowiecki, "Private Inequity," *New Yorker*, January 22, 2012, https://www.newyorker.com/magazine/2012/01/30/private-inequity.

38 *That November, a group:* Andrew Ross Sorkin, "HCA Buyout Highlights Era of Going Private," *New York Times*, July 25, 2006, https://www.nytimes.com/2006/07/25/business/25buyout.html.

38 *HCA returned:* Clare Baldwin and Alina Selyukh, "HCA Raises $3.79 Billion in Largest U.S. PE-Backed IPO," Reuters, March 9, 2011, https://www.reuters.com/article/us-hca-idUSTRE7280NV20110309/.

38 *The firms had figured out:* Julie Creswell and Reed Abelson, "A Giant Hospital Chain Is Blazing a Profit Trail," *New York Times*, August 14, 2012, https://www.nytimes.com/2012/08/15/business/hca-giant-hospital-chain-creates-a-windfall-for-private-equity.html.

39 *The same shifts:* "Private Equity Is Piling into Health Care," *Economist*, July 26, 2018, https://www.economist.com/finance-and-economics/2018/07/26/private-equity-is-piling-into-health-care.

39 *The third-largest deal:* Ellie Kincaid, "The Ten Biggest Private Equity Deals in Healthcare in 2018," *Forbes*, December 28, 2018, https://www.forbes.com/sites/elliekincaid/2018/12/28/the-ten-biggest-private-equity-deals-in-healthcare-in-2018/.

THREE: NATALIA

43 *There were three:* "Resurgimiento de El Heraldo de Tampico: Periódico Fantasma en el Norte," Stultifera Navis Institutom, accessed September 29, 2023, https://en.stultiferanavis.institute/resurgimiento-de-el-heraldo-de-tamp.

43 *The newspaper never:* Stultifera Navis Institutom, "Resurgimiento de El Heraldo de Tampico: Periódico Fantasma en el Norte."

44 *Advertising revenue plummeted:* Richard Pérez-Peña, "Papers Facing Worst Year for Ad Revenue," *New York Times*, June 23, 2008, https://www.nytimes.com/2008/06/23/business/media/23paper.html.

44 *That led to layoffs:* Pérez-Peña.

44 *In 2009, the* Baltimore Sun: "Sun Cuts 61 in News," *Baltimore Sun*, April 30, 2009, https://www.baltimoresun.com/news/bs-xpm-2009-04-30-0904290118-story.html.

44 *the parent company:* Keith J. Kelly, "It's Pink-Slip Time," *New York Post*, October 30, 2009, https://nypost.com/2009/10/30/its-pink-slip-time/.

44 *The* Los Angeles Times: Martin Zimmerman, "Times to Lay off 300, Consolidate Sections," *Los Angeles Times*, January 31, 2009, https://www.latimes.com/archives/la-xpm-2009-jan-31-fi-times31-story.html.

44 *In a single week:* Mark Potts, "Death of Almost 1,000 Cuts," Recovering Journalist, June 26, 2008, https://recoveringjournalist.typepad.com/recovering_journalist/2008/06/death-of-almost-1000-cuts.html.

45 *Even the vaunted:* Richard Pérez-Peña, "New York Times Moves to Trim 100 in Newsroom," *New York Times*, October 19, 2009, https://www.nytimes.com/2009/10/20/business/media/20times.html.

45 *Many economists:* "Journalism as a Public Good," UNESCO, accessed October 6, 2023, https://www.unesco.org/reports/world-media-trends/2021/en/journalism-public-good.

46 *For much of the twentieth century:* "We Were Wrong About the Bulletproof Franchise," Warren Buffett Archive, CNBC, May 6, 2006, https://buffett.cnbc.com/video/2006/05/06/2006-weve-got-to-believe-our-eyes.html.

46 *By the start of the twenty-first century:* "The Media Landscape," Federal Communications Commission, accessed October 21, 2024, https://transition.fcc.gov/osp/inc-report/INoC-1-Newspapers.pdf.

46 *Between 1975 and 1990:* Federal Communications Commission, "The Media Landscape."

46 *As recently as the early 2000s:* "Attorney General Approves Denver Rocky Mountain News and the Denver Post Joint Newspaper Operating Arrangement," U.S. Department of Justice, January 5, 2001, https://www.justice.gov/archive/opa/pr/2001/January/005at.htm.

49 *The paper was owned:* Kenneth N. Gilpin, "Scripps to Buy Harte-Hanks Media Assets," *New York Times*, May 20, 1997, https://www.nytimes.com/1997/05/20/business/scripps-to-buy-harte-hanks-media-assets.html.

49 *Scripps wasn't a big player:* "The Rise of a New Media Baron," UNC Hussman School of Journalism and Media, accessed October 11, 2023, https://newspaperownership.com/new-media-barons/.

49 *By 2008, the year before:* Federal Communications Commission, "The Media Landscape."

53 *Employment and classified ads:* Carolyn Micheli, "Scripps Reports Second-Quarter 2013 Results," Scripps, August 2, 2013, https://scripps.com/press-releases/893-scripps-reports-second-quarter-2013-results/.

53 *The fact that many journalists:* Lee Bernard Becker, Tudor Vlad, and Holly Anne Simpson, "2013 Annual Survey of Journalism Mass Communication Graduates: Enrollments Decline for Third Consecutive Year," *Journalism & Mass Communication Educator* 69, no. 4 (2014): 349–56, https://doi.org/10.1177/1077695814555432.

53 *the median entry-level salary:* Becker, Vlad, and Simpson.

53 *Overall revenue from Scripps's:* "2013 Annual Report," E. W. Scripps Company, accessed October 29, 2024, https://ir.scripps.com/static-files/7c76aaf4-7e2f-4c96 -9e91-f0a516c9b8fb.

53 *"During the past five years":* Scripps, "2013 Annual Report."

54 *In a press release:* Michael J. De La Merced, "E. W. Scripps and Journal Communica- tions to Merge, Then Spin Off Newspapers," *New York Times,* July 31, 2014, https:// dealbook.nytimes.com/2014/07/31/e-w-scripps-and-journal-communications-to -merge-then-spin-off-newspapers/.

54 *"The persistent financial demands":* David Carr, "Print Is Down, and Now Out," *New York Times,* August 10, 2014, https://www.nytimes.com/2014/08/11/business /media/media-companies-spin-off-newspapers-to-uncertain-futures.html.

55 *In April 2015:* Scripps, "E. W. Scripps Company Completes Merger, Spinoff Trans- action with Journal Communications," press release, April 1, 2015, https:// scripps.com/press-releases/873-ew-scripps-company-completes-merger-spinoff -transaction-with-journal-communications/.

55 *The move was part:* Carr, "Print Is Down, and Now Out."

55 Time *magazine dubbed him:* "The Press: The Chain That Isn't," *Time,* December 16, 1957, https://content.time.com/time/subscriber/article/0,33009,893804-2,00 .html.

55 *Tegna even got:* Christine Haughney and Michael J. De La Merced, "Gannett, Owner of USA Today, to Split Its Print and Broadcast Businesses," *New York Times,* August 5, 2014, https://dealbook.nytimes.com/2014/08/05/gannett-to -spin-off-its-print-business/.

56 *That October, the company:* Dana Cimilluca and Keach Hagey, "Gannett Reaches Deal to Buy Journal Media," *Wall Street Journal,* October 7, 2015, http://www .wsj.com/articles/gannett-nears-deal-to-buy-journal-media-1444252694.

56 *In a press release:* "Gannett to Acquire Journal Media Group for $12.00 per Share," Business Wire, October 7, 2015, https://www.businesswire.com/news /home/20151007006588/en/Gannett-to-Acquire-Journal-Media-Group-for -12.00-per-share.

56 *He took a special interest:* Ben Bagdikian, *The Media Monopoly* (Boston: Beacon Press, 1983), 67.

57 *Between 1966 and 1980:* Bagdikian, 84.

57 *Many began relying:* Bagdikian, 83.

57 *"The highest levels":* Bagdikian, 21.

FOUR: LOREN

61 *Shaul Kuba:* Peter Waldman, "An Entire Neighborhood Is Being Flipped by a Los Angeles Developer," Bloomberg, April 27, 2022, https://www.bloomberg .com/news/features/2022-04-27/gentrification-battle-comes-to-los-angeles -neighborhood.

61 *One day they happened to:* Stuart Pfeifer and David Zahniser, "CIM Lands in Pension-Fund Spotlight," *Los Angeles Times,* December 26, 2009, https://www .latimes.com/archives/la-xpm-2009-dec-26-la-fi-calpers-cim26-2009dec26-story .html.

61 *Like his older brother:* Bryan Burrough and John Helyar, *Barbarians at the Gate* (New York: Harper & Row, 1989), 140.

61 *But the scandal didn't taint:* Lawrence Delevingne, "Where Are They Now? The Drexel Alumni 25 Years Later," CNBC, February 13, 2015, https://www.cnbc.com/2015/02/13/where-are-they-now-the-drexel-alumni-25-years-later.html.

62 *They called their company:* Pfeifer and Zahniser, "CIM Lands in Pension-Fund Spotlight."

62 *In the early days:* Ronald W. Powell, "A Gaslamp Squeeze," *San Diego Union-Tribune*, April 10, 1998, https://advance.lexis.com/api/document?collection=news&id=urn:contentItem:4P7G-PYM0-TWDC-M4FK-00000-00&context=1519360.

62 *CIM had recently:* Jesus Sanchez, "Firm Building on Hollywood Revival," *Los Angeles Times*, August 3, 1999, https://www.latimes.com/archives/la-xpm-1999-aug-03-fi-62161-story.html.

62 *Crucially, those projects:* Pfeifer and Zahniser, "CIM Lands in Pension-Fund Spotlight."

62 *For the first six years:* Joel Chernoff, "Staff Bypassed: CalPERS Commits to Urban Real Estate Fund," *Pensions & Investments*, October 2, 2000, https://www.pionline.com/article/20001002/PRINT/10020729/staff-bypassed-calpers-commits-to-urban-real-estate-fund.

62 *Pensions are a key source:* Vrinda Mittal, "Desperate Capital Breeds Productivity Loss: Evidence from Public Pension Investments in Private Equity," Wharton Research Data Services, July 13, 2024, http://dx.doi.org/10.2139/ssrn.4283853.

63 *Many funds don't come close:* "Investing in Today to Meet the Needs of Our Members Tomorrow," California Public Employees' Retirement System, November 17, 2023, https://www.calpers.ca.gov/docs/forms-publications/acfr-2023.pdf.

63 *While a 2022 report:* "Private Equity Delivers the Strongest Returns for Retirees Across America," American Investment Council, July 2022, https://www.investmentcouncil.org/wp-content/uploads/2022/07/22AIC002_2022-Report_SA-2226.pdf.

63 *SEC "Risk Alert":* "Observations from Examinations of Private Fund Advisers," U.S. Securities and Exchange Commission, January 27, 2022, https://www.sec.gov/files/private-fund-risk-alert-pt-2.pdf.

63 *Initially, CalPERS's board balked:* Philip Boroff, "Who Makes Up CalPERS' Mind?," Bloomberg News, June 18, 2000, https://advance.lexis.com/api/document?collection=news&id=urn:contentItem:40MT-2K10-00SH-22S4-00000-00&context=1519360.

63 *Three months later:* Joel Chernoff, "Staff Bypassed: CalPERS Commits to Urban Real Estate Fund."

63 *Villalobos was later indicted:* U.S. Attorney's Office, Northern District of California, "Placement Agent Charged with Bribery in CalPERS Corruption Conspiracy," press release, August 7, 2014, https://www.justice.gov/usao-ndca/pr/placement-agent-charged-bribery-calpers-corruption-conspiracy.

63 *All the while, CalPERS:* Stuart Pfeifer and David Zahniser, "CIM Lands in Pension-Fund Spotlight."

63 *CIM bought Chicago's:* Alaina Griffin, "SCB Converts Chicago's Tribune Tower and Surrounding Media Complex into Luxury Residences," *Architect's Newspaper,* February 22, 2023, https://www.archpaper.com/2023/02/scb-converts-chicago-tribune-tower-and-surrounding-media-complex-into-luxury-residences/.

63 *It bought Jack London Square:* CIM Group, "CIM Group Completes Construction of Channel House Apartment Building at Jack London Square," press release, March 4, 2021, https://www.cimgroup.com/press-releases/cim-group-completes-construction-of-channel-house-apartment-building-at-jack-london-square.

63 *It developed Manhattan's:* Stefanos Chen, "Residents of Troubled Supertall Tower Seek $125 Million in Damages," *New York Times,* September 23, 2021, https://www.nytimes.com/2021/09/23/realestate/432-park-avenue-lawsuit.html.

64 *It also became a go-to partner:* Andrea Bernstein and Ilya Marritz, "Trump and Kushner's Little-Known Business Partner," WNYC News, May 25, 2017, https://www.wnyc.org/story/trump-kushner-little-known-business-partner/.

64 *Often, CIM developments:* CIM Group (@cimgroup), "CIM is a community-focused real estate and infrastructure owner, operator, lender and developer. Since 1994, we have qualified more than 120 thriving and transitional urban communities and invested in more than 70. Our first projects were in urban, southern California communities. Our reach has since expanded to communities of all sizes across the Americas, but enhancing urban communities is still integral to our purpose. Swipe right to learn more about our community focused work. #CIM #CIMGroup #EnhancingCommunities #CoreValues #Commuity #Discipline #CommunityRealEstate," Instagram photo, September 9, 2020, https://www.instagram.com/tv/CE7a9_Kj1g0/.

64 *In CIM's hometown:* Waldman, "An Entire Neighborhood Is Being Flipped by a Los Angeles Developer."

67 *She also wanted:* "Rhode Island Population by Race and Hispanic or Latino Origin, 2000–2010," Rhode Island Statewide Planning, accessed October 21, 2024, https://planning.ri.gov/sites/g/files/xkgbur826/files/documents/census/race_ethnicity/race_ethnicity_2000-2010.pdf.

68 *Home prices fell:* Michele Lerner, "10 Years Later: How the Housing Market Has Changed Since the Crash," *Washington Post,* October 4, 2018, https://www.washingtonpost.com/news/business/wp/2018/10/04/feature/10-years-later-how-the-housing-market-has-changed-since-the-crash/.

69 *The origins of the companies:* "A Brief History of the Housing Government-Sponsored Enterprises," Federal Home Finance Agency Office of Inspector General, accessed October 21, 2024, https://www.fhfaoig.gov/Content/Files/History%20of%20the%20Government%20Sponsored%20Enterprises.pdf.

69 *In at least one year:* Heather Vogell, "When Private Equity Becomes Your Landlord," ProPublica, February 7, 2022, https://www.propublica.org/article/when-private-equity-becomes-your-landlord.

69 *In 2017, private equity firm Greystar:* "NMHC 50 Largest Apartment Managers," National Multifamily Housing Council, accessed March 7, 2024, https://www.nmhc.org/research-insight/the-nmhc-50/top-50-lists/2023-top-managers-list/.

69 *And while federal law:* "12 U.S. Code § 4563—Multifamily Special Affordable Housing Goal," Cornell Law School, accessed March 7, 2024, https://www.law.cornell.edu/uscode/text/12/4563.

70 *By 2021, private equity firms were backing:* Vogell, "When Private Equity Becomes Your Landlord."

70 *In 2022, institutional investors:* Laurie Goodman, Amalie Zinn, Kathryn Reynolds, and Owen Noble, "A Profile of Institutional Investor–Owned Single-Family Rental Properties," Housing Finance Policy Center, April 2023, https://www.urban.org/sites/default/files/2023-08/A%20Profile%20of%20Institutional%20Investor%E2%80%93Owned%20Single-Family%20Rental%20Properties.pdf.

70 *Some 72,000 homes:* Brian Eason and John Perry, "American Dream for Rent: Investors Elbow Out Individual Home Buyers," *Atlanta Journal-Constitution*, February 9, 2023, https://www.ajc.com/american-dream/investor-owned-houses-atlanta/.

70 *One researcher found:* Brian An, "The Influence of Institutional Single-Family Investors on Homeownership: Who Gets Targeted and Pushed Out of the Local Market?," *Journal of Planning Education and Research*, March 21, 2023, http://dx.doi.org/10.2139/ssrn.4156851.

70 *More than 20 million:* "Factory-Built Housing for Affordability, Efficiency, and Resilience," Office of Policy Development and Research, accessed March 7, 2024, https://www.huduser.gov/portal/periodicals/em/WinterSpring20/highlight1.html.

71 *This recipe has made:* Julie Reynolds Martínez, "First They Came for the Newspapers. Then for Mobile Home Parks," Voices of Monterey Bay, September 25, 2022, https://voicesofmontereybay.org/2022/09/25/boundless-greed-first-they-came-for-the-newspapers-then-for-mobile-home-parks/.

71 *Most infamously, Frank Rolfe:* Anthony Effinger and Katherine Burton, "Goldman Alum Gives Up Funds to Become Trailer-Park Mogul," Bloomberg, April 10, 2014, https://www.bloomberg.com/news/articles/2014-04-10/trailer-parks-lure-investors-pursuing-double-wide-returns.

71 *Blackstone, which is:* Frank Cohen, A. J. Agarwal, Wesley LePatner, and Brian Kim, "2022 Year-End Stockholder Letter," Blackstone, January 26, 2023, https://www.breit.com/2022-year-end-stockholder-letter/.

71 *The firm has also poured:* Jordan Ash, "Helter Shelter," Private Equity Stakeholder Project, July 2024, p. 10, https://pestakeholder.org/wp-content/uploads/2024/07/PESP_Report_Helter_Shelter_2024.pdf.

71 *In 2019, a United Nations committee:* "Letter to Blackstone CEO from the UN Special Rapporteur on the right to adequate housing & UN Working Group on Business & Human Rights," Business & Human Rights Resource Centre, April 16, 2019, https://www.business-humanrights.org/en/latest-news/letter-to-blackstone-ceo-from-the-un-special-rapporteur-on-the-right-to-adequate-housing-un-working-group-on-business-human-rights/.

72 *710 units in Denver:* CIM Group, "CIM Group Acquires One of Denver's Largest Multifamily Properties The Lex at Lowry, a 710-Unit Apartment and Townhome Community," press release, June 30, 2021, https://cimgroup.com/press-releases

/cim-group-acquires-one-of-denvers-largest-multifamily-properties-the-lex-at
-lowry-a-710-unit-apartment-and-townhome-community.

72　*1,012 in Phoenix:* CIM Group, "CIM Group and Tides Equities Acquire Largest
Market Rate Apartment Community in Phoenix," press release, March 1, 2022,
https://cimgroup.com/press-releases/cim-group-and-tides-equities-acquire
-largest-market-rate-apartment-community-in-phoenix.

72　*301 in Washington, D.C.:* CIM Group, "CIM Group Expands Washington, D.C.
Multifamily Portfolio with Acquisition of The Vale, a Newly Constructed Apartment Community," press release, July 28, 2021, https://www.cimgroup.com
/press-releases/cim-group-expands-washington-d-c-multifamily-portfolio-with
-acquisition-of-the-vale-a-newly-constructed-apartment-community.

72　*In 2020, CIM paid:* Bryce Meyers, "Southern Towers Trades in Largest Apartment
Deal in DC-Area History," CoStar, August 25, 2020, https://www.costar.com
/article/1458874870/southern-towers-trades-in-largest-apartment-deal-in-dc
-area-history.

72　*$346 million:* Alex Nicoll, "A Band of Immigrant Tenants Went to War with Their
$31 Billion Landlord. It's a Sneak Peek at What's to Come Across America," *Busi-
ness Insider*, December 27, 2022, https://www.businessinsider.com/southern
-towers-apartment-tenants-battle-investor-landlord-2022-11.

FIVE: LIZ

79　*"You don't report":* Emily Stewart, "What Is Private Equity, and Why Is It Killing
Everything You Love?" Vox, January 6, 2020, https://www.vox.com/the-goods
/2020/1/6/21024740/private-equity-taylor-swift-toys-r-us-elizabeth-warren.

80　*Three percent of the average:* Jonathan Harvey, Helen Lucas, and Kate Gribbon,
"Private Equity Trends 2024," Investec, accessed October 21, 2024, https://
www.investec.com/content/dam/gated-content-assets/uk/focus/pe-trends
-report-2024.pdf.

80　*An oft-cited 2009 paper:* Andrew Metrick and Ayako Yasuda, "The Economics
of Private Equity Funds," *Review of Financial Studies* 23, no. 6 (2010): 2303–41,
https://doi.org/10.1093/rfs/hhq020.

80　*Former private equity executive:* Jeffrey C. Hooke, *The Myth of Private Equity* (New
York: Columbia Business School Publishing, 2021), 122.

81　*Kravis kept a framed:* Loomis, "Buyout Kings."

82　*"All the risk":* Dealbook, "Romney's Presidential Run Puts Spotlight on Bain Capital," *New York Times*, June 4, 2007, https://archive.nytimes.com/dealbook.nytimes
.com/2007/06/04/romneys-presidential-run-throws-spotlight-on-bain-capital/.

84　*KKR, Bain Capital, and Vornado:* Dan Primack, "Toys 'R' Us Not a Total Loss
for Private Equity Fund Managers," Axios, October 5, 2017, https://www
.axios.com/2017/12/15/toys-r-us-not-a-total-loss-for-private-equity-fund
-managers-1513305992.

84　*When a private equity fund:* Appelbaum and Batt, *Private Equity at Work*, 3.

85　*"If they didn't have":* Matt Levine, "Retail Bankruptcy and Insider Trading,"
Bloomberg, September 20, 2017, https://www.bloomberg.com/opinion
/articles/2017-09-20/retail-bankruptcy-and-insider-trading.

86 *Within a few months:* "Toys Master Lease Agreements May Create Intercompany Complexities for Right-Sizing Operations, Restructuring Efforts," Reorg, October 19, 2017, accessed October 21, 2024, https://www.reorg.com/articles/toys-master-lease-agreements-may-create-intercompany-complexities-for-right-sizing-operations-restructuring-efforts/.

90 *only the specialists:* U.S. Securities and Exchange Commission, "Toys 'R' Us, Inc. Announces Agreement to be Acquired by KKR, Bain Capital and Vornado for $26.75 Per Share in $6.6 Billion Transaction," press release, March 17, 2005, https://www.sec.gov/Archives/edgar/data/1005414/000119312505057773/dex991.htm.

90 *By 2021, those averaged:* "Our Facilities," Amazon, accessed October 21, 2024, https://www.aboutamazon.com/workplace/facilities.

90 *That strategy allowed:* Ashley Gale, "After a Woman's Dog Died, Pet Company Chewy Sent Her Flowers and a Card," *Newsweek*, June 16, 2022, https://www.newsweek.com/after-womans-dog-died-pet-company-chewy-sent-her-flowers-card-1716712.

91 *The only penalty:* Martin Wolk, "Toys 'R' Us Wins Suit Against Amazon.com," NBC News, March 2, 2006, https://www.nbcnews.com/id/wbna11641703.

92 *Two researchers later found:* Jamie Morgan and Muhammad Ali Nasir, "Financialised Private Equity Finance and the Debt Gamble: The Case of Toys R Us," *New Political Economy* 26, no. 3 (2020): 455–71, https://doi.org/10.1080/13563467.2020.1782366.

92 *Overall, the retail sector added:* Jim Baker, Maggie Corser, and Eli Vitulli, "Pirate Equity: How Wall Street Firms Are Pillaging American Retail," United for Respect, July 2019, https://united4respect.org/wp-content/uploads/2019/07/Pirate-Equity-How-Wall-Street-Firms-are-Pillaging-American-Retail-July-2019.pdf.

95 *Companies acquired:* Ayash and Rastad, "Leveraged Buyouts and Financial Distress."

95 *retail chains:* James Nani, "Repeat Chapter 11 Filers Dominate 2023 Bankruptcy Landscape," Bloomberg Law, January 10, 2024, https://news.bloomberglaw.com/bankruptcy-law/repeat-chapter-11-filers-dominate-2023-bankruptcy-landscape.

95 *Meanwhile, studies have found:* Ayash and Rastad, "Leveraged Buyouts and Financial Distress."

95 *Private equity–owned chains:* Baker, Corser, and Vitulli, "Pirate Equity."

96 *KKR, Bain, and Vornado:* Ben Unglesbee, "How Toys R Us' Bankruptcy Hopes Came Crashing Down," Retail Dive, March 15, 2018, https://www.retaildive.com/news/how-toys-r-us-bankruptcy-hopes-came-crashing-down/519230/.

98 *Headlines bemoaned:* Nathan Vardi, "The Big Investment Firms That Lost $1.3 Billion in the Toys 'R' Us Bankruptcy," *Forbes*, September 19, 2017, https://www.forbes.com/sites/nathanvardi/2017/09/19/the-big-investment-firms-that-lost-1-3-billion-on-the-toys-r-us-bankruptcy/.

98 *And that doesn't include:* Primack, "Toys 'R' Us Not a Total Loss for Private Equity Fund Managers."

SIX: ROGER

103 *University of California, Berkeley:* Richard M. Scheffler, Daniel R. Arnold, and
     Christopher M. Whaley, "Consolidation Trends in California's Health Care Sys-
     tem: Impacts On ACA Premiums And Outpatient Visit Prices," *Health Affairs* 37,
     no. 9 (2018): 1409–16, http://dx.doi.org/10.1377/hlthaff.2018.0472.

103 *In the New Haven area:* Reed Abelson, "When Hospitals Merge to Save Money,
     Patients Often Pay More," *New York Times*, November 14, 2018, https://www
     .nytimes.com/2018/11/14/health/hospital-mergers-health-care-spending.html.

103 *The commission in charge:* "Report to the Congress: Medicare Payment Policy,"
     Medicare Payment Advisory Commission, March 2020, https://www.medpac
     .gov/wp-content/uploads/import_data/scrape_files/docs/default-source
     /reports/mar20_entirereport_sec.pdf.

103 *Biden's executive order:* "Rural Hospital Closures: Affected Residents Had Reduced
     Access to Health Care Services," U.S. Government Accountability Office, De-
     cember 2020, https://www.gao.gov/assets/gao-21-93.pdf.

103 *In addition, they wrote:* Caitlin Carroll, Rhiannon Euhus, Nancy Beaulieu, and Mi-
     chael E. Chernew, "Hospital Survival in Rural Markets: Closures, Mergers, and
     Profitability," *Health Affairs* 42, no. 4 (2023): 498–507, https://doi.org/10.1377
     /hlthaff.2022.01191.

104 *Lander Regional Medical Center:* "Hospital Provider Cost Report," Centers for
     Medicare & Medicaid Services, accessed November 6, 2023, https://data.cms
     .gov/provider-compliance/cost-report/hospital-provider-cost-report/data/2013.

104 *In 2015, the first full year:* Centers for Medicare & Medicaid Services, "Hospital
     Provider Cost Report."

104 *"There's no way":* Wyoming News Exchange, "Riverton Hospital Will Not Re-
     open OB Unit as Planned," *Casper Star-Tribune*, June 18, 2018, https://trib.com
     /news/state-and-regional/riverton-hospital-will-not-reopen-ob-unit-as-planned
     /article_a0bd1b39-075f-5754-9c29-a4bcad405762.html.

105 *Medicaid reimburses:* "The Cost of Having a Baby in the United States," National
     Partnership, January 2013, https://nationalpartnership.org/wp-content/uploads
     /2023/02/the-cost-of-having-a-baby-in-the-us.pdf.

105 *A study in Louisiana:* Maeve Wallace, Lauren Dyer, Erica Felker-Kantor, Jia Benno,
     Dovile Vilda, Emily Harville, and Katherine Theall, "Maternity Care Deserts and
     Pregnancy-Associated Mortality in Louisiana," *Women's Health Issues* 31, no. 2
     (2021): 122–29, https://doi.org/10.1016/j.whi.2020.09.004.

105 *Fewer than half:* Claire Rush and Laura Ungar, "Rural Hospitals Are Closing
     Maternity Wards. People Are Seeking Options to Give Birth Closer to Home,"
     Associated Press, September 17, 2023, https://apnews.com/article/birthing
     -rural-hospitals-maternity-care-births-e67a91d927eb545459e83bc7b2b95a0d.

105 *Today, SageWest Lander employs:* "Find a Provider," SageWest Health Care, ac-
     cessed November 3, 2024, https://www.sagewesthealthcare.com/find-a-doctor/
     results?query=obstetrics.

106 *LifePoint CEO:* Paige Minemyer, "LifePoint Health, RCCH HealthCare Part-
     ners Announce Merger Plans," Fierce Healthcare, July 23, 2018, https://www

.fiercehealthcare.com/hospitals-health-systems/lifepoint-health-rcch-healthcare
-partners-announce-merger-plans.

106 *The acquisition wasn't:* Allison Prang, "LifePoint Health Agrees to Apollo Buyout," *Wall Street Journal*, July 23, 2018, https://www.wsj.com/articles/lifepoint
-health-agrees-to-apollo-buyout-1532347207.

107 *In 2018, the year LifePoint:* Bain & Company, "Healthcare Private Equity Delivers
Another Banner Year with Deal Values Surging by Almost Half to $63.1 Billion,"
press release, April 17, 2019, https://www.bain.com/about/media-center
/press-releases/2019/healthcare-private-equity-report/.

107 *Total spending on health care:* Joshua Barrett and Zoey Kernodle, "Private Equity
in Healthcare: Exploring the Challenges and Opportunities," Center for the
Business of Health, June 2023, https://cboh.unc.edu/wp-content/uploads
/2023/07/Private-Equity-in-Healthcare-07062023.pdf.

107 *The largest, KKR's buyout:* Kincaid, "The Ten Biggest Private Equity Deals in
Healthcare in 2018."

107 *Now the new company:* Jonathan Schwarzberg, "Apollo Extends Olive Branch to
Investors on LifePoint Loan," Reuters, November 16, 2018, https://www.reuters
.com/article/lifepoint-loan-idUSL2N1XR0R9.

108 *They found that on average:* Chapin White and Christopher M. Whaley, "Prices
Paid to Hospitals by Private Health Plans Are High Relative to Medicare and Vary
Widely: Findings from an Employer-Led Transparency Initiative," RAND Corporation, May 9, 2019, https://www.rand.org/pubs/research_reports/RR3033
.html.

108 *When the researchers:* Seth Klamann, "Hospitals in Wyoming Charging Significantly More than Medicare, National Study Finds," *Casper Star-Tribune*, June
10, 2019, https://trib.com/news/state-and-regional/govt-and-politics/health
/hospitals-in-wyoming-charging-significantly-more-than-medicare-national
-study/article_0ee7ea88-0964-596c-8cfd-6581e726367a.html.

108 *Data from 2020:* "Sage Transparency," Sage Transparency, accessed November 6,
2023, https://dashboard.sagetransparency.org/

108 *An administrator:* Seth Klamann, "Eastern Shoshone Tribe Accuses SageWest
Health of Overcharging Tribal Members to Inflate Profits," *Casper Star-Tribune*,
January 12, 2019, https://trib.com/news/local/govt-and-politics/eastern
-shoshone-tribe-accuses-sagewest-health-of-overcharging-tribal-members-to
-inflate-profits/article_cb2ca173-d2b4-5505-bd66-83101702b77e.html.

108 *By 2022, the last year:* Centers for Medicare & Medicaid Services, "Hospital Provider Cost Report."

109 *Roughly 7 out of 10 patients:* Seth Klamann, "Eastern Shoshone Decry Closure
of Lander Mental Health Unit," *Casper Star-Tribune*, April 24, 2019, https://
trib.com/news/state-and-regional/govt-and-politics/health/eastern-shoshone
-decry-closure-of-lander-mental-health-unit/article_96ad5c6b-ea1d-573d-b480
-c3d2f2b91ba8.html.

109 *SageWest CEO:* Seth Klamann, "Fremont County Hospital Group Confirms It
Will Close Lander Mental Health Unit," *Casper Star-Tribune*, February 21, 2019,
https://trib.com/news/state-and-regional/govt-and-politics/health/fremont

-county-hospital-group-confirms-it-will-close-lander-mental-health-unit
/article_844e50f6-1edb-56a4-9524-9c43865516f7.html.

109 *After Riverton's maternity ward:* SageWest Health Care, "Find a Provider."

110 *In November 2019, LifePoint:* Eileen O'Grady, "Private Equity Firms Reap Payouts After Hospital Chain Received $1.6 Billion in CARES Act Support," Private
Equity Stakeholder Project, September 2021, https://pestakeholder.org/wp
-content/uploads/2021/09/Apollo_Kindred_Lifepoint_PESP_September-2021
.pdf.

110 *SageWest's press release:* "SageWest Responds to Sale of Hospital Real Estate
to MPT," WyoToday, November 21, 2019, https://wyotoday.com/sagewest
-responds-to-sale-of-hospital-real-estate-to-mpt/.

110 *Medical Properties Trust, a publicly traded:* Brian Spegele, "How a Small Alabama
Company Fueled Private Equity's Push into Hospitals," *Wall Street Journal*, February 14, 2022, https://www.wsj.com/articles/hospitals-private-equity-reit-mpt
-steward-11644849598.

110 *major private equity players:* Spegele.

110 *real estate investment trusts:* Rosemary Batt and Eileen Appelbaum, with Tamar
Katz, "The Role of Public REITs in Financialization and Industry Restructuring,"
Institute for New Economic Thinking, July 9, 2022, https://www.ineteconomics
.org/uploads/papers/WP_189-Batt-Appelbaum-Public-REITS-2.pdf.

111 *But a month later:* Sabrina Willmer, "Private Equity Powerhouse Books $1.6 Bil-
lion Profit Selling Hospital Chain—to Itself," Bloomberg, July 29, 2021, https://
www.bloomberg.com/news/articles/2021-07-29/apollo-books-1-6-billion-gain
-selling-hospital-chain-to-itself.

111 *Soon after, LifePoint spun off:* Dave Muoio, "LifePoint Health to Create New
79-Hospital Company upon Close of Kindred Healthcare Acquisition," October 27, 2021, https://www.fiercehealthcare.com/hospitals/scionhealth-lifepoint
-health-to-create-new-79-hospital-company-upon-close-kindred.

114 *"If we acquiesce":* Joshua Wolfson, "Concerned About Hospital, Riverton Residents Band Together to Push for Changes," *Casper Star-Tribune*, August 29, 2018,
https://trib.com/news/state-and-regional/concerned-about-hospital-riverton
-residents-band-together-to-push-for-changes/article_a407af75-8604-521d-a68a
-fd8782f4ea09.html.

114 *SageWest was operating:* Amanda Gaudern, "Breaking: SageWest CEO Announces
Intentions for Riverton Hospital," County 10, September 7, 2018, https://
county10.com/breaking-sagewest-ceo-announces-intentions-for-riverton
-hospital/.

114 *Centers for Medicare:* Centers for Medicare & Medicaid Services, "Hospital Provider Cost Report."

115 *In 2020, a study:* Joseph D. Bruch, Suhas Gondi, and Zirui Song, "Changes in
Hospital Income, Use, and Quality Associated with Private Equity Acquisition,"
JAMA Internal Medicine 180, no. 11 (2020): 1428–35, https://jamanetwork.com
/journals/jamainternalmedicine/article-abstract/2769549.

115 *"We have to decide":* Shelby Livingston, "Surge in Private Equity Deals Causes
Some Alarm," Modern Healthcare, June 16, 2018, https://www.modernhealthcare

.com/article/20180616/NEWS/180619918/surge-in-private-equity-deals-causes
-some-alarm.

115 *Then, in late 2023, a landmark study:* Sneha Kannan, Joseph Dov Bruch, and Zirui
Song, "Changes in Hospital Adverse Events and Patient Outcomes Associated
with Private Equity Acquisition," *JAMA* 330, no. 24 (2023): 2365–75, https://
jamanetwork.com/journals/jama/fullarticle/2813379.

116 *Data from the Wyoming Department of Health:* Brian Spegele, "A City's Only Hospital Cut Services. How Locals Fought Back," *Wall Street Journal*, April 11, 2021,
https://www.wsj.com/articles/a-citys-only-hospital-cut-services-how-locals
-fought-back-11618133400.

116 *According to the state health department:* Carrie Haderlie, "State Tries to Tackle
Air Ambulance Problem," *Wyoming Business Report*, December 30, 2019,
https://www.wyomingnews.com/wbr/current_edition/state-tries-to-tackle-air
-ambulance-problem/article_3b4500cf-cebc-5da0-b2c2-3ba8bf8fdaa2.html.

116 *He also caused:* "Wyoming Health Survey," Wyoming Department of Health,
accessed October 15, 2024, https://ohlssurvey.health.wyo.gov/NonSecure
/PublicDisplay.aspx?SurveyId=7814.

116 *The woman died:* Vince Tropea, "Family of Eye Gouging Victim Files Lawsuit
Against Hospital," County 10, July 28, 2021, https://county10.com/family-of
-eye-gouging-victim-files-lawsuit-against-hospital/.

117 *"It had been known":* "Amended Complaint–Document #24 in Tillman v. Riverton
Memorial Hospital LLC (D. Wyo., 2:21-cv-00138)," CourtListener, accessed October 15, 2024, https://www.courtlistener.com/docket/60069124/24/tillman-v
-riverton-memorial-hospital-llc/.

SEVEN: NATALIA

121 *A masthead:* "Staff Directory," *Corpus Christi Caller-Times*, archived December 20,
2017, https://web.archive.org/web/20171220002441/https://www.caller.com
/contact/staff/.

121 *Gannett's rival GateHouse Media:* "List of Publications of GateHouse Media,
Inc.," accessed October 25, 2023, https://www.sec.gov/Archives/edgar/data
/1579684/000119312513380897/d603516dex992.htm.

122 *"They are very, very good":* "Big News—but Fewer Owners," *Chicago Tribune*, September 30, 1999, https://www.chicagotribune.com/news/ct-xpm-1999-09-30
-9909300254-story.html.

122 *Earnings jumped 30 percent:* Jeremy Mullman, "Liberty Grp. Publishing Refi-
nances," *Crain's Chicago Business*, January 27, 2005, accessed October 25, 2023,
https://www.chicagobusiness.com/article/20050127/NEWS01/200015297
/liberty-grp-publishing-refinances.

123 *With three hundred papers:* Dennis K. Berman, "Fortress Capital Will Buy Publisher Liberty Group," *Wall Street Journal*, May 11, 2005, https://www.wsj.com
/articles/SB111577592873230054.

123 *And cutting costs:* Davis, Haltiwanger, Handley, Lipsius, Lerner, and Miranda,
"The Economic Effects of Private Equity Buyouts."

124 *"This means that workers":* "Study Affirms the Key Role Private Equity Plays in

Creating Jobs and Increasing Productivity," *Financial Times*, October 14, 2019, https://www.ft.com/content/45a5bad2-ee7b-11e9-ad1e-4367d8281195.

125 *Just five years earlier:* "Notice of Exempt Solicitation (Voluntary Submission)," Securities and Exchange Commission, accessed October 15, 2024, https://www.sec.gov/Archives/edgar/data/1579684/000177316123000006/gcishareholderletter3.htm.

126 *The column called upon:* Robert McChesney, Russell Newman, and Ben Scott, *The Future of Media: Resistance and Reform in the 21st Century* (New York: Seven Stories Press, 2005), 42.

126 *Within several months:* "History," NewsGuild, November 5, 2020, https://newsguild.org/history/.

126 *In 1937, they were joined:* "About," Indianapolis NewsGuild, accessed October 27, 2023, https://indynewsguild.com/news/about/.

126 *Like 84 percent:* Jacob Liedke, "About One-in-Six U.S. Journalists at News Outlets Are Part of a Union; Many More Would Join One If They Could," Pew Research Center, August 4, 2022, https://www.pewresearch.org/short-reads/2022/08/04/about-one-in-six-u-s-journalists-at-news-outlets-are-part-of-a-union-many-more-would-join-one-if-they-could.

126 *An employee who:* "Contract Between Indianapolis Newspapers Inc. and the Indianapolis Newspaper Guild," Indianapolis Newspaper Guild, September 1, 2018, https://indynewsguild.com/wp-content/uploads/2018/12/3346_001.pdf.

126 *The union hadn't even won:* "Contract Between Indianapolis Newspapers Inc. and the Indianapolis Newspaper Guild," Indianapolis Newspaper Guild, August 25, 2014, https://indynewsguild.com/wp-content/uploads/2006/05/guild-contract-final.pdf.

127 *That meant less news:* Danny Hayes and Jennifer L. Lawless, *News Hole: The Demise of Local Journalism and Political Engagement* (Cambridge: Cambridge University Press, 2021): 27. https://doi.org/10.1017/9781108876940.

127 *more than 56 percent:* Hayes and Lawless.

127 *Just a few weeks:* Tom Jones, "Gannett Lays Off Journalists Across the Country," Poynter Institute, January 23, 2019, https://www.poynter.org/business-work/2019/gannett-lays-off-journalists-across-the-country/.

127 *The name that really mattered:* Cara Lombardo, "Hedge-Fund-Backed Media Group Makes Bid for Gannett," *Wall Street Journal*, January 14, 2019, https://www.wsj.com/articles/hedge-fund-backed-media-group-prepares-bid-for-gannett-11547427720.

128 *"whose office near":* Alison Leigh Cowan, "Company News; Bottom Fishing with R. D. Smith," *New York Times*, March 29, 1991, https://www.nytimes.com/1991/03/29/business/company-news-bottom-fishing-with-rd-smith.html.

128 *In the 1990s, a large painting:* Cynthia Cotts, "Vulture Press," *Village Voice*, April 20, 1999, https://www.villagevoice.com/vulture-press/.

128 *"So who is Randall Smith":* Rick Edmonds, "Who Is Investor Randall Smith and Why Is He Buying Up Newspaper Companies?," Poynter Institute, July 27, 2011, https://www.poynter.org/reporting-editing/2011/randall-smith-alden-global-capital-newspaper-companies/.

128 *the entirety of the company's website:* "Alden Global Capital," Alden Global Capital, accessed October 27, 2024, https://aldenglobal.com/.

129 *When a viewer slid:* "Editorial: As Vultures Circle, the Denver Post Must Be Saved," *Denver Post,* April 6, 2018, https://www.denverpost.com/2018/04/06 /as-vultures-circle-the-denver-post-must-be-saved/.

129 *In his statement:* Rick Edmonds, "Gannett Rejects Acquisition Bid, Says Digital First Would Be Unfit to Run Its Properties," Poynter Institute, February 4, 2019, https://www.poynter.org/business-work/2019/gannett-rejects-acquisition-bid -says-digital-first-would-be-unfit-to-run-its-properties/.

129 *He didn't mention:* Securities and Exchange Commission, "Notice of Exempt Solicitation."

129 *He left out:* John Russell, "Indianapolis Star Parent Gannett Offering Another Round of Buyouts," *Indianapolis Business Journal,* October 21, 2020, https:// www.ibj.com/articles/indy-star-parent-gannett-co-offering-another-round-of -buyouts.

129 *So Alden gave up:* Jonathan O'Connell, "Gannett Shareholders Reject Hedge Fund's Board Candidates," *Washington Post,* May 16, 2019, https://www.washingtonpost .com/business/2019/05/16/gannett-shareholders-reject-hedge-funds-board -candidates/.

130 *in fact, GateHouse closed:* Penelope Muse Abernathy, "The Expanding News Desert," UNC Hussman School of Media and Journalism, October 2018, https://www .cislm.org/wp-content/uploads/2018/10/The-Expanding-News-Desert-10_14 -Web.pdf.

130 *So GateHouse and Gannett:* Marc Tracy, "Gannett, Now Largest U.S. Newspaper Chain, Targets 'Inefficiencies,'" *New York Times,* November 19, 2019, https:// www.nytimes.com/2019/11/19/business/media/gannett-gatehouse-merger .html.

130 *When the ink dried:* Ken Doctor, "Newsonomics: The Perils—and Promises— of New Gannett," Nieman Lab, August 9, 2019, https://www.niemanlab .org/2019/08/newsonomics-the-perils-and-promises-of-new-gannett/.

131 *The previous year, Gannett:* Ken Doctor, "Newsonomics: It's Looking like Gan- nett Will Be Acquired by GateHouse—Creating a Newspaper Megachain like the U.S. Has Never Seen," Nieman Lab, July 18, 2019, https://www.niemanlab .org/2019/07/newsonomics-its-looking-like-gannett-will-be-acquired-by -gatehouse-creating-a-newspaper-megachain-like-the-u-s-has-never-seen/.

131 *In the beginning:* Joshua Benton, "On a Rough Day for American Newspapers, Investors Aren't Buying Gannett's Story and Tribune's Not Done Chopping," Nieman Lab, February 27, 2020, https://www.niemanlab.org/2020/02/on-a -rough-day-for-american-newspapers-investors-arent-buying-gannetts-story-and -tribunes-not-done-chopping/.

131 *"Do we need two people":* Tracy, "Gannett, Now Largest U.S. Newspaper Chain, Targets 'Inefficiencies.'"

132 *"Digital producers live":* "A Diverse Newsroom, Pay Equity, Job Security and Safety: Here's What We're Fighting for in Our Contract," Indianapolis News- paper Guild, December 8, 2020, https://indynewsguild.com/2020/12/08/a

-diverse-newsroom-pay-equity-job-security-and-safety-heres-what-were-fighting
-for-in-our-contract/.

132 *A round of layoffs:* Barbara Allen, "Gannett Layoffs Underway at Combined New Company," Poynter Institute, February 27, 2020, https://www.poynter.org /business-work/2020/gannett-layoffs-underway-at-combined-new-company/.

132 *30 percent:* Securities and Exchange Commission, "Notice of Exempt Solicitation."

133 *Thousands more had devolved:* Abernathy, "The Expanding News Desert."

134 *Record numbers of newsrooms:* Sara Fischer, "Record Number of Journalists Unionize during COVID Pandemic," Axios, April 20, 2021, https://www.axios .com/2021/04/20/journalists-unionize-digital-media.

134 *including at multiple:* Angela Fu, "Not Just a Wave, but a Movement: Journalists Unionize at Record Numbers," Poynter Institute, July 16, 2021, https://www .poynter.org/business-work/2021/not-just-a-wave-but-a-movement-journalists -unionize-at-record-numbers/.

134 *though just 16 percent:* Liedke, "About One-in-Six U.S. Journalists at News Outlets Are Part of a Union; Many More Would Join One If They Could."

134 *A month later, seven more:* Daryl Slusher, "Austin American-Statesman Lays Off Seven Reporters," Austin Independent, April 30, 2020, https://theaustinindependent .org/austin-american-statesman-lays-off-seven-reporters/.

134 *In February 2021, the remaining:* Kirk Ladendorf, "American-Statesman Journalists Vote to Unionize," *Austin American-Statesman*, February 24, 2021, https://www .statesman.com/story/business/2021/02/24/american-statesman-journalists -vote-unionize/4574228001/.

134 *In 2022, the average monthly rent:* Paulina Cachero, "These Are the Cities Where Rents Have Risen the Most," Bloomberg, July 19, 2022, https://www.bloomberg .com/news/articles/2022-07-18/where-is-rent-most-expensive-austin-nyc -apartment-prices-surge.

135 *The union's vice chair:* Haya Panjwani, "Austin American-Statesman Staff Strike over Low Pay," KUT Radio, June 5, 2023, https://www.kut.org/austin /2023-06-05/austin-american-statesman-staff-strike-over-low-pay.

135 *One full-time photographer:* Mikala Compton 🐝 (@MikalaCompton), "Just signed up to be a DoorDash driver because I don't make enough to live in Austin, the city I cover & care so deeply about. @Gannett should be ashamed of themselves. Thankful for @AustinNewsGuild fighting for what's right." Twitter (now X), February 24, 2023, https://twitter.com/MikalaCompton /status/1629147902999232520.

135 *a former reporter said:* Austin NewsGuild (@AustinNewsGuild), "Former reporter @rebeccahmac worked a second job while working at the Statesman before leaving for a better-paying job. 'I had two jobs. I was getting up at 4am as a curbside shopper for HEB. I knew I needed a second job just to have my ends meet.'" Twitter (now X), September 21, 2022, https://twitter.com/AustinNewsGuild /status/1572719323692638210.

135 *In 2021, Gannett CEO:* Securities and Exchange Commission, "Notice of Exempt Solicitation."

136 *But Fortress still owned:* Gannett, "Gannett Announces Opportunistic Debt Refinancing," press release, September 27, 2021, https://gannett2023cr.q4web.com/news/news-details/2021/Gannett-Announces-Opportunistic-Debt-Refinancing/default.aspx.

137 *In early 2024:* "We Did It: Indy News Guild Just Ratified a Two-Year Contract. See What We Won," Indianapolis Newspaper Guild, January 24, 2024, https://indynewsguild.com/2024/01/24/we-did-it-indy-news-guild-just-ratified-a-two-year-contract-see-what-we-won/.

137 *The Austin NewsGuild:* Austin NewsGuild (@AustinNewsGuild), "The Austin NewsGuild is pleased to announce a tentative agreement with @Gannett. Thank you to the community for its ongoing support. We're excited to continue doing what we do best: reporting the news." X, October 18, 2024, https://x.com/AustinNewsGuild/status/1847432115706875920.

137 *By the end of 2022:* Securities and Exchange Commission, "Notice of Exempt Solicitation."

137 *down from 24,338:* Joshua Benton, "The Scale of Local News Destruction in Gannett's Markets Is Astonishing," Nieman Lab, March 9, 2023, https://www.niemanlab.org/2023/03/the-scale-of-local-news-destruction-in-gannetts-markets-is-astonishing/.

EIGHT: LOREN

138 *Nearly 60 percent:* "Southern Towers," African Communities Together, accessed March 11, 2024, https://africans.us/southern-towers.

139 *Bell Partners' only response:* Eliza Tebo, "'No Job? No Rent': Residents at an Alexandria Apartment Complex Prepare to Strike," WAMU, April 8, 2020, https://wamu.org/story/20/04/08/no-job-no-rent-residents-at-an-alexandria-apartment-complex-prepare-to-strike/.

140 *A 2021 report found:* "Invested in Evictions," African Communities Together, April 2021, https://africans.us/sites/default/files/Invested%20in%20Evictions%20with%20hyperlinks_0.pdf.

140 *Thanks in part:* James Cullum, "City Providing Rent and Mortgage Relief as Protestors Demand Rent Cancellation," ALXnow, July 15, 2020, https://www.alxnow.com/2020/07/15/city-providing-rent-and-mortgage-relief-as-protestors-demand-rent-cancellation/.

140 *and the state:* "Virginia," Eviction Lab, accessed March 13, 2024, https://evictionlab.org/eviction-tracking/virginia/.

140 *CIM had said:* "Mitsui to Participate in CIM Group, LLC, a US Real Estate Asset Manager," Mitsui & Co., Ltd., February 20, 2017, https://www.mitsui.com/jp/en/release/2017/__icsFiles/afieldfile/2017/02/20/en_170220_attach.pdf.

140 *CIM management had told:* Vernon Miles, "Southern Towers Residents and Activists Protest Rent Increases and Lingering Health Issues," ALXnow, November 18, 2022, https://www.alxnow.com/2022/11/18/southern-towers-residents-and-activists-protest-rent-increases-and-lingering-health-issues/.

141 *nearly 30 percent of all Alexandria:* African Communities Together, "Invested in Evictions."

141 *average rent at Southern Towers:* Vernon Miles, "Southern Towers Residents Nervous as Landlord Steps Up Eviction Proceedings," ALXnow, April 14, 2021, https://www.alxnow.com/2021/04/14/southern-towers-residents-nervous-as-landlord-steps-up-eviction-proceedings/.

141 *The Korean Teachers' Credit Union:* Kang Doo-soon, Park Jae-young, and Cho Jeehyun, "Korean Teachers' Credit Union Partakes $700mn Real Estate Investment Project in U.S.," Pulse, September 2, 2020, https://pulsenews.co.kr/view.php?year=2020&no=904734.

143 *The spokesman added:* Miles, "Southern Towers Residents and Activists Protest Rent Increases and Lingering Health Issues."

143 *Councilwoman Alyia Gaskins:* "Alexandria Leaders View Maintenance Problems at Southern Towers," Annandale Today, September 21, 2023, https://annandaletoday.com/alexandria-leaders-view-maintenance-problems-at-southern-towers/.

144 *Just four senators:* "Private Equity & Investment Firms Recipients," OpenSecrets, 2022, accessed October 15, 2024, https://www.opensecrets.org/industries//summary?ind=F2600&recipdetail=A&sortorder=U&mem=Y&cycle=2020.

144 *In 2022, New York Democrat:* Taylor Giorno and Srijita Datta, "Private Equity and Hedge Fund Industries Pour Nearly $347.7 Million into 2022 Midterms," OpenSecrets, September 7, 2022, https://www.opensecrets.org/news/2022/09/private-equity-and-hedge-fund-industries-pour-nearly-347-7-million-into-2022-midterms/.

144 *Kyrsten Sinema, the Arizona:* Aime Williams and Caitlin Gilbert, "Kyrsten Sinema Is Significant Beneficiary of Private Equity Lobbying Machine," *Financial Times*, August 7, 2022, https://www.ft.com/content/64305c91-c7aa-427b-adb9-7a32d74d3490.

144 *The American Investment Council spends:* "Client Profile: American Investment Council," OpenSecrets, 2023, accessed October 15, 2024, https://www.opensecrets.org/federal-lobbying/clients/summary?cycle=2023&id=D000036835.

144 *its CEO, Drew Maloney:* Drew Maloney, "Raising Taxes on Investors Would Be a Mistake. Small Businesses Need Them to Grow," azcentral, July 6, 2021, https://www.azcentral.com/story/opinion/op-ed/2021/07/06/small-businesses-lose-when-their-investors-taxed-more/7831846002/.

144 *When Sinema did:* Sahil Kapur, "Krysten Sinema Delivers a 'Gift to Private Equity' in Democrats' Big Agenda Bill," NBC News, August 12, 2022, https://www.nbcnews.com/politics/congress/kyrsten-sinema-delivers-gift-private-equity-democrats-big-agenda-bill-rcna42394.

145 *No information about:* Sosseh Prom, "Request for Immediate Investigation into Predatory Practices of Federally-Funded Entity, the CIM Group," submitted to Sandra Thompson and Michael DeVito, November 8, 2022, https://africans.us/sites/default/files/Formal%20Complaint%20Against%20CIM%20Group.pdf.

145 *In response:* "Addendum to November 8, 2022 Complaint Filed by African Communities Together," African Communities Together, accessed October 29, 2024, https://africans.us/sites/default/files/Addendum%20-%20Formal%20Complaint%20Against%20CIM%20Group.pdf.

146 *if a family had to be:* Prom, "Request for Immediate Investigation into Predatory Practices of Federally-Funded Entity, the CIM Group."

146 *"Southern Towers is not now":* Roshan Abraham, "People Are Organizing to Fight

the Private Equity Firms Who Own Their Homes," *Vice*, May 16, 2023, https://
www.vice.com/en/article/jg5pek/people-are-organizing-to-fight-the-private
-equity-firms-who-own-their-homes.

150 *"And that's not":* James Cullum, "Southern Towers Apartment Complex Owner
at Odds with Residents over Living Conditions," ALXnow, November 8, 2023,
https://www.alxnow.com/2023/11/08/southern-towers-apartment-complex
-owner-is-at-odds-with-residents-over-living-conditions/.

NINE: LIZ

163 *office supply manufacturer in Indiana:* "Romney Economics: Job Loss and Bankruptcy at Ampad," YouTube video, posted by BarackObamadotcom, May 21,
2012, https://www.youtube.com/watch?v=TLatxTzVE4w.

163 *steel factory in Kansas City:* "Romney Economics: Bankruptcy and Bailouts at GST
Steel," YouTube video, posted by BarackObamadotcom, May 14, 2012, https://
www.youtube.com/watch?v=ZMndjLIQUFw.

165 *Just 4 percent of retail workers:* "Union Members—2023," Bureau of Labor Statistics, January 28, 2025, https://www.bls.gov/news.release/pdf/union2.pdf.

165 *at Costco, more than fifteen thousand:* Nate Delesline III, "Costco Workers at Virginia
Store Unionize," Retail Dive, December 22, 2023, https://www.retaildive.com
/news/costco-workers-at-virginia-store-unionize/703346/.

166 *News articles at the time:* Neil Irwin, "How Did Walmart Get Cleaner Stores
and Higher Sales? It Paid Its People More," *New York Times*, October 15, 2016,
https://www.nytimes.com/2016/10/16/upshot/how-did-walmart-get-cleaner
-stores-and-higher-sales-it-paid-its-people-more.html.

166 *As the* Washington Post *put it:* Lydia DePillis, "A Key Union Appears to Be Backing Away from One of Labor's Most Prominent Campaigns," *Washington Post*,
April 15, 2015, https://www.washingtonpost.com/news/wonk/wp/2015/04/15
/one-union-appears-to-be-backing-away-from-labors-most-prominent-campaign/.

167 *A&P, once the largest:* Lisa Fickenscher, "Bankrupt A&P Seeks to Slash Severance
so It Can Pay Creditors," *New York Post*, August 13, 2015, https://nypost.com
/2015/08/13/bankrupt-ap-seeks-to-slash-severance-so-it-can-pay-creditors/.

168 *"Amazon didn't kill":* Chris Isidore, "Amazon Didn't Kill Toys 'R' Us. Here's What
Did," CNN, March 15, 2018, https://money.cnn.com/2018/03/15/news
/companies/toys-r-us-closing-blame/index.html.

169 *Eighty-eight percent:* "Private Equity Delivers the Strongest Returns for Retirees
Across America," American Investment Council.

169 *About $3 billion:* "Private Equity Program (PEP) Fund Performance Review,"
CalPERS, accessed March 31, 2024, https://www.calpers.ca.gov/page/investments
/about-investment-office/investment-organization/pep-fund-performance.

169 *"To the extent":* "Blackstone Group Inc—10K—Annual Report—February 24,
2023," Fintel, accessed June 26, 2023, https://fintel.io/doc/sec-blackstone-inc
-1393818-10k-2023-february-24-19413-6057.

169 *Killing off Revlon's:* J. Adam Cobb, "Risky Business: The Decline of Defined Benefit
Pensions and Firms' Shifting of Risk," Wharton School, https://faculty.wharton
.upenn.edu/wp-content/uploads/2015/09/jac_pensions_FINAL_3.pdf.

170 *public pension funds:* Michelle Celarier, "Is Private Equity Overrated?," *New York Times*, December 4, 2021, https://www.nytimes.com/2021/12/04/business/is-private-equity-overrated.html.

170 *"capitalism's washing machine":* Hamilton Nolan, "Capitalism's Washing Machine," How Things Work, September 20, 2023, https://www.hamiltonnolan.com/p/capitalisms-washing-machine.

172 *Minnesota's $93 billion:* Neal St. Anthony, "Minnesota Pension Board Looks at Private Equity Strategy," *Star Tribune*, June 20, 2018, https://www.startribune.com/minnesota-pension-board-looks-at-private-equity-strategy/486085681/.

172 *"Did anyone at KKR":* Katrina Compoli, Melissa Mittelman, and Eliza Ronalds-Hannon, "State Pension Funds Question KKR on Role in Toys 'R' Us Demise," Bloomberg, June 22, 2018, https://www.bloomberg.com/news/articles/2018-06-22/state-pension-funds-question-kkr-on-role-in-toys-r-us-demise.

173 *KKR and Bain:* Anne D'Innocenzio, "Former Toys R Us Workers to Get $20M in Hardship Fund," Associated Press, November 20, 2018, https://apnews.com/general-news-f2a8f4088d704660afcc99f505e6de2f.

175 *The following year:* "Support Laid-off Organizers," GoFundMe, December 13, 2023, https://www.gofundme.com/f/support-laidoff-organizers.

175 *KKR's private equity portfolio:* "Portfolio," KKR, accessed April 11, 2024, https://www.kkr.com/invest/portfolio.

175 *Bain Capital:* "Our Portfolio," Bain Capital Private Equity, accessed April 11, 2024, https://www.baincapitalprivateequity.com/portfolio.

175 *Of the twenty largest retailers:* "Top 100 Retailers 2024 List," National Retail Federation, accessed October 16, 2024, https://nrf.com/research-insights/top-retailers/top-100-retailers/top-100-retailers-2024-list.

176 *In videos of the event:* Elizabeth Warren, "Stop Wall Street Looting Act Introduction," Facebook, July 18, 2019, https://www.facebook.com/watch/live/?ref=watch_permalink&v=1130702730460786.

177 *"Everyone is nervous":* Kate Kelly and Lisa Lerer, "As Warren Gains in Race, Wall Street Sounds the Alarm," New York Times, November 4, 2019, https://www.nytimes.com/2019/11/04/us/politics/elizabeth-warren-wall-street.html.

177 *The exact amount:* "Fact Sheet: Close the Carried Interest Loophole That Is a Tax Dodge for Super-Rich Private Equity Executives," Americans for Financial Reform, October 14, 2021, https://ourfinancialsecurity.org/2021/10/close-the-carried-interest-loophole-that-is-a-tax-dodge-for-super-rich-private-equity-executives/.

178 *Though the measure:* Tory Newmyer, "The Finance 202: Elizabeth Warren's Pitch to Upend Private Equity Rattles Industry," Washington Post, July 17, 2020, https://www.washingtonpost.com/news/powerpost/paloma/the-finance-202/2019/07/19/the-finance-202-elizabeth-warren-s-pitch-to-upend-private-equity-rattles-industry/5d30f77e1ad2e5592fc35a0a/.

178 *The American Families Plan:* Alan Rappeport, Emily Flitter, and Kate Kelly, "The Carried Interest Loophole Survives Another Political Battle," *New York Times*, August 5, 2022, https://www.nytimes.com/2022/08/05/business/carried-interest-senate-bill.html.

178 *Since then, no one:* "Fact Sheet: The President's Budget Cuts Taxes for Working

Families and Makes Big Corporations and the Wealthy Pay Their Fair Share," White House, March 11, 2024, https://bidenwhitehouse.archives.gov/omb /briefing-room/2024/03/11/fact-sheet-the-presidents-budget-cuts-taxes-for -working-families-and-makes-big-corporations-and-the-wealthy-pay-their-fair -share/.

TEN: ROGER

182 *Even small rural hospitals:* Kamila Kudelska, "Sublette County Gets Funding to Start Construction on Its First Hospital," Wyoming Public Media, March 3, 2023, https://www.wyomingpublicmedia.org/open-spaces/2023-03-03/sublette -county-gets-funding-to-start-construction-on-its-first-hospital.

182 *possibly apocryphally:* "Frequently Asked Questions about Mead/Bateson," Institute for Intercultural Studies, accessed February 14, 2024, http://www .interculturalstudies.org/faq.html.

183 *But many people:* "Wyoming Community Bank Welcomes Corte McGuffey to Its Board of Directors," County 10, March 10, 2020, https://county10.com /wyoming-community-bank-welcomes-corte-mcguffey-to-its-board-of-directors/.

183 *Better yet, they won:* "Riverton Wolverines Football: Year by Year," Wyoming -Football.com, January 11, 2018, https://wyoming-football.com/index.php /results/results-by-team/riverton-wolverines/.

183 *In the process:* "Corte McGuffey (1999)—Hall of Fame," National Football Foundation, accessed February 5, 2024, https://footballfoundation.org/hof_scholars .aspx?hof=225.

184 *In a town where:* "2024 Fremont County General Election Cumulative Report Official Results," Fremont County Clerk, November 7, 2024, https://cms9files .revize.com/fremontcounty/Government/Clerk/Elections/2024%20Election%20 Results/General%202024%20Official%20Results%20Abstract%20(1).pdf.

185 *As a result of all these:* U.S. Government Accountability Office, "Rural Hospital Closures: Affected Residents Had Reduced Access to Health Care Services."

185 *after the extra income:* Zachary Levinson, Jamie Godwin, and Scott Hulver, "Rural Hospitals Face Renewed Financial Challenges, Especially in States That Have Not Expanded Medicaid," KFF, February 23, 2023, https://www.kff.org/health -costs/issue-brief/rural-hospitals-face-renewed-financial-challenges-especially -in-states-that-have-not-expanded-medicaid/.

187 *a city slightly bigger:* "U.S. Census Bureau QuickFacts: Oskaloosa City, Iowa," U.S. Census Bureau, accessed February 12, 2024, https://www.census.gov/quickfacts /fact/table/oskaloosacityiowa/RHI725222.

187 *1.4 million health care workers:* Meg Anderson, "Amid Pandemic, Hospitals Lay Off 1.4M Workers in April," NPR, May 10, 2020, https://www.npr.org /2020/05/10/853524764/amid-pandemic-hospitals-lay-off-1-4m-workers-in-april.

187 *By 2023, it was making:* "Mahaska Health Leadership Talks About the Financial Future of the Hospital," *Oskaloosa News*, July 30, 2022, http://oskynews.org /mahaska-health-leadership-talks-about-the-financial-future-of-the-hospital/.

187 *"There's a culture":* Channing Rucks, "Mahaska Health Welcomes New Providers, Expands Care," *Oskaloosa Herald*, September 25, 2023, https://www.oskaloosa

.com/news/local_news/mahaska-health-welcomes-new-providers-expands
-care/article_8bf8601c-5bbd-11ee-adcf-e399bccaa9ad.html.

188 *Riverton's population grew:* "U.S. Census Bureau QuickFacts: Riverton City, Wyoming," U.S. Census Bureau, accessed February 12, 2024, https://www.census.gov/quickfacts/fact/table/rivertoncitywyoming/PST045223.

191 *That meant LifePoint:* Ayla Ellison, "LifePoint Received $1.5B in COVID-19 Relief Aid," *Becker's Hospital Review*, September 14, 2020, https://www.beckershospitalreview.com/finance/lifepoint-received-1-5b-in-covid-19-relief-aid.html.

193 *It was the largest:* "Riverton Medical District Takes Major Step Toward New Hospital," Riverton Medical District, archived April 6, 2023, https://web.archive.org/web/20230406031459/https://rivertonmedicaldistrict.com/wp-content/uploads/2022/04/USDAapproval.pdf.

194 *A half-cent:* "$10M Grant from State of Wyoming to Riverton Medical District Completes Funding Needed for New Hospital," Riverton Medical District, archived April 6, 2023, https://web.archive.org/web/20230406031459/https://rivertonmedicaldistrict.com/wp-content/uploads/2022/11/PressReleaseNov2022.pdf.

195 *Across the country:* Private Equity Stakeholder Project, "PESP Private Equity Hospital Tracker."

195 *During the Biden administration:* "Agency Profile: Department of Agriculture (USDA)," USASpending.gov, accessed October 16, 2024, https://www.usaspending.gov/agency/department-of-agriculture?fy=2024.

195 *Thirty-three states:* "The Corporate Practice of Medicine 50-State Guide," Permit Health, January 16, 2025, https://www.permithealth.com/post/the-corporate-practice-of-medicine-50-state-guide.

196 *In late 2023, delegates:* Shannon Firth, "AMA Delegates Divided on Federal Ban of the Corporate Practice of Medicine," MedPageToday, November 13, 2023, https://www.medpagetoday.com/meetingcoverage/ama/107314.

ELEVEN: NATALIA

197 *The goal:* Nu Yang, "Lesson Plans," *Editor & Publisher*, archived November 14, 2019, https://web.archive.org/web/20191114232349/https://www.editorandpublisher.com/a-section/lesson-plans/.

199 *it didn't publish:* Lisa Snedeker, "The Emerging Online-Only Local Paper," *Media Life*, archived March 24, 2010, https://web.archive.org/web/20100324075119/http://www.medialifemagazine.com/artman2/publish/Newspapers_24/The_emerging_online-only_local_paper.asp.

200 *The site's first major grant:* "Not for Profit? The Voice of San Diego Experiment," Columbia Journalism School, Knight Case Studies Initiative, accessed October 21, 2024, https://ccnmtl.columbia.edu/projects/caseconsortium/casestudies/51/casestudy/files/global/51/Voice%20of%20San%20Diego%20Experiment_wm.pdf.

200 *In 2009, the Texas Tribune:* Richard Pérez-Peña, "Web News Start-Up Has Its Eye on Texas," *New York Times*, July 17, 2009, https://www.nytimes.com/2009/07/18/business/media/18texas.html.

200 *"The apostles Peter and Luke":* John Thornton, "What If: The Non-Profit Media Model," HuffPost, August 30, 2009, https://www.huffpost.com/entry/what-if-the-non-profit-me_b_248284.

200 *When GateHouse bought Gannett:* Tracy, "Gannett, Now Largest U.S. Newspaper Chain, Targets 'Inefficiencies.'"

200 *Alden Global Capital:* Marc Tracy, "Gannett Counters the Latest Move by Its Hedge Fund-Backed Rival," *New York Times*, May 16, 2019, https://www.nytimes.com/2019/05/16/business/media/gannett-medianews-newspapers.html.

201 *In 2020, a small:* McClatchy, "McClatchy Acquired by Chatham Asset Management, LLC," press release, September 4, 2020, https://www.mcclatchy.com/about/news/mcclatchy-acquired-by-chatham-asset-management-llc.

201 *"I would love our team":* Sarah Ellison, "Heath Freeman Is the Hedge Fund Guy Who Says He Wants to Save Local News. Somehow, No One's Buying It," *Washington Post*, June 11, 2020, https://www.washingtonpost.com/lifestyle/media/heath-freeman-is-the-hedge-fund-guy-who-says-he-wants-to-save-local-news-somehow-no-ones-buying-it/2020/06/11/9850a15c-884a-11ea-8ac1-bfb250876b7a_story.html.

201 *the company's earnings grew:* Business Wire, "Gannett Announces Third Quarter 2023 Results & Updated Full Year Outlook," press release, November 2, 2023, https://www.businesswire.com/news/home/20231102658064/en/Gannett-Announces-Third-Quarter-2023-Results-Updated-Full-Year-Outlook.

202 *Twenty Lake flipped:* Jonathan O'Connell and Emma Brown, "A Hedge Fund's 'Mercenary' Strategy: Buy Newspapers, Slash Jobs, Sell the Buildings," *Washington Post*, February 11, 2019, https://www.washingtonpost.com/business/economy/a-hedge-funds-mercenary-strategy-buy-newspapers-slash-jobs-sell-the-buildings/2019/02/11/f2c0c78a-1f59-11e9-8e21-59a09ff1e2a1_story.html.

202 *The only loser:* Dillon Davis, "Asheville Citizen Times Building, Home to Local Journalists for 80 Years, Is Sold," *Citizen-Times*, April 5, 2018, https://www.citizen-times.com/story/news/local/2018/04/05/asheville-citizen-times-building-sold-dlb-properties-gannett/380910002/.

202 *When a company goes public:* Matthew Goldstein, "Private Equity Firms Are Piling On Debt to Pay Dividends," *New York Times*, February 19, 2021, https://www.nytimes.com/2021/02/19/business/private-equity-dividend-loans.html.

202 *the payments can help:* Appelbaum and Batt, *Private Equity at Work*, 69.

202 *After the Gannett-GateHouse merger:* Aron Pilhofer, "The Gannett/Gatehouse Deal Is Even More Depressing Than I Imagined," Medium, August 11, 2019, https://medium.com/@pilhofer/the-gannett-gatehouse-deal-is-even-more-depressing-than-i-imagined-c0af9701d5b6.

202 *All they had to do:* Ellison, "Heath Freeman Is the Hedge Fund Guy Who Says He Wants to Save Local News. Somehow, No One's Buying It."

205 *Nearly a quarter:* "INN Index: The State of Nonprofit News—2018 Survey Report," Institute for Nonprofit News, October 2018, https://inn.org/wp-content/uploads/2021/04/INN.Index2018FinalFullReport.pdf.

205 *Two and a half newspapers:* "More than Half of U.S. Counties Have No Access or Very Limited Access to Local News," Medill School of Journalism, November 16,

2023, https://www.medill.northwestern.edu/news/2023/more-than-half-of-us -counties-have-no-access-or-very-limited-access-to-local-news.html.

205 *"You have to look at Gannett"*: Michael Hardy, "Austin's Daily Newspaper Is Being Starved to Death," *Texas Monthly*, January 29, 2024, https://www.texasmonthly .com/news-politics/austin-american-statesman-cuts-gannett.

205 *In 2018, a report*: Institute for Nonprofit News, "INN Index: The State of Non- profit News—2018 Survey Report."

205 *In February 2019*: "American Journalism Project Launches Major Effort to Re- invigorate Local News with $42 Million in Founding Commitments," American Journalism Project, February 26, 2019, http://www.theajp.org/american -journalism-project-to-reinvigorate-local-news-with-42-million/.

206 *"Many of the practices"*: Garry W. Jenkins, "Who's Afraid of Philanthrocapitalism?," *Case Western Reserve Law Review* 61, no. 3 (2011), https://scholarlycommons.law .case.edu/cgi/viewcontent.cgi?article=3504&context=caselrev.

207 *The American Journalism Project boasts*: Sarabeth Berman, "How Our Venture Philan- thropy Is Impacting Local News," American Journalism Project, March 28, 2022, https://www.theajp.org/news-insights/insights/how-our-venture-philanthropy -is-impacting-local-news/.

207 *Of the 225 counties*: Penelope Muse Abernathy, "Texas," in "The Expanding News Desert," UNC Hussman School of Journalism and Media, accessed January 25, 2024, https://www.usnewsdeserts.com/states/texas/.

207 *As many as 20*: Penelope Muse Abernathy, "The Rise of the Ghost Newspaper," in "The Expanding News Desert," UNC Hussman School of Journalism and Media, accessed October 16, 2024, https://www.usnewsdeserts.com/reports /expanding-news-desert/loss-of-local-news/the-rise-of-the-ghost-newspaper/.

207 *the median household income*: Erin Karter, "As Newspapers Close, Struggling Communities Are Hit Hardest by the Decline in Local Journalism," North- western Now, June 29, 2022, https://news.northwestern.edu/stories/2022/06 /newspapers-close-decline-in-local-journalism/.

207 *According to a NewsGuild filing*: Securities and Exchange Commission, "Notice of Exempt Solicitation."

207 *The Statesman had a single*: "Newsroom Directory," *Austin American-Statesman*, accessed January 25, 2024, https://www.statesman.com/contact/staff/.

208 *Just 8 percent*: Emily Tomasik and Jeffrey Gottfried, "U.S. Journalists' Beats Vary Widely by Gender and Other Factors," Pew Research Center, April 4, 2023, https://www.pewresearch.org/short-reads/2023/04/04/us-journalists-beats -vary-widely-by-gender-and-other-factors/.

208 *compared to 19 percent*: "U.S. Census Bureau QuickFacts: United States," U.S. Cen- sus Bureau, accessed September 25, 2023, https://www.census.gov/quickfacts /fact/table/US/PST045222.

208 *40 percent*: "U.S. Census Bureau QuickFacts: Texas," U.S. Census Bureau, accessed September 25, 2023, https://www.census.gov/quickfacts/fact/table/TX /RHI225222.

208 *In a state where*: "American Community Survey (ACS)," U.S. Census Bureau, accessed September 25, 2023, https://www.census.gov/programs-surveys/acs/.

209 *As AJP executive:* Megan Greenwell, "Solutions Oriented: How Foundation Money Is Transforming Local News," *Columbia Journalism Review*, October 16, 2023, https://www.cjr.org/local_news/solutions-oriented-cleveland-documentars-community-foundation.php.

209 *On Election Day:* Maria Mendez and Yuriko Schumacher, "Here's How to Vote in Texas' Midterm Elections," Votebeat Texas, October 15, 2022, https://www.votebeat.org/texas/2022/10/15/23405143/how-to-vote-in-texas-midterm-elections/.

209 *When conspiracy-minded:* Natalia Contreras, "Texas Republicans Want to Hand Count 2024 Primary Ballots. Experts Say It's 'a Recipe for Disaster,'" Votebeat Texas, December 21, 2023, https://www.votebeat.org/texas/2023/12/21/gillespie-county-texas-hand-counting-ballots-2024-primary-election/.

210 *Stewart Bainum, the chairman:* Katie Robertson, "Is Baltimore Big Enough for the Two of Them?," *New York Times*, July 1, 2022, https://www.nytimes.com/2022/07/01/business/media/baltimore-banner-the-sun.html.

210 *He lost out:* Marc Tracy, "The Executive Who Tried to Buy the Baltimore Sun Plans a Rival News Outlet," *New York Times*, October 14, 2021, https://www.nytimes.com/2021/10/14/business/stewart-bainum-baltimore-news-outlet.html.

210 *"There's no industry":* McKay Coppins, "A Secretive Hedge Fund Is Gutting Newsrooms," *Atlantic*, October 14, 2021, https://www.theatlantic.com/magazine/archive/2021/11/alden-global-capital-killing-americas-newspapers/620171/.

211 *"a bunch of financial titans":* Thornton, "What If: The Non-Profit Media Model."

211 *Votebeat, meanwhile:* "Support Truthful Reporting About Voting Across America," Votebeat, accessed March 2, 2025, https://votebeat.fundjournalism.org/donate/?campaign=701Pc000004g1a9IAA.

211 *There appear to be:* "Our Portfolio," American Journalism Project, accessed October 21, 2024, https://www.theajp.org/our-portfolio/.

211 *"Of course, we entertained":* Corinne Colbert, "Does Big Philanthropy Really Care about Our Smaller News Markets?," Local News Blues, January 18, 2024, https://www.localnewsblues.com/does-big-philanthropy-really-care-about-our-smaller-news-markets/.

211 *Having a strong:* Josh Stearns, "How We Know Journalism Is Good for Democracy," Democracy Fund, September 15, 2022, accessed January 9, 2024, https://democracyfund.org/idea/how-we-know-journalism-is-good-for-democracy/.

211 *Research shows that towns:* Pengjie Gao, Chang Lee, and Dermot Murphy, "Financing Dies in Darkness? The Impact of Newspaper Closures on Public Finance," Hutchins Center, September 2018, https://www.brookings.edu/wp-content/uploads/2018/09/WP44.pdf.

212 *NPR and PBS:* "Public Radio Finances," NPR, accessed August 15, 2023, https://www.npr.org/about-npr/178660742/public-radio-finances.

212 *As media scholar Nikki Usher:* Nikki Usher, *News for the Rich, White, and Blue: How Place and Power Distort American Journalism* (New York: Columbia University Press, 2021), 32.

212 *"It is time we accepted":* Steven Waldman, "The Collapse of California's News Industry Is So Severe It'll Require Taxpayer Support to Rebuild," CalMatters,

January 26, 2024, http://calmatters.org/commentary/2024/01/collapse-news
-taxpayer-support-rebuild/.

213 *The $30 million program:* Joseph Spector, "Tax Breaks to Hire Local Journalists
Approved in New York, a National First," *Politico*, April 21, 2024, https://www
.politico.com/news/2024/04/21/new-york-journalism-tax-breaks-00153482.

213 *"We missed something":* Jon Campbell, "New York's $90M Tax Break for Local
News Outlets Leaves Out TV and Nonprofits," Gothamist, May 16, 2024, https://
gothamist.com/news/new-yorks-90m-tax-break-for-local-news-outlets-leaves
-out-tv-and-nonprofits.

213 *In 2023, California's lower house:* Helen Li, "Meta Threatens to Pull News from
Facebook, Instagram If California Bill Passes," *Los Angeles Times*, June 1, 2023,
https://www.latimes.com/business/story/2023-06-01/meta-threatens-to-pull
-news-from-facebook-instagram-if-california-bill-passes.

213 *The agreement also funded:* Trân Nguyễn, "Google Agreed to Pay Millions for California News. Journalists Call It a Bad Deal," Associated Press, August 23, 2024,
https://apnews.com/article/california-google-news-funding-87d423a8a8bfe273
0b27ee3e59f4f454.

214 *In a tweet:* Natalia Contreras (@NataliaECG), "I should clarify and say that
I am for the first time, finally, working in a healthy, supportive and uplifting
workplace and I just want the same for everyone. It can be done. Starts with
management." X, September 8, 2023, https://x.com/NataliaECG/status
/1700129352162193686.

214 *In South Texas:* U.S. Census Bureau, "Language Spoken at Home,"https://
www.census.gov/acs/www/about/why-we-ask-each-question/language/,
accessed March 2, 2025.

214 *What she found:* Natalia Contreras, "How This Texas Elections Official Keeps
the Peace with Right-Wing Voting Activists," Texas Tribune, November 14,
2022, https://www.texastribune.org/2022/11/14/heider-garcia-tarrant-county
-election-transparency/.

215 *This American Life:* Natalia Contreras and Zoe Chace, *This American Life*,
podcast, "Flies, Meet Honey," in episode 785, "Through the Looking Glass,"
November 25, 2022, https://www.thisamericanlife.org/785/through-the
-looking-glass/act-one-9.

215 *Garcia was asked:* Natalia Contreras, "Heider Garcia Set to Become New Dallas
County Elections Chief," Votebeat Texas, October 18, 2023, https://www
.votebeat.org/texas/2023/10/18/23921683/heider-garcia-appointed-dallas
-county-election-administrator/.

215 *She wrote for Votebeat:* Natalia Contreras, "I'm an Elections Reporter—and I Just
Cast My First Vote as a Naturalized U.S. Citizen," Texas Tribune, March 5, 2024,
https://www.texastribune.org/2024/03/05/texas-election-reporter-votes-us
-citizen/.

TWELVE: LOREN

216 *That summer, during a record-breaking:* Max Marcilla, "Alexandria Apartment Complex Without AC amid Record-Setting Heat Wave," DC News Now, July 16,

2024, https://www.dcnewsnow.com/news/local-news/virginia/alexandria
/alexandria-apartment-complex-without-ac-amid-record-setting-heat-wave/.

218 *They wrote that:* Senator Mark R. Warner, "Warner, Kaine Push for Accountability
Following Reports of Inadequate Living Conditions at Affordable Housing Complex in Alexandria," press release, June 27, 2023, https://www.warner.senate
.gov/public/index.cfm/2023/6/warner-kaine-push-for-accountability-following
-reports-of-inadequate-living-conditions-at-affordable-housing-complex-in
-alexandria.

218 *In a response:* Anna Chen, "Warner, Kaine Push for Affordable Housing Accountability," DC News Now, June 27, 2023, https://www.dcnewsnow.com/news
/local-news/virginia/alexandria/warner-kaine-push-for-affordable-housing
-accountability/.

218 *He is one of the richest:* Russ Choma and Ian Gordon, "These Are Congress' Biggest
Private Equity Investors," *Mother Jones*, May 9, 2022, https://www.motherjones
.com/politics/2022/05/congress-private-equity-scott-warner-delbene-blumenthal
-romney/.

218 *For the last five years:* "Sen. Mark Warner—Campaign Finance Summary,"
OpenSecrets, accessed March 26, 2024, https://www.opensecrets.org/members
-of-congress/mark-warner/summary?cid=N00002097.

219 *during the 2024 election cycle:* Chris Cumming, "Republicans Lead Race for Private
Equity's 2024 Dollars," *Wall Street Journal*, September 21, 2023, https://www.wsj
.com/articles/republicans-lead-race-for-private-equitys-2024-dollars-ba152e12.

219 *The company, Ellison alleged:* Susan Du, "Amended Summons and Complaint
(62-cv-22-780)," State of Minnesota, District Court, August 10, 2022, https://
www.documentcloud.org/documents/24483316-mcro_62-cv-22-780_amended
-summons-and-complaint_2022-08-10_20240315102814?responsive=1&title=1.

219 *Most surprisingly, Pretium:* "Attorney General Ellison Reaches Landmark Settle-
ment with Single-Family Rental-Home Landlords," Office of Minnesota Attorney General Keith Ellison, March 15, 2024, https://www.ag.state.mn.us/Office
/Communications/2024/03/15_HavenBrookHomes.asp.

220 *"the heart of African American commerce":* Karen Robinson-Jacobs, "Noticing a
Latin Flavor in Crenshaw," *Los Angeles Times*, May 2, 2001, https://www.latimes
.com/archives/la-xpm-2001-may-02-fi-58221-story.html.

221 *"There are very few":* Roger Vincent, "Sale of Baldwin Hills Crenshaw Plaza
May Bring Offices, Not Housing, to the Mall," *Los Angeles Times*, April 29, 2020,
https://www.latimes.com/business/story/2020-04-29/baldwin-hills-crenshaw
-plaza-to-be-sold-to-cim-group.

221 *"What CIM proposes":* Roger Vincent, "Developer Drops Plan to Buy Baldwin
Hills Crenshaw Plaza and Add Offices, Not Housing," *Los Angeles Times*, June 15,
2020, https://www.latimes.com/business/story/2020-06-15/developer-drops
-plan-to-buy-baldwin-hills-crenshaw-plaza-and-add-offices-not-housing.

221 *More than ten thousand people:* "Send a Message for Community Ownership of
the Crenshaw Mall," Downtown Crenshaw, archived May 29, 2023, https://
web.archive.org/web/20230529114113/https://www.downtowncrenshaw.com
/petition.

221	*CIM announced in an Instagram post:* CIM Group (@cimgroup), "CIM helps communities achieve their goals and supports minority-owned businesses . . ." Instagram, June 14, 2020, https://instagram.com/cimgroup/p/CBb_Ba3jBnz/.

221	*The following year:* Roger Vincent, "Baldwin Hills Crenshaw Plaza Gets a New Owner with Plans to Modernize the Center," *Los Angeles Times*, August 25, 2021, https://www.latimes.com/business/story/2021-08-25/baldwin-hills-crenshaw -plaza-gets-a-new-owner-with-plans-to-modernize-the-center.

222	*Its goal:* "About CII," Council of Institutional Investors, accessed April 8, 2024, https://www.cii.org/about.

223	*As decision-makers:* "Southern Towers Tenant Speaks at Council for Institutional Investors Conference about Problems at CIM Group Apartment Complex," Private Equity Stakeholder Project, November 23, 2022, https://pestakeholder .org/news/southern-towers-tenant-speaks-at-council-for-institutional-investors -conference-about-problems-at-cim-group-apartment-complex/.

223	*a representative:* "CIM Infrastructure Fund III—Public IM," Commonwealth of Pennsylvania, accessed October 16, 2024, https://www.psers.pa.gov/About /Board/Resolutions/Documents/2022/CIM%20Infrastructure%20Fund%20 III%20-%20Public%20IM.pdf.

223	*Soon afterward, CIM leaders:* Alex Nicoll, "A Band of Immigrant Tenants Went to War with Their $31 Billion Landlord. It's a Sneak Peek at What's to Come Across America," *Business Insider*, December 27, 2022, https://www.businessinsider .com/southern-towers-apartment-tenants-battle-investor-landlord-2022-11.

223	*She told them:* K Agbebiyi, "Flooding in CIM Group's Southern Towers Profiled in Local News Outlets," Private Equity Stakeholder Project, November 7, 2023, https://pestakeholder.org/news/flooding-in-southern-towers-profiled-in-local -news-outlets/.

223	*Across the country, a handful:* Heather Gillers, "Some Public Pension Funds Are Pulling Back on Private Equity," *Wall Street Journal*, March 20, 2023, https:// www.wsj.com/articles/some-public-pension-funds-are-pulling-back-on-private -equity-dd8caa65.

224	*In 1992, Congress assigned:* "A Brief History of the Housing Government-Sponsored Enterprises," Federal Housing Finance Agency, accessed October 21, 2024, https://www.fhfaoig.gov/Content/Files/History%20of%20the%20 Government%20Sponsored%20Enterprises.pdf.

224	*The exact number:* "Housing and Economic Recovery Act of 2008," Sec. 1331, July 30, 2008, https://www.govinfo.gov/content/pkg/PLAW-110publ289/pdf /PLAW-110publ289.pdf.

224	*And while Fannie and Freddie:* Alejandra Cancino, "In Rare Move, Freddie Mac Files Suit Against South Side Landlord," Block Club Chicago, August 8, 2023, http://blockclubchicago.org/2023/08/08/in-rare-move-freddie-mac-files-suit -against-south-side-landlord/.

224	*"Freddie Mac is using":* Prom, "Request for Immediate Investigation into Predatory Practices of Federally-Funded Entity, the CIM Group."

224	*In its request:* "Tenant Protections for Enterprise-Backed Multifamily Properties: Request for Input," Federal Housing Financing Agency, May 2023, https://www

.fhfa.gov/Media/PublicAffairs/PublicAffairsDocuments/Multifamily-Tenant
-Protections-RFI.pdf.

225 *"Require good cause":* Sherrod Brown et al., "Brown Letter to FHFA on Tenant Protections," United States Senate, July 31, 2023, https://www.banking.senate .gov/imo/media/doc/brown_letter_to_fhfa_on_tenant_protections.pdf.

225 *But it did require:* Federal Housing Finance Agency, "FHFA Announces Multifamily Tenant Protections," news release, July 12, 2024, https://www.fhfa.gov /news/news-release/fhfa-announces-multifamily-tenant-protections-july-2024.

226 *When a ProPublica journalist:* Heather Vogell, "When Private Equity Becomes Your Landlord."

226 *In December 2023:* Adam Smith and Jeff Merkley, "S.3402—118th Congress (2023– 2024): End Hedge Fund Control of American Homes Act," Congress.gov, December 5, 2023, https://www.congress.gov/bill/118th-congress/senate-bill/3402 /text?s=1&r=14.

227 *"Wall Street":* "Rep. Smith Joins MSNBC to Discuss New Housing Bill: End Hedge Fund Control of American Homes Act," YouTube video, posted by RepAdam Smith, January 9, 2024, https://www.youtube.com/watch?v=Dk2EgPf03ik.

227 *Fewer than one in three:* "Report on the Economic Well-Being of U.S. Households in 2022–May 2023," Board of Governors of the Federal Reserve System, accessed April 1, 2024, https://www.federalreserve.gov/publications/2023-economic -well-being-of-us-households-in-2022-housing.htm.

228 *In Maine:* Robert B. Hunt, "First Special Session—2023," 131st Maine Legislature, House of Representatives, May 15, 2023, https://legislature.maine.gov /backend/App/services/getDocument.aspx?documentId=99990.

228 *In New York:* James Skoufis, "NY State Senate Bill 2023-S7381," New York State Senate, May 22, 2023, accessed April 1, 2024, https://www.nysenate.gov /legislation/bills/2023/S7381.

228 *Not a single park:* "Where They Are," ROC USA, accessed April 1, 2024, https:// rocusa.org/whats-a-roc/where-they-are/.

229 *The creation of America's:* Sara Katherine Copeland, "'Down with the Landlords': Tenant Activism in New York City, 1917–1920" (master's thesis, Massachusetts Institute of Technology, 2000), https://dspace.mit.edu/bitstream /handle/1721.1/65254/47911995-MIT.pdf.

229 *In 1971, shortly after:* "About STPCV–TA," Stuyvesant Town–Peter Cooper Village Tenants Association, accessed April 3, 2024, https://www.stpcvta.org/about_us.

229 *When Blackstone:* Dana Schulz, "Blackstone Buys Stuy Town for $5.3 Billion, Will Preserve Affordable Housing," 6sqft, October 20, 2015, https://www.6sqft.com /blackstone-buys-stuy-town-for-5-3-billion-will-preserve-affordable-housing/.

229 *The tenants' association sued:* Mihir Zaveri, "Blackstone Loses Rent Dispute at Manhattan's Biggest Apartment Complex," *New York Times*, January 6, 2023, https://www.nytimes.com/2023/01/06/nyregion/nyc-apartments-blackstone -rent-dispute.html.

229 *In San Diego:* Roshan Abraham, "Tenants of America's Biggest Landlord Form Union to Fight Evictions, Rent Hikes," *Vice*, March 31, 2023, https://www.vice .com/en/article/epvdzw/blackstone-tenants-union-san-diego-evictions-rent.

230 *Two years later, the city:* Lisa Halverstadt, "City Council Approves New Tenant Protections," Voice of San Diego, April 26, 2023, http://voiceofsandiego.org/2023/04/26/city-council-approves-new-tenant-protections/.

230 *In Kansas City, Missouri, a tenant association:* Charlotte Alter, "Renters Are in Revolt. This Tenant Union Plans to Get Them Organized," *Time*, October 26, 2023, https://time.com/6325516/kc-tenants-union-time-documentary/.

230 *In Minneapolis, the nonprofit:* Abraham, "People Are Organizing to Fight the Private Equity Firms Who Own Their Homes."

230 *including Washington, D.C.:* "§ 42–3505.06. Right of Tenants to Organize," Council of the District of Columbia, accessed April 8, 2024, https://code.dccouncil.us/us/dc/council/code/sections/42-3505.06.

230 *Seattle:* "Subtitle II—Housing Code," Municipal Code, Seattle, Washington, Municode Library, accessed April 8, 2024, https://library.municode.com/wa/seattle/codes/municipal_code?nodeId=TIT22BUCOCO_SUBTITLE_IIHOCO_CH22.206HABU_SUBCHAPTER_VIDUOWTE_22.206.180PRACOW.

230 *San Francisco:* "File No. 211096: Administrative Code—Tenant Organizing," Legistar, accessed April 8, 2024, https://sfgov.legistar.com/View.ashx?M=F&ID=10514976&GUID=1E551549-F00F-493B-B2DB-4C5CFBB8880C.

230 *In 2018, Oxfam:* "Best and Worst States to Work in the US," Oxfam, accessed April 3, 2024, https://www.oxfamamerica.org/explore/countries/united-states/poverty-in-the-us/best-states-to-work/.

230 *Oxfam's 2023 ranking:* Oxfam, "Best and Worst States to Work in the US."

230 *2021 law:* Mel Borja, "How Public-Sector Workers Are Building Power in Virginia," Economic Policy Institute, February 18, 2022, https://www.epi.org/blog/how-public-sector-workers-are-building-power-in-virginia/.

230 *After Princeton University's Eviction Lab:* Emily Badger and Quoctrung Bui, "In 83 Million Eviction Records, a Sweeping and Intimate New Look at Housing in America," *New York Times*, April 7, 2018, https://www.nytimes.com/interactive/2018/04/07/upshot/millions-of-eviction-records-a-sweeping-new-look-at-housing-in-america.html.

230 *the state spent:* Ben Finley, "Shame Put Virginia on Course to Stronger Tenant Protections," Associated Press, August 22, 2021, https://apnews.com/article/health-coronavirus-pandemic-virginia-b22cd7738d74e2651674911f749c1127.

230 *Republican governor Glenn Youngkin:* Dean Mirshahi, "After Bipartisan Vote, Tenant Protection Bill Fails in Virginia House Panel," WAVY.com, January 26, 2023, https://www.wavy.com/news/politics/virginia-politics/after-bipartisan-vote-tenant-protection-bill-fails-in-virginia-house-panel/.

CONCLUSION

233 *Steward boasted:* Steward Health Care, "Team of Steward Doctors Acquire Controlling Stake of Steward Health Care," press release, June 3, 2020, https://www.steward.org/newsroom/2020-06-03/team-steward-doctors-acquire-controlling-stake-steward.

233 *But then the owner:* Medical Properties Trust, "Medical Properties Trust Pro-

vides Update on Steward Health Care," press release, January 4, 2024, https://medicalpropertiestrust.gcs-web.com/node/15791/pdf.

233 *Massachusetts governor Maura Healey:* Commonwealth of Massachusetts, "Governor Healey Demands Financial Transparency and Patient Safety from Steward Health Care," press release, February 20, 2024, https://www.mass.gov/news/governor-healey-demands-financial-transparency-and-patient-safety-from-steward-health-care.

234 *In 2020:* Melanie Evans and Jonathan Weil, "A Bat Infestation, Postponed Surgeries and Unpaid Bills: A Hospital Chain in Crisis," *Wall Street Journal,* March 20, 2024, https://wsj.com/health/healthcare/hospital-chain-financial-crisis-steward-mpt-45be8bfb.

234 *"transformational moment":* Rebecca Ostriker and Catherine Carlock, "House of Cards: How a Real Estate Firm and Steward Health Care Grew in Tandem, in Part by Keeping Steward's Shaky Finances Secret," *Boston Globe,* October 8, 2024, https://apps.bostonglobe.com/metro/investigations/spotlight/2024/09/steward-hospitals/steward-mpt/.

234 *The* Globe *found fifteen cases:* Liz Kowalczyk, Chris Serres, Jessica Bartlett, Elizabeth Koh, Mark Arsenault, and Yoohyun Jung, "Practice of Neglect Led to Indignity, Death," *Boston Globe,* September 6, 2024, https://apps.bostonglobe.com/metro/investigations/spotlight/2024/09/steward-hospitals/steward-for-profit-hospitals-investigation/.

234 *At the time of the bankruptcy:* Dietrich Knauth, "Bankrupt Steward Health Puts Its Hospitals Up for Sale, Discloses $9 Bln in Debt," Reuters, May 7, 2024, https://www.reuters.com/business/healthcare-pharmaceuticals/bankrupt-steward-health-puts-its-hospitals-up-sale-discloses-9-bln-debt-2024-05-07/.

234 *The company even hired corporate spies:* Khadija Sharife and Tom Stocks, "U.S. Healthcare Firm Embroiled in Malta Corruption Scandal Spent Millions on Private Spies," Organized Crime and Corruption Reporting Project, July 1, 2024, https://www.occrp.org/en/investigation/us-healthcare-firm-embroiled-in-malta-corruption-scandal-spent-millions-on-private-spies.

234 *Cerberus Capital Management:* Cerberus, "Statement from Cerberus on Massachusetts Congressional Delegation's Hearing Related to Steward Health Care," press release, April 3, 2024, https://www.cerberus.com/media/statement-from-cerberus-on-massachusetts-congressional-delegations-hearing-related-to-steward-health-care/.

234 *A $3 million donation:* Jonathan Weil, "The CEO Who Made a Fortune While His Hospital Chain Collapsed," *Wall Street Journal,* August 18, 2024, https://www.wsj.com/business/steward-health-ceo-ralph-de-la-torre-deabfe4b.

235 *Donald Berwick:* When Health Care Becomes Wealth Care: How Corporate Greed Puts Patient Care and Health Workers at Risk: Hearing Before the Subcomm. on Primary Health and Retirement Security of the Comm. on Health, Education, Labor, and Pensions, 118th Cong., 2nd sess., April 3, 2024, https://www.govinfo.gov/content/pkg/CHRG-118shrg55874/pdf/CHRG-118shrg55874.pdf.

235 *"No individual can coerce":* Friedman, "A Friedman Doctrine."

236 *More than half of Republicans:* "Americans and Billionaires Survey," Harris Poll

Thought Leadership Practice, August 2024, https://theharrispoll.com/wp
-content/uploads/2024/07/Americans-and-Billionaires-Survey-August-2024
.pdf.

237 *Just five years earlier:* "From Businesses and Banks to Colleges and Churches:
Americans' Views of U.S. Institutions," Pew Research Center, February 1, 2024,
https://www.pewresearch.org/politics/2024/02/01/small-and-large-businesses
-banks-and-technology-companies/.

INDEX

meeting/wedding, 10–11

moves, 11–12, 18, 83, 84

Marin, Liz/Toys R Us

Babies R Us, 18–19, 87, 88, 89, 92, 93–94, 95, 96–97

bankruptcy consequences, 97–98, 99–100

beginnings, 12, 18, 79

customers and, 19, 88, 96–97, 167

giraffes/Geoffrey the Giraffe and, 5, 18

schedule, 83, 84

store situation and, 84, 89, 92, 93–94, 95, 96–97

tattoo, 18

training new employees and, 89, 92

transfer to other stores and, 18

wages, 83, 89, 97–98

work of/as employee, 5, 83, 88, 89, 91

See also Toys R Us

Marin, Liz/Toys R Us demise

activism of, 164, 165, 168, 171–172, 173, 174

job loss, 162

views on, 161

Martore, Gracia, 56

Massey, Jack, 32

Mead, Margaret, 182

Means, Gardiner, xiv–xv, xxi

Media Monopoly, The (Bagdikian), 56

MediaNews Group, 128

Medicaid/patients, 37, 104–105, 116, 185

medical insurance

Affordable Care Act, 39

Clinton administration/universal health care and, 36

debate (early 1900s), 23–24

socialism question, 23–24

See also specific types

Medical Properties Trust, 110, 233

Medicare for All, 180, 186, 196, 219–220

Medicare/patients, 33, 37, 38–39, 103, 108, 185, 189

medicine/health care

expenses increasing, 23

first medical school, 23

generalists/specialists, 30

history (overview), 23–25

hospitalists, 30

"just cause," 186

workplace injuries (early 1900s), 23–24

See also hospitals; specific components/individuals

medicine/health care and private equity

beginnings, 38–39

dominance/reasons, 106–107, 115

research findings on, 115–117

shareholder value philosophy and, 36, 39

Merkley, Jeff, 226–227

Metrick, Andrew, 80

Metropolitan Museum of Art, xiii

Milken, Michael, 61

minimum price laws, 12

Mirror Indy, 206–207

MIT computing school, xiii

mobile homes/parks, 70–71, 227–228

Modern Corporation and Private Property, The (Berle and Means), xiv–xix

Montgomery Ward, 6

Morgan, Neil, 199

Mount Sinai Hospital, xiii

Muilenburg, Robert

as Contreras, Natalia mentor, 44, 119–120

Contreras, Natalia relationship, 119–120, 136, 203, 204, 215

Del Mar Community College, 44, 119–120

Nassar, Larry, 125

Natalia. See Contreras, Natalia

National Sport Shop, 6, 7

New Deal, 69

Newe (Eastern Shoshone), 28, 108, 109, 189–190, 192–193, 194–195

Newlands, Francis, 7

NewsGuild, 207

newspaper industry

advertising revenue decrease beginnings, 46, 199